History of William Collins

In 1819, millworker William Collins from Glasgow, Scotland, set up a company for printing and publishing pamphlets, sermons, hymn books, and prayer books. That company was Collins and was to mark the birth of HarperCollins Publishers as we know it today. The long tradition of Collins dictionary publishing can be traced back to the first dictionary William co-published in 1825, *Greek and English Lexicon*. Indeed, from 1840 onwards, he began to produce illustrated dictionaries and even obtained a licence to print and publish the Bible.

Soon after, William published the first Collins novel; however, it was the time of the Long Depression, where harvests were poor, prices were high, potato crops had failed, and violence was erupting in Europe. As a result, many factories across the country were forced to close down and William chose to retire in 1846, partly due to the hardships he was facing.

Aged 30, William's son, William II, took over the business. A keen humanitarian with a warm heart and a generous spirit, William II was truly "Victorian" in his outlook. He introduced new, up-to-date steam presses and published affordable editions of Shakespeare's works and *The Pilgrim's Progress*, making them available to the masses for the first time.

A new demand for educational books meant that success came with the publication of travel books, scientific books, encyclopedias, and dictionaries. This demand to be educated led to the later publication of atlases, and Collins also held the monopoly on scripture writing at the time.

In the 1860s Collins began to expand and diversify and the idea of "books for the millions" was developed, although the phrase wasn't coined until 1907. Affordable editions of classical literature were published, and in 1903 Collins introduced 10 titles in their Collins Handy Illustrated Pocket Novels. These proved so popular that a few years later this had increased to an output of 50 volumes, selling nearly half a million in their year of publication. In the same year, The Everyman's Library was also instituted, with the idea of publishing an affordable library of the most important classical works, biographies, religious and philosophical treatments, plays, poems, travel, and adventure. This series eclipsed all competition at the time, and the introduction of paperback books in the 1950s helped to open that market and marked a high point in the industry.

HarperCollins is and has always been a champion of the classics, and the current Collins Classics series follows in this tradition—publishing classical literature that is affordable and available to all. Beautifully packaged, highly collectible, and intended to be reread and enjoyed at every opportunity.

DOWN AND OUT IN PARIS AND LONDON

'O scathful harm, condition of poverte!'

—*Chaucer*

I

The rue du Coq d'Or, Paris, seven in the morning. A succession of furious, choking yells from the street. Madame Monce, who kept the little hotel opposite mine, had come out on to the pavement to address a lodger on the third floor. Her bare feet were stuck into sabots and her grey hair was streaming down.

Madame Monce: '*Salope! Salope!* How many times have I told you not to squash bugs on the wallpaper? Do you think you've bought the hotel, eh? Why can't you throw them out of the window like everyone else? *Putain! Salope!*'

The woman on the third floor: '*Vache!*'

Thereupon a whole variegated chorus of yells, as windows were flung open on every side and half the street joined in the quarrel. They shut up abruptly ten minutes later, when a squadron of cavalry rode past and people stopped shouting to look at them.

I sketch this scene, just to convey something of the spirit of the rue du Coq d'Or. Not that quarrels were the only thing that happened there—but still, we seldom got through the morning without at least one outburst of this description. Quarrels, and the desolate cries of street hawkers, and the shouts of children chasing orange-peel over the cobbles, and at night loud singing and the sour reek of the refuse-carts, made up the atmosphere of the street.

It was a very narrow street—a ravine of tall, leprous houses, lurching towards one another in queer attitudes, as though they had all been frozen in the act of collapse. All the houses were hotels and packed to the tiles with lodgers, mostly Poles, Arabs and Italians. At the foot of the hotels were tiny *bistros*, where you could be drunk for the equivalent of a shilling. On Saturday nights about a third of the male population of the quarter was drunk. There was fighting over women, and the Arab navvies who lived in the cheapest hotels used to conduct mysterious feuds, and fight them out with chairs and occasionally revolvers. At night the policemen would only come through the street two together. It was a fairly rackety place. And yet amid the noise and dirt lived the usual respectable French shopkeepers, bakers and laundresses and the like, keeping themselves to themselves and quietly piling up small fortunes. It was quite a representative Paris slum.

My hotel was called the Hôtel des Trois Moineaux. It was a dark, rickety warren of five storeys, cut up by wooden partitions into forty rooms. The rooms were small and inveterately dirty, for there was no maid, and Madame F., the *patronne*, had no time to do any sweeping. The walls were as thin as matchwood, and to hide the cracks they had been covered with layer after layer of pink paper, which had come loose and housed innumerable bugs. Near the ceiling long lines of bugs marched all day like columns of soldiers, and at night came down ravenously hungry, so that one had to get up every few hours and kill them in hecatombs. Sometimes when the bugs got too bad one used to burn sulphur and drive them into the next room; whereupon the lodger next door would retort by having *his* room sulphured, and drive the bugs back. It was a dirty place, but homelike, for Madame F. and her husband were good sorts. The rent of the rooms varied between thirty and fifty francs a week.

The lodgers were a floating population, largely foreigners, who used to turn up without luggage, stay a week and then disappear again. They were of every trade—cobblers, bricklayers, stonemasons, navvies, students, prostitutes, rag-pickers. Some of them were fantastically poor. In one of the attics there was a Bulgarian student who made fancy shoes for the American market. From six to twelve he sat on his bed, making a dozen pairs of shoes and earning thirty-five francs; the rest of the day he attended lectures at the Sorbonne. He was studying for the Church, and books of theology lay face-down on his leather-strewn floor. In another room lived a Russian woman and her son, who called himself an artist. The mother worked sixteen hours a day, darning socks at twenty-five centimes a sock, while the son, decently dressed, loafed in the Montparnasse cafés. One room was let to two different lodgers, one a day worker and the other a night worker. In another room a widower shared the same bed with his two grown-up daughters, both consumptive.

There were eccentric characters in the hotel. The Paris slums are a gathering-place for eccentric people—people who have fallen into solitary, half-mad grooves of life and given up trying to be normal or decent. Poverty frees them from ordinary standards of behaviour, just as money frees people from work. Some of the lodgers in our hotel lived lives that were curious beyond words.

There were the Rougiers, for instance, an old, ragged, dwarfish couple who plied an extraordinary trade. They used to sell postcards on the Boulevard St Michel. The curious thing was that the postcards were sold in sealed packets as pornographic ones, but were actually photographs of chateaux on the Loire; the buyers did not discover this till too late, and of course never complained. The Rougiers earned about a hundred francs a week, and by strict economy managed to be always half starved and half drunk. The filth of their room was such that one could smell it on the floor below. According to Madame F., neither of the Rougiers had taken off their clothes for four years.

Or there was Henri, who worked in the sewers. He was a tall, melancholy man with curly hair, rather romantic-looking in his long, sewer-man's boots. Henri's peculiarity was that he did not speak, except for the purposes of work, literally for days together. Only a year before he had been a chauffeur in good employ and saving money. One day he fell in love, and when the girl refused him he lost his temper and kicked her. On being kicked the girl fell desperately in love with Henri, and for a fortnight they lived together and spent a thousand francs of Henri's money. Then the girl was unfaithful; Henri planted a knife in her upper arm and was sent to prison for six months. As soon as she had been stabbed the girl fell more in love with Henri than ever, and the two made up their quarrel and agreed that when Henri came out of jail he should buy a taxi and they would marry and settle down. But a fortnight later the girl was unfaithful again, and when Henri came out she was with child. Henri did not stab her again. He drew out all his savings and went on a drinking-bout that ended in another month's imprisonment; after that he went to work in the sewers. Nothing would induce Henri to talk. If you asked him why he worked in the sewers he never answered, but simply crossed his wrists to signify handcuffs, and jerked his head southward, towards the prison. Bad luck seemed to have turned him half-witted in a single day.

Or there was R., an Englishman, who lived six months of the year in Putney with his parents and six months in France. During his time in France he drank four litres of wine a day, and six litres on Saturdays; he had once travelled as far as the Azores, because the wine there is cheaper than anywhere in Europe. He was a gentle, domesticated creature,

DOWN AND OUT IN PARIS AND LONDON

never rowdy or quarrelsome, and never sober. He would lie in bed till midday, and from then till midnight he was in his corner of the *bistro*, quietly and methodically soaking. While he soaked he talked, in a refined, womanish voice, about antique furniture. Except myself, R. was the only Englishman in the quarter.

There were plenty of other people who lived lives just as eccentric as these: Monsieur Jules, the Roumanian, who had a glass eye and would not admit it, Furex the Limousin stonemason, Roucolle the miser—he died before my time, though—old Laurent the rag-merchant, who used to copy his signature from a slip of paper he carried in his pocket. It would be fun to write some of their biographies, if one had time. I am trying to describe the people in our quarter, not for the mere curiosity, but because they are all part of the story. Poverty is what I am writing about, and I had my first contact with poverty in this slum. The slum, with its dirt and its queer lives, was first an object-lesson in poverty, and then the background of my own experiences. It is for that reason that I try to give some idea of what life was like there.

II

Life in the quarter. Our *bistro*, for instance, at the foot of the Hôtel des Trois Moineaux. A tiny brick-floored room, half underground, with wine-sodden tables, and a photograph of a funeral inscribed '*Crédit est mort*'; and red-sashed workmen carving sausage with big jack-knives; and Madame F., a splendid Auvergnat peasant woman with the face of a strong-minded cow, drinking Malaga all day 'for her stomach'; and games of dice for *apéritifs*; and songs about '*Les Fraises et Les Framboises*', and about Madelon, who said, '*Comment épouser un soldat, moi qui aime tout le régiment?*'; and extraordinarily public love-making. Half the hotel used to meet in the *bistro* in the evenings. I wish one could find a pub in London a quarter as cheery.

One heard queer conversations in the *bistro*. As a sample I give you Charlie, one of the local curiosities, talking.

Charlie was a youth of family and education who had run away from home and lived on occasional remittances. Picture him very pink and young, with the fresh cheeks and soft brown hair of a nice little boy, and lips excessively red and wet, like cherries. His feet are tiny, his arms abnormally short, his hands dimpled like a baby's. He has a way of dancing and capering while he talks, as though he were too happy and too full of life to keep still for an instant. It is three in the afternoon, and there is no one in the *bistro* except Madame F. and one or two men who are out of work; but it is all the same to Charlie whom he talks to, so long as he can talk about himself. He declaims like an orator on a barricade, rolling the words on his tongue and gesticulating with his short arms. His small, rather piggy eyes glitter with enthusiasm. He is, somehow, profoundly disgusting to see.

He is talking of love, his favourite subject.

'*Ah, l'amour, l'amour! Ah, que les femmes m'ont tué!* Alas, *messieurs et dames*, women have been my ruin, beyond all hope my ruin. At twenty-two I am utterly worn out and finished. But what things I have learned, what abysses of wisdom have I not plumbed! How great a thing it is to have acquired the true wisdom, to have become in the highest sense of the word a civilized man, to have become *raffiné, vicieux*,' etc. etc.

'*Messieurs et dames*, I perceive that you are sad. *Ah, mais la vie est belle*—you must not be sad. Be more gay, I beseech you!

> 'Fill high ze bowl vid Samian vine,
> Ve vill not sink of semes like zese!

'*Ah, que la vie est belle!* Listen, *messieurs et dames*, out of the fullness of my experience I will discourse to you of love. I will explain to you what is the true meaning of love—what is the true sensibility, the higher, more refined pleasure which is known to civilized men alone. I will tell you of the happiest day of my life. Alas, but I am past the time when I could know such happiness as that. It is gone for ever—the very possibility, even the desire for it, are gone.

'Listen, then. It was two years ago; my brother was in Paris—he is a lawyer—and my parents had told him to find me and take me out to dinner. We hate each other, my brother and I, but we preferred not to disobey my parents. We dined, and at dinner he grew very drunk upon three bottles of Bordeaux. I took him back to his hotel, and on the way I bought a bottle of brandy, and when we had arrived I made my brother drink a tumblerful of it—I told him it was something to make him sober. He drank it, and immediately he fell down like somebody in a fit, dead drunk. I lifted him up and propped his back against the bed; then I went through his pockets. I found eleven hundred francs, and with that I hurried down the stairs, jumped into a taxi, and escaped. My brother did not know my address—I was safe.

'Where does a man go when he has money? To the *bordels*, naturally. But you do not suppose that I was going to waste my time on some vulgar debauchery fit only for navvies? Confound it, one is a civilized man! I was fastidious, exigeant, you understand, with a thousand francs in my pocket. It was midnight before I found what I was looking for. I had fallen in with a very smart youth of eighteen, dressed *en smoking* and with his hair cut *à l'américaine*, and we were talking in a quiet *bistro* away from the boulevards. We understood one another well, that youth and I. We talked of this and that, and discussed ways of diverting oneself. Presently we took a taxi together and were driven away.

'The taxi stopped in a narrow, solitary street with a single gas-lamp flaring at the end. There were dark puddles among the stones. Down one side ran the high, blank wall of a convent. My guide led me to a tall, ruinous house with shuttered windows, and knocked several times at the door. Presently there was a sound of footsteps and a shooting of bolts, and the door opened a little. A hand came round the edge of it; it was a large, crooked hand, that held itself palm upwards under our noses, demanding money.

'My guide put his foot between the door and the step. "How much do you want?" he said.

'"A thousand francs," said a woman's voice. "Pay up at once or you don't come in."

'I put a thousand francs into the hand and gave the remaining hundred to my guide: he said good night and left me. I could hear the voice inside counting the notes, and then a thin old crow of a woman in a black dress put her nose out and regarded me suspiciously before letting me in. It was very dark inside: I could see nothing except a flaring gas-jet that illuminated a patch of plaster wall, throwing everything else into deeper shadow. There was a smell of rats and dust. Without speaking, the old woman lighted a candle at the gas-jet, then hobbled in front of me down a stone passage to the top of a flight of stone steps.

'"*Voilà!*" she said; "go down into the cellar there and do what you like. I shall see nothing, hear nothing, know nothing. You are free, you understand—perfectly free."

'Ha, *messieurs*, need I describe to you—*forcément*, you know it yourselves—that shiver, half of terror and half of joy, that goes through one at these moments? I crept down, feeling my way; I could hear my breathing and the scraping of my shoes on the stones, otherwise all was silence. At the bottom of the stairs my hand met an electric switch. I turned it, and a great electrolier of twelve red globes flooded the cellar with a red light. And behold, I was not in a cellar, but in a bedroom, a great, rich, garish bedroom, coloured blood red from top to bottom. Figure it to yourselves, *messieurs et dames*! Red carpet on the floor, red paper on the walls, red plush on the chairs, even the ceiling red; everywhere red, burning into the eyes. It was a heavy, stifling red, as though the light were shining through bowls of blood. At the far end stood a huge, square bed, with quilts red like the rest, and on it a girl was lying, dressed in a frock of red velvet. At the sight of me she shrank away and tried to hide her knees under the short dress.

'I had halted by the door. "Come here, my chicken," I called to her.

'She gave a whimper of fright. With a bound I was beside the bed; she tried to elude me, but I seized her by the throat— like this, do you see?—tight! She struggled, she began to cry out for mercy, but I held her fast, forcing back her head and staring down into her face. She was twenty years old, perhaps; her face was the broad, dull face of a stupid child, but it was coated with paint and powder, and her blue, stupid eyes, shining in the red light, wore that shocked, distorted look that one sees nowhere save in the eyes of these women. She was some peasant girl, doubtless, whom her parents had sold into slavery.

'Without another word I pulled her off the bed and threw her on to the floor. And then I fell upon her like a tiger! Ah, the joy, the incomparable rapture of that time! There, *messieurs et dames*, is what I would expound to you; *voilà l'amour*! There is the true love, there is the only thing in the world worth striving for; there is the thing beside which all your arts and ideals, all your philosophies and creeds, all your fine words and high attitudes, are as pale and profitless as ashes. When one has experienced love— the true love—what is there in the world that seems more than a mere ghost of joy?

'More and more savagely I renewed the attack. Again and again the girl tried to escape; she cried out for mercy anew, but I laughed at her.

'"Mercy!" I said, "do you suppose I have come here to show mercy? Do you suppose I have paid a thousand francs for that?" I swear to you, *messieurs et dames*, that if it were not for that accursed law that robs us of our liberty, I would have murdered her at that moment.

'Ah, how she screamed, with what bitter cries of agony.

But there was no one to hear them; down there under the streets of Paris we were as secure as at the heart of a pyramid. Tears streamed down the girl's face, washing away the powder in long, dirty smears. Ah, that irrecoverable time! You, *messieurs et dames*, you who have not cultivated the finer sensibilities of love, for you such pleasure is almost beyond conception. And I too, now that my youth is gone—ah, youth!—shall never again see life so beautiful as that. It is finished.

'Ah yes, it is gone—gone for ever. Ah, the poverty, the shortness, the disappointment of human joy! For in reality— *car en réalité*, what is the duration of the supreme moment of love. It is nothing, an instant, a second perhaps. A second of ecstasy, and after that—dust, ashes, nothingness.

'And so, just for one instant, I captured the supreme happiness, the highest and most refined emotion to which human beings can attain. And in the same moment it was finished, and I was left—to what? All my savagery, my passion, were scattered like the petals of a rose. I was left cold and languid, full of vain regrets; in my revulsion I even felt a kind of pity for the weeping girl on the floor. Is it not nauseous, that we should be the prey of such mean emotions? I did not look at the girl again; my sole thought was to get away. I hastened up the steps of the vault and out into the street. It was dark and bitterly cold, the streets were empty, the stones echoed under my heels with a hollow, lonely ring. All my money was gone, I had not even the price of a taxi fare. I walked back alone to my cold, solitary room.

'But there, *messieurs et dames*, that is what I promised to expound to you. That is Love. That was the happiest day of my life.'

He was a curious specimen, Charlie. I describe him, just to show what diverse characters could be found flourishing in the Coq d'Or quarter.

III

I lived in the Coq d'Or quarter for about a year and a half. One day, in summer, I found that I had just four hundred and fifty francs left, and beyond this nothing but thirty-six francs a week, which I earned by giving English lessons. Hitherto I had not thought about the future, but I now realized that I must do something at once. I decided to start looking for a job, and—very luckily, as it turned out—I took the precaution of paying two hundred francs for a month's rent in advance. With the other two hundred and fifty francs, besides the English lessons, I could live a month, and in a month I should probably find work. I aimed at becoming a guide to one of the tourist companies, or perhaps an interpreter. However, a piece of bad luck prevented this.

One day there turned up at the hotel a young Italian who called himself a compositor. He was rather an ambiguous person, for he wore side whiskers, which are the mark either of an apache or an intellectual, and nobody was quite certain in which class to put him. Madame F. did not like the look of him, and made him pay a week's rent in advance. The Italian paid the rent and stayed six nights at the hotel. During this time he managed to prepare some duplicate keys, and on the last night he robbed a dozen rooms, including mine.

Luckily, he did not find the money that was in my pockets, so I was not left penniless. I was left with just forty-seven francs—that is, seven and tenpence.

This put an end to my plans of looking for work. I had now got to live at the rate of about six francs a day, and from the start it was too difficult to leave much thought for anything else. It was now that my experiences of poverty began—for six francs a day, if not actual poverty, is on the fringe of it. Six francs is a shilling, and you can live on a shilling a day in Paris if you know how. But it is a complicated business.

It is altogether curious, your first contact with poverty. You have thought so much about poverty—it is the thing you have feared all your life, the thing you knew would happen to you sooner or later; and it is all so utterly and prosaically different. You thought it would be quite simple; it is extraordinarily complicated. You thought it would be terrible; it is merely squalid and boring. It is the peculiar *lowness* of poverty that you discover first; the shifts that it puts you to, the complicated meanness, the crust-wiping.

You discover, for instance, the secrecy attaching to poverty. At a sudden stroke you have been reduced to an income of six francs a day. But of course you dare not admit it—you have got to pretend that you are living quite as usual. From the start it tangles you in a net of lies, and even with the lies you can hardly manage it. You stop sending clothes to the laundry, and the laundress catches you in the street and asks you why; you mumble something, and she, thinking you are sending the clothes elsewhere, is your enemy for life. The tobacconist keeps asking why you have cut down your smoking. There are letters you want to answer, and cannot, because stamps are too expensive. And then there are your meals—meals are the worst difficulty of all. Every day at meal-times you go out, ostensibly to a restaurant, and loaf an hour in the Luxembourg Gardens, watching the pigeons. Afterwards you smuggle your food home in your pockets. Your food is bread and margarine, or bread and wine, and even the nature of the food is governed by lies. You have to buy rye bread instead of household bread, because the rye loaves, though dearer, are round and can be smuggled in your pockets. This wastes you a franc a day. Sometimes, to keep up appearances, you have to spend sixty centimes on a drink, and go correspondingly short of food. Your linen gets filthy, and you run out of soap and razor-blades. Your hair wants cutting, and you try to cut it yourself, with such fearful results that you have to go to the barber after all, and spend the equivalent of a day's food. All day you are telling lies, and expensive lies.

You discover the extreme precariousness of your six francs a day. Mean disasters happen and rob you of food. You have spent your last eighty centimes on half a litre of milk, and are boiling it over the spirit lamp. While it boils a bug runs down your forearm; you give the bug a flick with your nail, and it falls, plop! straight into the milk. There is nothing for it but to throw the milk away and go foodless.

You go to the baker's to buy a pound of bread, and you wait while the girl cuts a pound for another customer. She is clumsy, and cuts more than a pound. '*Pardon, monsieur,*' she says, 'I suppose you don't mind paying two sous extra?' Bread is a franc a pound, and you have exactly a franc. When you think that you too might be asked to pay two sous extra, and would have to confess that you could not, you bolt in panic. It is hours before you dare venture into a baker's shop again.

You go to the greengrocer's to spend a franc on a kilogram of potatoes. But one of the pieces that make up the franc is a Belgian piece, and the shopman refuses it. You slink out of the shop, and can never go there again.

You have strayed into a respectable quarter, and you see a prosperous friend coming. To avoid him you dodge into the nearest café. Once in the café you must buy something, so you spend your last fifty centimes on a glass of black coffee with a dead fly in it. Once could multiply these disasters by the hundred. They are part of the process of being hard up.

You discover what it is like to be hungry. With bread and margarine in your belly, you go out and look into the shop windows. Everywhere there is food insulting you in huge, wasteful piles; whole dead pigs, baskets of hot loaves, great yellow blocks of butter, strings of sausages, mountains of potatoes, vast Gruyère cheeses like grindstones. A snivelling self-pity comes over you at the sight of so much food. You plan to grab a loaf and run, swallowing it before they catch you; and you refrain, from pure funk.

You discover the boredom which is inseparable from poverty; the times when you have nothing to do and, being underfed, can interest yourself in nothing. For half a day at a time you lie on your bed, feeling like the *jeune squelette* in Baudelaire's poem. Only food could rouse you. You discover that a man who has gone even a week on bread and margarine is not a man any longer, only a belly with a few accessory organs.

This—one could describe it further, but it is all in the same style—is life on six francs a day. Thousands of people in Paris live it—struggling artists and students, prostitutes when their luck is out, out-of-work people of all kinds. It is the suburbs, as it were, of poverty.

I continued in this style for about three weeks. The forty-seven francs were soon gone, and I had to do what I could on thirty-six francs a week from the English lessons. Being inexperienced, I handled the money badly, and sometimes I was a day without food. When this happened I used to sell a few of my clothes, smuggling them out of the hotel in small packets and taking them to a secondhand shop in the rue de la Montagne St Geneviève. The shopman was a red-haired Jew, an extraordinary disagreeable man, who used to fall into furious rages at the sight of a client. From his manner one would have supposed that we had done him some injury by coming to him. '*Merde!*' he used to shout, '*you* here again?

What do you think this is? A soup kitchen?' And he paid incredibly low prices. For a hat which I had bought for twenty-five shillings and scarcely worn he gave five francs; for a good pair of shoes, five francs; for shirts, a franc each. He always preferred to exchange rather than buy, and he had a trick of thrusting some useless article into one's hand and then pretending that one had accepted it. Once I saw him take a good overcoat from an old woman, put two white billiard-balls into her hand, and then push her rapidly out of the shop before she could protest. It would have been a pleasure to flatten the Jew's nose, if only one could have afforded it.

These three weeks were squalid and uncomfortable, and evidently there was worse coming, for my rent would be due before long. Nevertheless, things were not a quarter as bad as I had expected. For, when you are approaching poverty, you make one discovery which outweighs some of the others. You discover boredom and mean complications and the beginnings of hunger, but you also discover the great redeeming feature of poverty: the fact that it annihilates the future. Within certain limits, it is actually true that the less money you have, the less you worry. When you have a hundred francs in the world you are liable to the most craven panics. When you have only three francs you are quite indifferent; for three francs will feed you till tomorrow, and you cannot think further than that. You are bored, but you are not afraid. You think vaguely, 'I shall be starving in a day or two—shocking, isn't it?' And then the mind wanders to other topics. A bread and margarine diet does, to some extent, provide its own anodyne.

And there is another feeling that is a great consolation in poverty. I believe everyone who has been hard up has experienced it. It is a feeling of relief, almost of pleasure, at knowing yourself at last genuinely down and out. You have talked so often of going to the dogs—and well, here are the dogs, and you have reached them, and you can stand it. It takes off a lot of anxiety,

IV

One day my English lessons ceased abruptly. The weather was getting hot and one of my pupils, feeling too lazy to go on with his lessons, dismissed me. The other disappeared from his lodgings without notice, owing me twelve francs. I was left with only thirty centimes and no tobacco. For a day and a half I had nothing to eat or smoke, and then, too hungry to put it off any longer, I packed my remaining clothes into my suitcase and took them to the pawnshop. This put an end to all pretence of being in funds, for I could not take my clothes out of the hotel without asking Madame F.'s leave. I remember, however, how surprised she was at my asking her instead of removing the clothes on the sly, shooting the moon being a common trick in our quarter.

It was the first time that I had been in a French pawn-shop. One went through grandiose stone portals (marked, of course, '*Liberté, Égalité, Fraternité*'—they write that even over the police stations in France) into a large, bare room like a school classroom, with a counter and rows of benches. Forty or fifty people were waiting. One handed one's pledge over the counter and sat down. Presently, when the clerk had assessed its value he would call out, '*Numéro* such and such, will you take fifty francs?' Sometimes it was only fifteen francs, or ten, or five—whatever it was, the whole room knew it. As I came in the clerk called with an air of offence, '*Numéro* 83—here!' and gave a little whistle and a beckon, as though calling a dog. *Numéro* 83 stepped to the counter; he was an old bearded man, with an overcoat buttoned up at the neck and frayed trouser-ends. Without a word the clerk shot the bundle across the counter—evidently it was worth nothing. It fell to the ground and came open, displaying four pairs of men's woollen pants. No one could help laughing. Poor *Numéro* 83 gathered up his pants and shambled out, muttering to himself.

The clothes I was pawning, together with the suitcase, had cost over twenty pounds, and were in good condition. I thought they must be worth ten pounds, and a quarter of this (one expects quarter value at a pawnshop) was two hundred and fifty or three hundred francs. I waited without anxiety, expecting two hundred francs at the worst.

At last the clerk called my number: '*Numéro* 97!'

'Yes,' I said, standing up.

'Seventy francs?'

Seventy francs for ten pounds' worth of clothes! But it was no use arguing; I had seen someone else attempt to argue, and the clerk had instantly refused the pledge. I took the money and the pawnticket and walked out. I had now no clothes except what I stood up in—the coat badly out at the elbow—an overcoat, moderately pawnable, and one spare shirt. Afterwards, when it was too late, I learned that it was wiser to go to a pawnshop in the afternoon. The clerks are French, and, like most French people, are in a bad temper till they have eaten their lunch.

When I got home, Madame F. was sweeping the *bistro* floor. She came up the steps to meet me. I could see in her eye that she was uneasy about my rent.

'Well,' she said, 'what did you get for your clothes? Not much, eh?'

'Two hundred francs,' I said promptly.

'*Tiens*!' she said, surprised; 'well, *that's* not bad. How expensive those English clothes must be!'

The lie saved a lot of trouble, and, strangely enough, it came true. A few days later I did receive exactly two hundred francs due to me for a newspaper article, and, though it hurt to do it, I at once paid every penny of it in rent. So, though I came near to starving in the following weeks, I was hardly ever without a roof.

It was now absolutely necessary to find work, and I remembered a friend of mine, a Russian waiter named Boris, who might be able to help me. I had first met him in the public ward of a hospital, where he was being treated for arthritis in the left leg. He had told me to come to him if I were ever in difficulties.

I must say something about Boris, for he was a curious character and my close friend for a long time. He was a big, soldierly man of about thirty-five, and had been good looking, but since his illness he had grown immensely fat from lying in bed. Like most Russian refugees, he had had an adventurous life. His parents, killed in the Revolution, had been rich people, and he had served through the war in the Second Siberian Rifles, which, according to him, was the best regiment in the Russian Army. After the war he had first worked in a brush factory, then as a porter at Les Halles, then had become a dishwasher, and had finally worked his way up to be a waiter. When he fell ill he was at the Hôtel Scribe, and taking a hundred francs a day in tips. His ambition was to become a *maître d'hôtel*, save fifty thousand francs, and set up a small, select restaurant on the Right Bank.

Boris always talked of the war as the happiest time of his life. War and soldiering were his passion; he had read innumerable books of strategy and military history, and could tell you all about the theories of Napoleon, Kutuzof, Clausewitz, Moltke and Foch. Anything to do with soldiers pleased him. His favourite café was the Closerie des Lilas in Montparnasse, simply because the statue of Marshal Ney stands outside it. Later on, Boris and I sometimes went to the rue du Commerce together. If we went by Métro, Boris always got out at Cambronne station instead of Commerce, though Commerce was nearer; he liked the association with General Cambronne, who was called on to surrender at Waterloo, and answered simply, '*Merde!*'

The only things left to Boris by the Revolution were his medals and some photographs of his old regiment; he had kept these when everything else went to the pawnshop. Almost every day he would spread the photographs out on the bed and talk about them:

'*Voilà, mon ami.* There you see me at the head of my company. Fine big men, eh? Not like these little rats of Frenchmen. A captain at twenty—not bad, eh? Yes, a captain in the Second Siberian Rifles; and my father was a colonel.

'*Ah, mais, mon ami*, the ups and downs of life! A captain in the Russian Army, and then, piff! the Revolution—every penny gone. In 1916 I stayed a week at the Hôtel Édouard Sept; in 1920 I was trying for a job as night watchman there. I have been night watchman, cellarman, floor scrubber, dishwasher, porter, lavatory attendant. I have tipped waiters, and I have been tipped by waiters.

'Ah, but I have known what it is to live like a gentleman, *mon ami.* I do not say it to boast, but the other day I was trying to compute how many mistresses I have had in my life, and I made it out to be over two hundred. Yes, at least two hundred . . . Ah, well, *ça reviendra.* Victory is to him who fights the longest. Courage!' etc. etc.

Boris had a queer, changeable nature. He always wished himself back in the army, but he had also been a waiter long enough to acquire the waiter's outlook. Though he had never saved more than a few thousand francs, he took it for granted that in the end he would be able to set up his own restaurant and grow rich. All waiters, I afterwards found, talk and think of this; it is what reconciles them to being waiters. Boris used to talk interestingly about hotel life:

'Waiting is a gamble,' he used to say; 'you may die poor, you may make your fortune in a year. You are not paid wages, you depend on tips—ten per cent of the bill, and a commission from the wine companies on champagne corks. Sometimes the tips are enormous. The barman at Maxim's, for instance, makes five hundred francs a day. More than five hundred, in the season . . . I have made two hundred francs a day myself. It was at a hotel in Biarritz, in the season. The whole staff, from the manager down to the *plongeurs*, was working twenty-one hours a day. Twenty-one hours' work and two and a half hours in bed, for a month on end. Still, it was worth it, at two hundred francs a day.

'You never know when a stroke of luck is coming. Once when I was at the Hôtel Royal an American customer sent for me before dinner and ordered twenty-four brandy cocktails. I brought them all together on a tray, in twenty-four glasses. "Now, *garçon*," said the customer (he was drunk), "I'll drink twelve and you'll drink twelve, and if you can walk to the door afterwards you get a hundred francs." I walked to the door, and he gave me a hundred francs. And every night for six days he did the same thing; twelve brandy cocktails, then a hundred francs. A few months later I heard he had been extradited by the American Government—embezzlement. There is something fine, do you not think, about these Americans?'

I liked Boris, and we had interesting times together, playing chess and talking about war and hotels. Boris used often to suggest that I should become a waiter. 'The life would suit you,' he used to say; 'when you are in work, with a hundred francs a day and a nice mistress, it's not bad. You say you go in for writing. Writing is bosh. There is only one way to make money at writing, and that is to marry a publisher's daughter. But you would make a good waiter if you shaved that moustache off. You are tall and you speak English—those are the chief things a waiter needs. Wait till I can bend this accursed leg, *mon ami*. And then, if you are ever out of a job, come to me.'

Now that I was short of my rent, and getting hungry, I remembered Boris's promise, and decided to look him up at once. I did not hope to become a waiter so easily as he had promised, but of course I knew how to scrub dishes, and no doubt he could get me a job in the kitchen. He had said that dishwashing jobs were to be had for the asking during the summer. It was a great relief to remember that I had after all one influential friend to fall back on.

V

A short time before, Boris had given me an address in the rue du Marché des Blancs Manteaux. All he had said in his letter was that 'things were not marching too badly', and I assumed that he was back at the Hôtel Scribe, touching his hundred francs a day. I was full of hope, and wondered why I had been fool enough not to go to Boris before. I saw myself in a cosy restaurant, with jolly cooks singing love-songs as they broke eggs into the pan, and five solid meals a day. I even squandered two francs fifty on a packet of Gaulois Bleu, in anticipation of my wages.

In the morning I walked down to the rue du Marché des Blancs Manteaux; with a shock, I found it a slummy back street as bad as my own. Boris's hotel was the dirtiest hotel in the street. From its dark doorway there came out a vile, sour odour, a mixture of slops and synthetic soup—it was Bouillon Zip, twenty-five centimes a packet. A misgiving came over me. People who drink Bouillon Zip are starving, or near it. Could Boris possibly be earning a hundred francs a day? A surly *patron*, sitting in the office, said to me, Yes, the Russian was at home—in the attic. I went up six flights of narrow, winding stairs, the Bouillon Zip growing stronger as one got higher. Boris did not answer when I knocked at his door, so I opened it and went in.

The room was an attic, ten feet square, lighted only by a skylight, its sole furniture a narrow iron bedstead, a chair, and a washhand-stand with one game leg. A long S-shaped chain of bugs marched slowly across the wall above the bed. Boris was lying asleep, naked, his large belly making a mound under the grimy sheet. His chest was spotted with insect bites. As I came in he woke up, rubbed his eyes, and groaned deeply.

'Name of Jesus Christ!' he exclaimed, 'oh, name of Jesus Christ, my back! Curse it, I believe my back is broken!'

'What's the matter?' I exclaimed.

'My back is broken, that is all. I have spent the night on the floor. Oh, name of Jesus Christ! If you knew what my back feels like!'

'My dear Boris, are you ill?'

'Not ill, only starving—yes, starving to death if this goes on much longer. Besides sleeping on the floor, I have lived on two francs a day for weeks past. It is fearful. You have come at a bad moment, *mon ami.*'

It did not seem much use to ask whether Boris still had his job at the Hôtel Scribe. I hurried downstairs and bought a loaf of bread. Boris threw himself on the bread and ate half of it, after which he felt better, sat up in bed, and told me what was the matter with him. He had failed to get a job after leaving the hospital, because he was still very lame, and he had spent all his money and pawned everything, and finally starved for several days. He had slept a week on the quay under the Pont d'Austerlitz, among some empty wine barrels. For the past fortnight he had been living in this room, together with a Jew, a mechanic. It appeared (there was some complicated explanation) that the Jew owed Boris three hundred francs, and was repaying this by letting him sleep on the floor and allowing him two francs a day for food. Two francs would buy a bowl of coffee and three rolls. The Jew went to work at seven in the mornings, and after that Boris would leave his sleeping-place (it was beneath the skylight, which let in the rain) and get into the bed. He could not sleep much even there owing to the bugs, but it rested his back after the floor.

It was a great disappointment, when I had come to Boris for help, to find him even worse off than myself. I explained that I had only about sixty francs left and must get a job immediately. By this time, however, Boris had eaten the rest of the bread and was feeling cheerful and talkative. He said carelessly:

'Good heavens, what are you worrying about? Sixty francs—why, it's a fortune! Please hand me that shoe, *mon ami*. I'm going to smash some of those bugs if they come within reach.'

'But do you think there's any chance of getting a job?'

'Chance? It's a certainty. In fact, I have got something already. There is a new Russian restaurant which is to open in a few days in the rue du Commerce. It is *une chose entendue* that I am to be *maître d'hôtel*. I can easily get you a job in the kitchen. Five hundred francs a month and your food—tips, too, if you are lucky.'

'But in the meantime? I've got to pay my rent before long.'

'Oh, we shall find something. I have got a few cards up my sleeve. There are people who owe me money, for instance—Paris is full of them. One of them is bound to pay up before long. Then think of all the women who have been my mistress! A woman never forgets, you know—I have only to ask and they will help me. Besides, the Jew tells me he is going to steal some magnetos from the garage where he works, and he will pay us five francs a day to clean them before he sells them. That alone would keep us. Never worry, *mon ami*. Nothing is easier to get than money.'

'Well, let's go out now and look for a job.'

'Presently, *mon ami*. We shan't starve, don't you fear. This is only the fortune of war—I've been in a worse hole scores of times. It's only a question of persisting. Remember Foch's maxim: "*Attaquez! Attaquez! Attaquez!*"'

It was midday before Boris decided to get up. All the clothes he now had left were one suit, with one shirt, collar and tie, a pair of shoes almost worn out, and a pair of socks all holes. He had also an overcoat which was to be pawned in the last extremity. He had a suitcase, a wretched twenty-franc cardboard thing, but very important, because the *patron* of the hotel believed that it was full of clothes—without that, he would probably have turned Boris out of doors. What it actually contained were the medals and photographs, various odds and ends, and huge bundles of love-letters. In spite of all this Boris managed to keep a fairly smart appearance. He shaved without soap and with a razor-blade two months old, tied his tie so that the holes did not show, and carefully stuffed the soles of his shoes with newspaper. Finally, when he was dressed, he produced an ink-bottle and inked the skin of his ankles where it showed through his socks. You would never have thought, when it was finished, that he had recently been sleeping under the Seine bridges.

We went to a small café off the rue de Rivoli, a well-known rendezvous of hotel managers and employees. At the back was a dark, cave-like room where all kinds of hotel workers were sitting—smart young waiters, others not so smart and clearly hungry, fat pink cooks, greasy dishwashers, battered old scrubbing-women. Everyone had an untouched glass of black coffee in front of him. The place was, in effect, an employment bureau, and the money spent on drinks was the *patron's* commission. Sometimes a stout, important-looking man, obviously a restaurateur, would come in and speak to the barman, and the barman would call to one of the people at the back of the café. But he never called to Boris or me, and we left after two hours, as the etiquette was that you could only stay two hours for one drink. We learned afterwards, when it was too late, that the dodge was to bribe the barman; if you could afford twenty francs he would generally get you a job.

We went to the Hôtel Scribe and waited an hour on the pavement, hoping that the manager would come out, but he never did. Then we dragged ourselves down to the rue du Commerce, only to find that the new restaurant, which was being redecorated, was shut up and the *patron* away. It was now night. We had walked fourteen kilometres over pavement, and we were so tired that we had to waste one franc fifty on going home by Métro. Walking was agony to Boris with his game leg, and his optimism wore thinner and thinner as the day went on. When he got out of the Métro at the Place d'Italie he was in despair. He began to say that it was no use looking for work—there was nothing for it but to try crime.

'Sooner rob than starve, *mon ami*. I have often planned it. A fat, rich American—some dark corner down Montparnasse way—a cobblestone in a stocking—bang! And then go through his pockets and bolt. It is feasible, do you not think? I would not flinch—I have been a soldier, remember.'

He decided against the plan in the end, because we were both foreigners and easily recognized.

When we had got back to my room we spent another one franc fifty on bread and chocolate. Boris devoured his share, and at once cheered up like magic; food seemed to act on his system as rapidly as a cocktail. He took out a pencil and began making a list of the people who would probably give us jobs. There were dozens of them, he said.

'Tomorrow we shall find something, *mon ami*, I know it in my bones. The luck always changes. Besides, we both have brains—a man with brains can't starve.

'What things a man can do with brains! Brains will make

money out of anything. I had a friend once, a Pole, a real man of genius; and what do you think he used to do? He would buy a gold ring and pawn it for fifteen francs. Then—you know how carelessly the clerks fill up the tickets—where the clerk had written "*en or*" he would add "*et diamants*" and he would change "fifteen francs" to "fifteen thousand". Neat, eh? Then, you see, he could borrow a thousand francs on the security of the ticket. That is what I mean by brains . . .'

For the rest of the evening Boris was in a hopeful mood, talking of the times we should have together when we were waiters together at Nice or Biarritz, with smart rooms and enough money to set up mistresses. He was too tired to walk the three kilometres back to his hotel, and slept the night on the floor of my room, with his coat rolled round his shoes for a pillow.

VI

We again failed to find work the next day, and it was three weeks before the luck changed. My two hundred francs saved me from trouble about the rent, but everything else went as badly as possible. Day after day Boris and I went up and down Paris, drifting at two miles an hour through the crowds, bored and hungry, and finding nothing. One day, I remember, we crossed the Seine eleven times. We loitered for hours outside service doorways, and when the manager came out we would go up to him ingratiatingly, cap in hand. We always got the same answer: they did not want a lame man, nor a man without experience. Once we were very nearly engaged. While we spoke to the manager Boris stood straight upright, not supporting himself with his stick, and the manager did not see that he was lame. 'Yes,' he said, 'we want two men in the cellars. Perhaps you would do. Come inside.' Then Boris moved, the game was up. 'Ah,' said the manager, 'you limp. *Malheureusement—*'

We enrolled our names at agencies and answered advertisements, but walking everywhere made us slow, and we seemed to miss every job by half an hour. Once we very nearly got a job swabbing out railway trucks, but at the last moment they rejected us in favour of Frenchmen. Once we answered an advertisement calling for hands at a circus. You had to shift benches and clean up litter, and, during the performance, stand on two tubs and let a lion jump through your legs. When we got to the place, an hour before the time named, we found a queue of fifty men already waiting. There is some attraction in lions, evidently.

Once an agency to which I had applied months earlier sent me a *petit bleu*, telling me of an Italian gentleman who wanted English lessons. The *petit bleu* said 'Come at once' and promised twenty francs an hour. Boris and I were in despair. Here was a splendid chance, and I could not take it, for it was impossible to go to the agency with my coat out at the elbow. Then it occurred to us that I could wear Boris's coat—it did not match my trousers, but the trousers were grey and might pass for flannel at a short distance. The coat was so much too big for me that I had to wear it unbuttoned and keep one hand in my pocket. I hurried out, and wasted seventy-five centimes on a bus fare to get to the agency. When I got there I found that the Italian had changed his mind and left Paris.

Once Boris suggested that I should go to Les Halles and try for a job as a porter. I arrived at half-past four in the morning, when the work was getting into its swing. Seeing a short, fat man in a bowler hat directing some porters, I went up to him and asked for work. Before answering he seized my right hand and felt the palm.

'You are strong, eh?' he said.

'Very strong,' I said untruly.

'*Bien.* Let me see you lift that crate.'

It was a huge wicker basket full of potatoes. I took hold of it, and found that, so far from lifting it, I could not even move it. The man in the bowler hat watched me, then shrugged his shoulders and turned away. I made off. When I had gone some distance I looked back and saw *four* men lifting the basket on to a cart. It weighed three hundredweight, possibly. The man had seen that I was no use, and taken this way of getting rid of me.

Sometimes in his hopeful moments Boris spent fifty centimes on a stamp and wrote to one of his ex-mistresses, asking for money. Only one of them ever replied. It was a woman who, besides having been his mistress, owed him two hundred francs. When Boris saw the letter waiting and recognized the handwriting, he was wild with hope. We seized the letter and rushed up to Boris's room to read it, like a child with stolen sweets. Boris read the letter, then handed it silently to me. It ran:

My Little Cherished Wolf,

With what delight did I open thy charming letter, reminding me of the days of our perfect love, and of the so dear kisses which I have received from thy lips. Such memories linger for ever in the heart, like the perfume of a flower that is dead.

As to thy request for two hundred francs, alas! it is impossible. Thou dost not know, my dear one, how I am desolated to hear of thy embarrassments. But what wouldst thou? In this life which is so sad, trouble comes to everyone. I too have had my share. My little sister has been ill (ah, the poor little one, how she suffered!) and we are obliged to pay I know not what to the doctor. All our money is gone and we are passing, I assure thee, very difficult days.

Courage, my little wolf, always the courage! Remember that the bad days are not for ever, and the trouble which seems so terrible will disappear at last.

Rest assured, my dear one, that I will remember thee always. And receive the most sincere embraces of her who has never ceased to love thee, thy

Yvonne

This letter disappointed Boris so much that he went straight to bed and would not look for work again that day.

My sixty francs lasted about a fortnight. I had given up the pretence of going out to restaurants, and we used to eat in my room, one of us sitting on the bed and the other on the chair. Boris would contribute his two francs and I three or four francs, and we would buy bread, potatoes, milk and cheese, and make soup over my spirit lamp. We had a saucepan and a coffee-bowl and one spoon; every day there was a polite squabble as to who should eat out of the saucepan and who out of the coffee-bowl (the saucepan held more), and every day, to my secret anger, Boris gave in first and had the saucepan. Sometimes we had more bread in the evening, sometimes not. Our linen was getting filthy, and it was three weeks since I had had a bath; Boris, so he said, had not had a bath for months. It was tobacco that made everything tolerable. We had plenty of tobacco, for some time before Boris had met a soldier (the soldiers are given their tobacco free) and bought twenty or thirty packets at fifty centimes each.

All this was far worse for Boris than for me. The walking and sleeping on the floor kept his leg and back in constant pain, and with his vast Russian appetite he suffered torments of hunger, though he never seemed to grow thinner. On the whole he was surprisingly gay, and he had vast capacities for hope. He used to say seriously that he had a patron saint who watched over him, and when things were very bad he would search the gutter for money, saying that the saint often dropped a two-franc piece there. One day we were waiting in the rue Royale; there was a Russian restaurant near by, and we were going to ask for a job there. Suddenly, Boris made up his mind to go into the Madeleine and burn a fifty-centime candle to his *patron* saint. Then, coming out, he said that he would be on the safe side, and solemnly put a match to a fifty-centime stamp, as a sacrifice to the immortal gods.

Perhaps the gods and the saints did not get on together; at any rate, we missed the job.

On some mornings Boris collapsed in the most utter despair. He would lie in bed almost weeping, cursing the Jew with whom he lived. Of late the Jew had become restive about paying the daily two francs, and, what was worse, had begun putting on intolerable airs of patronage. Boris said that I, as an Englishman, could not conceive what torture it was to a Russian of family to be at the mercy of a Jew.

'A Jew, *mon ami*, a veritable Jew! And he hasn't even the decency to be ashamed of it. To think that I, a captain in the Russian Army—have I ever told you, *mon ami*, that I was a captain in the Second Siberian Rifles? Yes, a captain, and my father was a colonel. And here I am, eating the bread of a Jew. A Jew . . .

'I will tell you what Jews are like. Once, in the early months of the war, we were on the march, and we had halted at a village for the night. A horrible old Jew, with a red beard like Judas Iscariot, came sneaking up to my billet. I asked him what he wanted. "Your honour," he said, "I have brought a girl for you, a beautiful young girl only seventeen. It will only be fifty francs." "Thank you," I said, "you can take her away again. I don't want to catch any diseases." "Diseases!" cried the Jew, "*mais, monsieur le capitaine*, there's no fear of that. It's my own daughter!" That is the Jewish national character for you.

'Have I ever told you, *mon ami*, that in the old Russian Army it was considered bad form to spit on a Jew? Yes, we thought a Russian officer's spittle was too precious to be wasted on Jews . . .' etc. etc.

On these days Boris usually declared himself too ill to go out and look for work. He would lie till evening in the greyish, verminous sheets, smoking and reading old newspapers. Sometimes we played chess. We had no board, but we wrote down the moves on a piece of paper, and afterwards we made a board from the side of a packing-case, and a set of men from buttons, Belgian coins and the like. Boris, like many Russians, had a passion for chess. It was a saying of his that the rules of chess are the same as the rules of love and war, and that if you can win at one you can win at the others. But he also said that if you have a chessboard you do not mind being hungry, which was certainly not true in my case.

VII

My money oozed away—to eight francs, to four francs, to one franc, to twenty-five centimes; and twenty-five centimes is useless, for it will buy nothing except a newspaper. We went several days on dry bread, and then I was two and a half days with nothing to eat whatever. This was an ugly experience. There are people who do fasting cures of three weeks or more, and they say that fasting is quite pleasant after the fourth day; I do not know, never having gone beyond the third day. Probably it seems different when one is doing it voluntarily and is not underfed at the start.

The first day, too inert to look for work, I borrowed a rod and went fishing in the Seine, baiting with bluebottles. I hoped to catch enough for a meal, but of course I did not. The Seine is full of dace, but they grew cunning during the siege of Paris, and none of them has been caught since, except in nets. On the second day I thought of pawning my overcoat, but it seemed too far to walk to the pawnshop, and I spent the day in bed, reading the *Memoirs of Sherlock Holmes*. It was all that I felt equal to, without food. Hunger reduces one to an utterly spineless, brainless condition, more like the after-effects of influenza than anything else. It is as though one had been turned into a jellyfish, or as though all one's blood had been pumped out and luke-warm water substituted. Complete inertia is my chief memory of hunger; that, and being obliged to spit very frequently, and the spittle being curiously white and flocculent, like cuckoo-spit. I do not know the reason for this, but everyone who has gone hungry several days has noticed it.

On the third morning I felt very much better. I realized that I must do something at once, and I decided to go and ask Boris to let me share his two francs, at any rate for a day or two. When I arrived I found Boris in bed, and furiously angry. As soon as I came in he burst out, almost choking:

'He has taken it back, the dirty thief! He has taken it back!'

'Who's taken what?' I said.

'The Jew! Taken my two francs, the dog, the thief! He robbed me in my sleep!'

It appeared that on the previous night the Jew had flatly refused to pay the daily two francs. They had argued and argued, and at last the Jew had consented to hand over the money; he had done it, Boris said, in the most offensive manner, making a little speech about how kind he was, and extorting abject gratitude. And then in the morning he had stolen the money back before Boris was awake.

This was a blow. I was horribly disappointed, for I had allowed my belly to expect food, a great mistake when one is hungry. However, rather to my surprise, Boris was far from despairing. He sat up in bed, lighted his pipe and reviewed the situation.

'Now listen, *mon ami*, this is a tight corner. We have only twenty-five centimes between us, and I don't suppose the Jew will ever pay my two francs again. In any case his behaviour is becoming intolerable. Will you believe it, the other night he had the indecency to bring a woman in here, while I was there on the floor. The low animal! And I have a worse thing to tell you. The Jew intends clearing out of here. He owes a week's rent, and his idea is to avoid paying that and give me the slip at the same time. If the Jew shoots the moon I shall be left without a roof, and the *patron* will take my suitcase in lieu of rent, curse him! We have got to make a vigorous move.'

'All right. But what can we do? It seems to me that the only thing is to pawn our overcoats and get some food.'

'We'll do that, of course, but I must get my possessions out of this house first. To think of my photographs being seized! Well, my plan is ready. I'm going to forestall the Jew and shoot the moon myself. *F— le camp*—retreat, you understand. I think that is the correct move, eh?'

'But, my dear Boris, how can you, in daytime? You're bound to be caught.'

'Ah well, it will need strategy, of course. Our *patron* is on the watch for people slipping out without paying their rent; he's been had that way before. He and his wife take it in turns all day to sit in the office—what misers, these Frenchmen! But I have thought of a way to do it, if you will help.'

I did not feel in a very helpful mood, but I asked Boris what his plan was. He explained it carefully.

'Now listen. We must start by pawning our overcoats. First go back to your room and fetch your overcoat, then come back here and fetch mine, and smuggle it out under cover of yours. Take them to the pawnshop in the rue des Francs Bourgeois. You ought to get twenty francs for the two, with luck. Then go down to the Seine bank and fill your pockets with stones, and bring them back and put them in my suitcase. You see the idea? I shall wrap as many of my things as I can carry in a newspaper, and go down and ask the *patron* the way to the nearest laundry. I shall be very brazen and casual, you understand, and of course the *patron* will think the bundle is nothing but dirty linen. Or, if he does suspect anything, he will do what he always does, the mean sneak; he will go up to my room and feel the weight of my suitcase. And when he feels the weight of stones he will think it is still full. Strategy, eh? Then afterwards I can come back and carry my other things out in my pockets.'

'But what about the suitcase?'

'Oh, that? We shall have to abandon it. The miserable thing only cost about twenty francs. Besides, one always abandons something in a retreat. Look at Napoleon at the Beresina! He abandoned his whole army.'

Boris was so pleased with this scheme (he called it *une ruse de guerre*) that he almost forgot being hungry. Its main weakness—that he would have nowhere to sleep after shooting the moon—he ignored.

At first the *ruse de guerre* worked well. I went home and fetched my overcoat (that made already nine kilometres, on an empty belly) and smuggled Boris's coat out successfully. Then a hitch occurred. The receiver at the pawnshop, a nasty, sour-faced, interfering, little man—a typical French official—refused the coats on the ground that they were not wrapped up in anything. He said that they must be put either in a valise or a cardboard box. This spoiled everything, for we had no box of any kind, and with only twenty-five centimes between us we could not buy one.

I went back and told Boris the bad news. '*Merde!*' he said, 'that makes it awkward. Well, no matter, there is always a way. We'll put the overcoats in my suitcase.'

'But how are we to get the suitcase past the *patron*? He's sitting almost in the door of the office. It's impossible!'

'How easily you despair, *mon ami*! Where is that English obstinacy that I have read of? Courage! We'll manage it.'

Boris thought for a little while, and then produced another cunning plan. The essential difficulty was to hold the *patron's* attention for perhaps five seconds, while we could slip past with the suitcase. But, as it happened, the *patron* had just one weak spot—that he was interested in *Le Sport*, and was ready to talk if you approached him on this subject. Boris read an article about bicycle races in an old copy of the *Petit Parisien*, and then, when he had reconnoitred the stairs, went down and managed to set the *patron* talking. Meanwhile, I waited at the foot of the stairs, with the overcoats under one arm and the suitcase under the other. Boris was to give a cough when he thought the moment favourable. I waited trembling, for at any moment the *patron's* wife might come out of the door opposite the office, and then the game was up. However, presently Boris coughed. I sneaked rapidly past the office and out into the street, rejoicing that my shoes did not creak. The plan might have failed if Boris had been thinner, for his big shoulders blocked the doorway of the office. His nerve was splendid, too; he went on laughing and talking in the most casual way, and so loud that he quite covered any noise I made. When I was well away he came and joined me round the corner, and we bolted.

And then, after all our trouble, the receiver at the pawn-shop again refused the overcoats. He told me (one could see his French soul revelling in the pedantry of it) that I had not sufficient papers of identification; my *carte d'identité* was not enough, and I must show a passport or addressed envelopes. Boris had addressed envelopes by the score, but his *carte d'identité* was out of order (he never renewed it, so as to avoid the tax), so we could not pawn the overcoats in his name. All we could do was to trudge up to my room, get the necessary papers, and take the coats to the pawnshop in the Boulevard Port Royal.

I left Boris at my room and went down to the pawnshop. When I got there I found that it was shut and would not open till four in the afternoon. It was now about half-past one, and I had walked twelve kilometres and had no food for sixty hours. Fate seemed to be playing a series of extraordinarily unamusing jokes.

Then the luck changed as though by a miracle. I was walking home through the Rue Broca when suddenly, glittering on the cobbles, I saw a five-sou piece. I pounced on it, hurried home, got our other five-sou piece and bought a pound of potatoes. There was only enough alcohol in the stove to parboil them, and we had no salt, but we wolfed them, skins and all. After that we felt like new men, and sat playing chess till the pawnshop opened.

At four o'clock I went back to the pawnshop. I was not hopeful, for if I had only got seventy francs before, what could I expect for two shabby overcoats in a cardboard suitcase? Boris had said twenty francs, but I thought it would be ten francs, or even five. Worse yet, I might be refused altogether, like poor *Numéro* 83 on the previous occasion. I sat on the front bench, so as not to see people laughing when the clerk said five francs.

At last the clerk called my number: '*Numéro* 117!'

'Yes,' I said, standing up.

'Fifty francs?'

It was almost as great a shock as the seventy francs had been the time before. I believe now that the clerk had mixed my number up with someone else's, for one could not have sold the coats outright for fifty francs. I hurried home and walked into my room with my hands behind my back, saying nothing. Boris was playing with the chessboard. He looked up eagerly.

'What did you get?' he exclaimed. 'What, not twenty francs? Surely you got ten francs, anyway? *Nom de Dieu*, five francs—that is a bit too thick. *Mon ami, don't* say it was five francs. If you say it was five francs I shall really begin to think of suicide.'

I threw the fifty-franc note on to the table. Boris turned white as chalk, and then, springing up, seized my hand and gave it a grip that almost broke the bones. We ran out, bought bread and wine, a piece of meat and alcohol for the stove, and gorged.

After eating, Boris became more optimistic than I had ever known him. 'What did I tell you?' he said. 'The fortune of war! This morning with five sous, and now look at us. I have always said it, there is nothing easier to get than money. And that reminds me, I have a friend in the rue Fondary whom we might go and see. He has cheated me of four thousand francs, the thief. He is the greatest thief alive when he is sober, but it is a curious thing, he is quite honest when he is drunk. I should think he would be drunk by six in the evening. Let's go and find him. Very likely he will pay up a hundred on account. *Merde!* He might pay two hundred. *Allons-y!*'

We went to the rue Fondary and found the man, and he was drunk, but we did not get our hundred francs. As soon as he and Boris met there was a terrible altercation on the pavement. The other man declared that he did not owe Boris a penny, but that on the contrary Boris owed *him* four thousand francs, and both of them kept appealing to me for my opinion. I never understood the rights of the matter. The two argued and argued, first in the street, then in a *bistro*, then in a *prix fixe* restaurant where we went for dinner, then in another *bistro*. Finally, having called one another thieves for two hours, they went off together on a drinking bout that finished up the last sou of Boris's money.

Boris slept the night at the house of a cobbler, another Russian refugee, in the Commerce quarter. Meanwhile, I had eight francs left, and plenty of cigarettes, and was stuffed to the eyes with food and drink. It was a marvellous change for the better after two bad days.

VIII

We had now twenty-eight francs in hand, and could start looking for work once more. Boris was still sleeping, on some mysterious terms, at the house of the cobbler, and he had managed to borrow another twenty francs from a Russian friend. He had friends, mostly ex-officers like himself, here and there all over Paris. Some were waiters or dishwashers, some drove taxis, a few lived on women, some had managed to bring money away from Russia and owned garages or dancing-halls. In general, the Russian refugees in Paris are hard-working people, and have put up with their bad luck far better than one can imagine Englishmen of the same class doing. There are exceptions, of course. Boris told me of an exiled Russian duke whom he had once met, who frequented expensive restaurants. The duke would find out if there was a Russian officer among the waiters, and, after he had dined, call him in a friendly way to his table.

'Ah,' the duke would say, 'so you are an old soldier, like myself? These are bad days, eh? Well, well, the Russian soldier fears nothing. And what was your regiment?'

'The so-and-so, sir,' the waiter would answer.

'A very gallant regiment! I inspected them in 1912. By the way, I have unfortunately left my notecase at home. A

Russian officer will, I know, oblige me with three hundred francs.'

If the waiter had three hundred francs he would hand it over, and, of course, never see it again. The duke made quite a lot in this way. Probably the waiters did not mind being swindled. A duke is a duke, even in exile.

It was through one of these Russian refugees that Boris heard of something which seemed to promise money. Two days after we had pawned the overcoats, Boris said to me rather mysteriously:

'Tell me, *mon ami*, have you any political opinions?'

'No,' I said.

'Neither have I. Of course, one is always a patriot; but still—Did not Moses say something about spoiling the Egyptians? As an Englishman you will have read the Bible. What I mean is, would you object to earning money from Communists?'

'No, of course not.'

'Well, it appears that there is a Russian secret society in Paris who might do something for us. They are Communists; in fact they are agents for the Bolsheviks. They act as a friendly society, get in touch with exiled Russians, and try to get them to turn Bolshevik. My friend has joined their society, and he thinks they would help us if we went to them.'

'But what can they do for us? In any case they won't help me, as I'm not a Russian.'

'That is just the point. It seems that they are correspondents for a Moscow paper, and they want some articles on English politics. If we got to them at once they may commission you to write the articles.'

'Me? But I don't know anything about politics.'

'*Merde!* Neither do they. Who *does* know anything about politics? It's easy. All you have to do is to copy it out of the English papers. Isn't there a Paris *Daily Mail*? Copy it from that.'

'But the *Daily Mail* is a Conservative paper. They loathe the Communists.'

'Well, say the opposite of what the *Daily Mail* says, then you can't be wrong. We mustn't throw this chance away, *mon ami*. It might mean hundreds of francs.'

I did not like the idea, for the Paris police are very hard on Communists, especially if they are foreigners, and I was already under suspicion. Some months before, a detective had seen me come out of the office of a Communist weekly paper, and I had had a great deal of trouble with the police. If they caught me going to this secret society, it might mean deport-ation. However, the chance seemed too good to be missed. That afternoon Boris's friend, another waiter, came to take us to the rendezvous. I cannot remember the name of the street—it was a shabby street running south from the Seine bank, somewhere near the Chamber of Deputies. Boris's friend insisted on great caution. We loitered casually down the street, marked the doorway we were to enter—it was a laundry—and then strolled back again, keeping an eye on all the windows and cafés. If the place were known as a haunt of Communists it was probably watched, and we intended to go home if we saw anyone at all like a detective. I was fright-ened, but Boris enjoyed these conspiratorial proceedings, and quite forgot that he was about to trade with the slayers of his parents.

When we were certain that the coast was clear we dived quickly into the doorway. In the laundry was a Frenchwoman ironing clothes, who told us that 'the Russian gentlemen' lived up a staircase across the courtyard. We went up several flights of dark stairs and emerged on to a landing. A strong, surly-looking young man, with hair growing low on his head, was standing at the top of the stairs. As I came up he looked at me suspiciously, barred the way with his arm and said something in Russian.

'*Mot d'ordre!*' he said sharply when I did not answer.

I stopped, startled. I had not expected passwords.

'*Mot d'ordre!*' repeated the Russian.

Boris's friend, who was walking behind, now came forward and said something in Russian, either the password or an explanation. At this, the surly young man seemed satisfied, and led us into a small, shabby room with frosted windows. It was like a very poverty-stricken office, with propaganda posters in Russian lettering and a huge, crude picture of Lenin tacked on the walls. At the table sat an unshaven Russian in shirt sleeves, addressing newspaper wrappers from a pile in front of him. As I came in he spoke to me in French, with a bad accent.

'This is very careless!' he exclaimed fussily. 'Why have you come here without a parcel of washing?'

'Washing?'

'Everybody who comes here brings washing. It looks as though they were going to the laundry downstairs. Bring a good, large bundle next time. We don't want the police on our tracks.'

This was even more conspiratorial than I had expected. Boris sat down in the only vacant chair, and there was a great deal of talking in Russian. Only the unshaven man talked; the surly one leaned against the wall with his eyes on me, as though he still suspected me. It was queer, standing in the little secret room with its revolutionary posters, listening to a conversation of which I did not understand a word. The Russians talked quickly and eagerly, with smiles and shrugs of the shoulders. I wondered what it was all about. They would be calling each other 'little father', I thought, and 'little dove', and 'Ivan Alexandrovitch', like the characters in Russian novels. And the talk would be of revolutions. The unshaven man would be saying firmly, 'We never argue. Controversy is a bourgeois pastime. Deeds are our arguments.' Then I gathered that it was not this exactly. Twenty francs was being demanded, for an entrance fee apparently, and

Boris was promising to pay it (we had just seventeen francs in the world). Finally Boris produced our precious store of money and paid five francs on account.

At this the surly man looked less suspicious, and sat down on the edge of the table. The unshaven one began to question me in French, making notes on a slip of paper. Was I a Communist? he asked. By sympathy, I answered; I had never joined any organization. Did I understand the political situation in England? Oh, of course, of course. I mentioned the names of various Ministers, and made some contemptuous remarks about the Labour Party. And what about *Le Sport*? Could I do articles on *Le Sport*? (Football and Socialism have some mysterious connexion on the Continent.) Oh, of course, again. Both men nodded gravely. The unshaven one said:

'*Évidemment*, you have a thorough knowledge of conditions in England. Could you undertake to write a series of articles for a Moscow weekly paper? We will give you the particulars.'

'Certainly.'

'Then, comrade, you will hear from us by the first post tomorrow. Or possibly the second post. Our rate of pay is a hundred and fifty francs an article. Remember to bring a parcel of washing next time you come. *Au revoir*, comrade.'

We went downstairs, looked carefully out of the laundry to see if there was anyone in the street, and slipped out. Boris was wild with joy. In a sort of sacrificial ecstasy he rushed into the nearest tobacconist's and spent fifty centimes on a cigar. He came out thumping his stick on the pavement and beaming.

'At last! At last! Now, *mon ami*, out fortune really is made. You took them in finely. Did you hear him call you comrade? A hundred and fifty francs an article—*nom de Dieu*, what luck!'

Next morning when I heard the postman I rushed down

to the *bistro* for my letter; to my disappointment, it had not come. I stayed at home for the second post; still no letter. When three days had gone by and I had not heard from the secret society, we gave up hope, deciding that they must have found somebody else to do their articles.

Ten days later we made another visit to the office of the secret society, taking care to bring a parcel that looked like washing. And the secret society had vanished! The woman in the laundry knew nothing—she simply said that '*ces messieurs*' had left some days ago, after trouble about the rent. What fools we looked, standing there with our parcel! But it was a consolation that we had paid only five francs instead of twenty.

And that was the last we ever heard of the secret society. Who or what they really were, nobody knew. Personally I do not think they had anything to do with the Communist Party; I think they were simply swindlers, who preyed upon Russian refugees by extracting entrance fees to an imaginary society. It was quite safe, and no doubt they are still doing it in some other city. They were clever fellows, and played their part admirably. Their office looked exactly as a secret Communist office should look, and as for that touch about bringing a parcel of washing, it was genius.

IX

For three more days we continued traipsing about looking for work, coming home for diminishing meals of soup and bread in my bedroom. There were now two gleams of hope. In the first place, Boris had heard of a possible job at the Hôtel X, near the Place de la Concorde, and in the second, the *patron* of the new restaurant in the rue du Commerce had at last come back. We went down in the afternoon and saw him. On the way Boris talked of the vast fortunes we should make if we got this job, and on the importance of making a good impression on the *patron*.

'Appearance—appearance is everything, *mon ami*. Give me a new suit and I will borrow a thousand francs by dinner-time. What a pity I did not buy a collar when we had money. I turned my collar inside out this morning; but what is the use, one side is as dirty as the other. Do you think I look hungry, *mon ami*?'

'You look pale.'

'Curse it, what can one do on bread and potatoes? It is fatal to look hungry. It makes people want to kick you. Wait.'

He stopped at a jeweller's window and smacked his cheeks sharply to bring the blood into them. Then, before the flush had faded, we hurried into the restaurant and introduced ourselves to the *patron*.

The *patron* was a short, fattish, very dignified man with wavy grey hair, dressed in a smart, double-breasted flannel suit and smelling of scent. Boris told me that he too was an ex-colonel of the Russian Army. His wife was there too, a horrid, fat Frenchwoman with a dead-white face and scarlet lips, reminding me of cold veal and tomatoes. The *patron* greeted Boris genially, and they talked together in Russian for a few minutes. I stood in the background, preparing to tell some big lies about my experience as a dishwasher.

Then the *patron* came over towards me. I shuffled uneasily, trying to look servile. Boris had rubbed it into me that a *plongeur* is a slave's slave, and I expected the *patron* to treat me like dirt. To my astonishment, he seized me warmly by the hand.

'So you are an Englishman!' he exclaimed. 'But how charming! I need not ask, then, whether you are a golfer?'

'*Mais certainement*,' I said, seeing that this was expected of me.

'All my life I have wanted to play golf. Will you, my dear *monsieur*, be so kind as to show me a few of the principal strokes?'

Apparently this was the Russian way of doing business. The *patron* listened attentively while I explained the difference between a driver and an iron, and then suddenly informed me that it was all *entendu*; Boris was to be *maître d'hôtel* when the restaurant opened, and I *plongeur*, with a chance of rising to lavatory attendant if trade was good. When would the restaurant open? I asked. 'Exactly a fortnight from today,' the *patron* answered grandly (he had a manner of waving his hand and flicking off his cigarette ash at the same time, which looked very grand), 'exactly a fortnight from today, in time for lunch.' Then, with obvious pride, he showed us over the restaurant.

It was a smallish place, consisting of a bar, a dining-room, and a kitchen no bigger than the average bathroom. The *patron* was decorating it in a trumpery 'picturesque' style (he called it '*le Normand*'; it was a matter of sham beams stuck on the plaster, and the like) and proposed to call it the Auberge de Jehan Cottard, to give a medieval effect. He had a leaflet printed, full of lies about the historical associations of the quarter, and this leaflet actually claimed, among other things, that there had once been an inn on the site of the restaurant which was frequented by Charlemagne. The *patron* was very pleased with this touch. He was also having the bar decorated with indecent pictures by an artist from the Salon. Finally he gave us each an expensive cigarette, and after some more talk he went home.

I felt strongly that we should never get any good from this restaurant. The *patron* had looked to me like a cheat, and, what was worse, an incompetent cheat, and I had seen two unmistakable duns hanging about the back door. But Boris, seeing himself a *maître d'hôtel* once more, would not be discouraged.

'We've brought it off—only a fortnight to hold out. What is a fortnight? *Je m'en f—*. To think that in only three weeks I shall have my mistress! Will she be dark or fair, I wonder? I don't mind, so long as she is not too thin.'

Two bad days followed. We had only sixty centimes left, and we spent it on half a pound of bread, with a piece of garlic to rub it with. The point of rubbing garlic on bread is that the taste lingers and gives one the illusion of having fed recently. We sat most of that day in the Jardin des Plantes. Boris had shots with stones at the tame pigeons, but always missed them, and after that we wrote dinner menus on the backs of envelopes. We were too hungry even to try and think of anything except food. I remember the dinner Boris finally selected for himself. It was: a dozen oysters, bortch soup (the red, sweet, beetroot soup with cream on top), crayfishes, a young chicken *en casserole*, beef with stewed plums, new potatoes, a salad, suet pudding and Roquefort cheese, with a litre of Burgundy and some old brandy. Boris had international tastes in food. Later on, when we were prosperous, I occasionally saw him eat meals almost as large without difficulty.

When our money came to an end I stopped looking for work, and was another day without food. I did not believe that the Auberge de Jehan Cottard was really going to open, and I could see no other prospect, but I was too lazy to do anything but lie in bed. Then the luck changed abruptly. At night, at about ten o'clock, I heard an eager shout from the street. I got up and went to the window. Boris was there, waving his stick and beaming. Before speaking he dragged a bent loaf from his pocket and threw it up to me.

'*Mon ami, mon cher ami*, we're saved! What do you think?'

'Surely you haven't got a job!'

'At the Hôtel X, near the Place de la Concorde—five hundred francs a month, and food. I have been working there today. Name of Jesus Christ, how I have eaten!'

After ten or twelve hours' work, and with his game leg, his first thought had been to walk three kilometres to my hotel and tell me the good news! What was more, he told me to meet him in the Tuileries the next day during his afternoon interval, in case he should be able to steal some food for me. At the appointed time I met Boris on a public bench. He undid his waistcoat and produced a large, crushed, newspaper packet; in it were some minced veal, a wedge of Camembert cheese, bread and an éclair, all jumbled together.

'*Voilà!*' said Boris, 'that's all I could smuggle out for you. The doorkeeper is a cunning swine.'

It is disagreeable to eat out of a newspaper on a public seat, especially in the Tuileries, which are generally full of pretty girls, but I was too hungry to care. While I ate, Boris explained that he was working in the cafeterie of the hotel—that is, in English, the stillroom. It appeared that the cafeterie was the very lowest post in the hotel, and a dreadful come-down for a waiter, but it would do until the Auberge de Jehan Gottard opened. Meanwhile I was to meet Boris every day in the Tuileries, and he would smuggle out as much food as he dared. For three days we continued with this arrangement, and I lived entirely on the stolen food. Then all our troubles came to an end, for one of the *plongeurs* left the Hôtel X, and on Boris's recommendation I was given a job there myself.

X

The Hôtel X was a vast, grandiose place with a classical façade, and at one side a little, dark doorway like a rat-hole, which was the service entrance. I arrived at a quarter to seven in the morning. A stream of men with greasy trousers were hurrying in and being checked by a doorkeeper who sat in a tiny office. I waited, and presently the *chef du personnel*, a sort of assistant manager, arrived and began to question me. He was an Italian, with a round, pale face, haggard from overwork. He asked whether I was an experienced dish-washer, and I said that I was; he glanced at my hands and saw that I was lying, but on hearing that I was an Englishman he changed his tone and engaged me.

'We have been looking for someone to practise our English on,' he said. 'Our clients are all Americans, and the only English we know is—' He repeated something that little boys write on the walls in London. 'You may be useful. Come downstairs.'

He led me down a winding staircase into a narrow passage, deep underground, and so low that I had to stoop in places. It was stiflingly hot and very dark, with only dim, yellow bulbs several yards apart. There seemed to be miles of dark labyrinthine passages—actually, I suppose, a few hundred yards in all—that reminded one queerly of the lower decks of a liner; there were the same heat and cramped space and warm reek of food, and a humming, whirring noise (it came from the kitchen furnaces) just like the whir of engines. We passed doorways which let out sometimes a shouting of oaths, sometimes the red glare of a fire, once a shuddering draught from an ice chamber. As we went along, something struck me violently in the back. It was a hundred-pound block of ice, carried by a blue-aproned porter. After him came a boy with a great slab of veal on his shoulder, his cheek pressed into the damp, spongy flesh. They shoved me aside with a cry of '*Range-toi, idiot!*' and rushed on. On the wall, under one of the lights, someone had written in a very neat hand: 'Sooner will you find a cloudless sky in winter, than a woman at the Hôtel X who has her maidenhead.' It seemed a queer sort of place.

One of the passages branched off into a laundry, where an old, skull-faced woman gave me a blue apron and a pile of dishcloths. Then the *chef du personnel* took me to a tiny underground den—a cellar below a cellar, as it were—where there were a sink and some gas-ovens. It was too low for me to stand quite upright, and the temperature was perhaps 110 degrees Fahrenheit. The *chef du personnel* explained that my job was to fetch meals for the higher hotel employees, who fed in a small dining-room above, clean their room and wash their crockery. When he had gone, a waiter, another Italian, thrust a fierce, fuzzy head into the doorway and looked down at me.

'English, eh?' he said. 'Well, I'm in charge here. If you work well'—he made the motion of up-ending a bottle and sucked noisily. 'If you don't'—he gave the doorpost several vigorous kicks. 'To me, twisting your neck would be no more than spitting on the floor. And if there's any trouble, they'll believe me, not you. So be careful.'

After this I set to work rather hurriedly. Except for about

an hour, I was at work from seven in the morning till a quarter past nine at night; first at washing crockery, then at scrubbing the tables and floors of the employees' dining-room, then at polishing glasses and knives, then at fetching meals, then at washing crockery again, then at fetching more meals and washing more crockery. It was easy work, and I got on well with it except when I went to the kitchen to fetch meals. The kitchen was like nothing I had ever seen or imagined—a stifling, low-ceilinged inferno of a cellar, red-lit from the fires, and deafening with oaths and the clanging of pots and pans. It was so hot that all the metal-work except the stoves had to be covered with cloth. In the middle were furnaces, where twelve cooks skipped to and fro, their faces dripping sweat in spite of their white caps. Round that were counters where a mob of waiters and *plongeurs* clamoured with trays. Scullions, naked to the waist, were stoking the fires and scouring huge copper saucepans with sand. Everyone seemed to be in a hurry and a rage. The head cook, a fine, scarlet man with big moustachios, stood in the middle booming continuously, '*Ça marche deux œufs brouillés! Ça marche un Chateaubriand aux pommes sautées!*' except when he broke off to curse at a *plongeur*. There were three counters, and the first time I went to the kitchen I took my tray unknowingly to the wrong one. The head cook walked up to me, twisted his moustaches, and looked me up and down. Then he beckoned to the breakfast cook and pointed at me.

'Do you see *that*? That is the type of *plongeur* they send us nowadays. Where do you come from, idiot? From Charenton, I suppose?' (There is a large lunatic asylum at Charenton.)

'From England,' I said.

'I might have known it. Well, *mon cher monsieur l'Anglais*, may I inform you that you are the son of a whore? And now — the camp to the other counter, where you belong.'

I got this kind of reception every time I went to the kitchen, for I always made some mistake; I was expected to know the work, and was cursed accordingly. From curiosity I counted the number of times I was called *maquereau* during the day, and it was thirty-nine.

At half past four the Italian told me that I could stop working, but that it was not worth going out, as we began at five. I went to the lavatory for a smoke; smoking was strictly forbidden, and Boris had warned me that the lavatory was the only safe place. After that I worked again till a quarter past nine, when the waiter put his head into the doorway and told me to leave the rest of the crockery. To my astonishment, after calling me pig, mackerel, etc., all day, he had suddenly grown quite friendly. I realized that the curses I had met with were only a kind of probation.

'That'll do, *mon p'tit*,' said the waiter. '*Tu n'es pas débrouillard*, but you work all right. Come up and have your dinner. The hotel allows us two litres of wine each, and I've stolen another bottle. We'll have a fine booze.'

We had an excellent dinner from the leavings of the higher employees. The waiter, grown mellow, told me stories about his love-affairs, and about two men whom he had stabbed in Italy, and about how he had dodged his military service. He was a good fellow when one got to know him; he reminded me of Benvenuto Cellini, somehow. I was tired and drenched with sweat, but I felt a new man after a day's solid food. The work did not seem difficult, and I felt that this job would suit me. It was not certain, however, that it would continue, for I had been engaged as an 'extra' for the day only, at twenty-five francs. The sour-faced doorkeeper counted out the money, less fifty centimes which he said was for insurance (a lie, I discovered afterwards). Then he stepped out into the passage, made me take off my coat, and carefully prodded me all over, searching for stolen food. After this the *chef du personnel* appeared and spoke to me. Like the waiter, he had grown more genial on seeing that I was willing to work.

'We will give you a permanent job if you like,' he said. 'The head waiter says he would enjoy calling an Englishman names. Will you sign on for a month?'

Here was a job at last, and I was ready to jump at it. Then I remembered the Russian restaurant, due to open in a fortnight. It seemed hardly fair to promise working a month, and then leave in the middle. I said that I had other work in prospect—could I be engaged for a fortnight? But at that the *chef du personnel* shrugged his shoulders and said that the hotel only engaged men by the month. Evidently I had lost my chance of a job.

Boris, by arrangement, was waiting for me in the Arcade of the Rue de Rivoli. When I told him what had happened, he was furious. For the first time since I had known him he forgot his manners and called me a fool.

'Idiot! Species of idiot! What's the good of my finding you a job when you go and chuck it up the next moment? How could you be such a fool as to mention the other restaurant? You'd only to promise you would work for a month.'

'It seemed more honest to say I might have to leave,' I objected.

'Honest! Honest! Who ever heard of a *plongeur* being honest? *Mon ami*—suddenly he seized my lapel and spoke very earnestly—'*mon ami*, you have worked here all day. You see what hotel work is like. Do you think a *plongeur* can afford a sense of honour?'

'No, perhaps not.'

'Well, then, go back quickly and tell the *chef du personnel* you are quite ready to work for a month. Say you will throw the other job over. Then, when our restaurant opens, we have only to walk out.'

'But what about my wages if I break my contract?'

Boris banged his stick on the pavement and cried out at

such stupidity. 'Ask to be paid by the day, then you won't lose a sou. Do you suppose they would prosecute a *plongeur* for breaking his contract? A *plongeur* is too low to be prosecuted.'

I hurried back, found the *chef du personnel*, and told him that I would work for a month, whereat he signed me on. This was my first lesson in *plongeur* morality. Later I realized how foolish it had been to have any scruples, for the big hotels are quite merciless towards their employees. They engage or discharge men as the work demands, and they all sack ten per cent or more of their staff when the season is over. Nor have they any difficulty in replacing a man who leaves at short notice, for Paris is thronged by hotel employees out of work.

XI

As it turned out, I did not break my contract, for it was six weeks before the Auberge de Jehan Cottard even showed signs of opening. In the meantime I worked at the Hôtel X, four days a week in the cafeterie, one day helping the waiter on the fourth floor, and one day replacing the woman who washed up for the dining-room. My day off, luckily, was Sunday, but sometimes another man was ill and I had to work that day as well. The hours were from seven in the morning till two in the afternoon, and from five in the evening till nine—eleven hours; but it was a fourteen-hour day when I washed up for the dining-room. By the ordinary standards of a Paris *plongeur*, these are exceptionally short hours. The only hardship of life was the fearful heat and stuffiness of these labyrinthine cellars. Apart from this the hotel, which was large and well organized, was considered a comfortable one.

Our cafeterie was a murky cellar measuring twenty feet by seven by eight high, and so crowded with coffee-urns, breadcutters and the like that one could hardly move without banging against something. It was lighted by one dim electric bulb, and four or five gas-fires that sent out a fierce red breath. There was a thermometer there, and the temperature never fell below 110 degrees Fahrenheit—it neared 130 at some times of the day. At one end were five service lifts, and at the other an ice cupboard where we stored milk and butter. When you went into the ice cupboard you dropped a hundred degrees of temperature at a single step; it used to remind me of the hymn about Greenland's icy mountains and India's coral strand. Two men worked in the cafeterie besides Boris and myself. One was Mario, a huge, excitable Italian— he was like a city policeman with operatic gestures—and the other, a hairy, uncouth animal whom we called the Magyar; I think he was a Transylvanian, or something even more remote. Except the Magyar we were all big men, and at the rush hours we collided incessantly.

The work in the cafeterie was spasmodic. We were never idle, but the real work only came in bursts of two hours at a time—we called each burst '*un coup de feu*'. The first *coup de feu* came at eight, when the guests upstairs began to wake up and demand breakfast. At eight a sudden banging and yelling would break out all through the basement; bells rang on all sides, blue-aproned men rushed through the passages, our service lifts came down with a simultaneous crash, and the waiters on all five floors began shouting Italian oaths down the shafts. I don't remember all our duties, but they included making tea, coffee and chocolate, fetching meals from the kitchen, wines from the cellar and fruit and so forth from the dining-room, slicing bread, making toast, rolling pats of butter, measuring jam, opening milk-cans, counting lumps of sugar, boiling eggs, cooking porridge, pounding ice, grinding coffee—all this for from a hundred to two hundred customers. The kitchen was thirty yards away, and the dining-room sixty or seventy yards. Everything we sent up in the service lifts had to be covered by a voucher, and the vouchers had to be carefully filed, and there was trouble if even a lump of sugar was lost. Besides this, we had to supply the staff with bread and coffee, and fetch the meals for the waiters upstairs. All in all, it was a complicated job.

I calculated that one had to walk and run about fifteen miles during the day, and yet the strain of the work was more mental than physical. Nothing could be easier, on the face of it, than this stupid scullion work, but it is astonishingly hard when one is in a hurry. One has to leap to and fro between a multitude of jobs—it is like sorting a pack of cards against the clock. You are, for example, making toast, when bang! down comes a service lift with an order for tea, rolls and three different kinds of jam, and simultaneously bang! down comes another demanding scrambled eggs, coffee and grapefruit; you run to the kitchen for the eggs and to the dining-room for the fruit, going like lightning so as to be back before your toast burns, and having to remember about the tea and coffee, besides half a dozen other orders that are still pending; and at the same time some waiter is following you and making trouble about a lost bottle of soda-water, and you are arguing with him. It needs more brains than one might think. Mario said, no doubt truly, that it took a year to make a reliable cafetier.

The time between eight and half past ten was a sort of delirium. Sometimes we were going as though we had only five minutes to live; sometimes there were sudden lulls when the orders stopped and everything seemed quiet for a moment. Then we swept up the litter from the floor, threw down fresh sawdust, and swallowed gallipots of wine or coffee or water—anything, so long as it was wet. Very often we used to break off chunks of ice and suck them while we worked. The heat among the gas-fires was nauseating; we swallowed quarts of drink during the day, and after a few hours even our aprons were drenched with sweat. At times we were hopelessly behind with the work, and some of the customers would have gone without their breakfast, but Mario always pulled us through. He had worked fourteen years in the cafeterie, and he had the skill that never wastes a second between jobs. The Magyar was very stupid and I was

61

inexperienced, and Boris was inclined to shirk, partly because of his lame leg, partly because he was ashamed of working in the cafeterie after being a waiter; but Mario was wonderful. The way he would stretch his great arms right across the cafeterie to fill a coffee-pot with one hand and boil an egg with the other, at the same time watching toast and shouting directions to the Magyar, and between whiles singing snatches from *Rigoletto*, was beyond all praise. The *patron* knew his value, and he was paid a thousand francs a month, instead of five hundred like the rest of us.

The breakfast pandemonium stopped at half past ten. Then we scrubbed the cafeterie tables, swept the floor and polished the brasswork, and, on good mornings, went one at a time to the lavatory for a smoke. This was our slack time— only relatively slack, however, for we had only ten minutes for lunch, and we never got through it uninterrupted. The customers' luncheon hour, between twelve and two, was another period of turmoil like the breakfast hour. Most of our work was fetching meals from the kitchen, which meant constant *engueulades* from the cooks. By this time the cooks had sweated in front of their furnaces for four or five hours, and their tempers were all warmed up.

At two we were suddenly free men. We threw off our aprons and put on our coats, hurried out of doors, and, when we had money, dived into the nearest *bistro*. It was strange, coming up into the street from those firelit cellars. The air seemed blindingly clear and cold, like arctic summer; and how sweet the petrol did smell, after the stenches of sweat and food! Sometimes we met some of our cooks and waiters in the *bistros*, and they were friendly and stood us drinks. Indoors we were their slaves, but it is an etiquette in hotel life that between hours everyone is equal, and the *engueulades* do not count.

At a quarter to five we went back to the hotel. Till half-past six there were no orders, and we used this time to polish silver, clean out the coffee-urns, and do other odd jobs. Then the grand turmoil of the day started—the dinner hour. I wish I could be Zola for a little while, just to describe that dinner hour. The essence of the situation was that a hundred or two hundred people were demanding individually different meals of five or six courses, and that fifty or sixty people had to cook and serve them and clean up the mess afterwards; anyone with experience of catering will know what that means. And at this time when the work was doubled, the whole staff was tired out, and a number of them were drunk. I could write pages about the scene without giving a true idea of it. The chargings to and fro in the narrow passages, the collisions, the yells, the struggling with crates and trays and blocks of ice, the heat, the darkness, the furious festering quarrels which there was no time to fight out—they pass description. Anyone coming into the basement for the first time would have thought himself in a den of maniacs. It was only later, when I understood the working of a hotel, that I saw order in all this chaos.

At half past eight the work stopped very suddenly. We were not free till nine, but we used to throw ourselves full length on the floor, and lie there resting our legs, too lazy even to go to the ice cupboard for a drink. Sometimes the *chef du personnel* would come in with bottles of beer, for the hotel stood us an extra beer when we had had a hard day. The food we were given was no more than eatable, but the *patron* was not mean about drink; he allowed us two litres of wine a day each, knowing that if a *plongeur* is not given two litres he will steal three. We had the heeltaps of bottles as well, so that we often drank too much—a good thing, for one seemed to work faster when partially drunk.

Four days of the week passed like this; of the other two working days, one was better and one worse. After a week of this life I felt in need of a holiday. It was Saturday night, so the people in our *bistro* were busy getting drunk, and with a free day ahead of me I was ready to join them. We all went to bed, drunk, at two in the morning, meaning to sleep till noon. At half past five I was suddenly awakened. A night-watchman, sent from the hotel, was standing at my bedside. He stripped the clothes back and shook me roughly.

'Get up!' he said. '*Tu t'es bien saoulé la gueule, eh?* Well, never mind that, the hotel's a man short. You've got to work today.'

'Why should I work?' I protested. 'This is my day off.'

'Day off, nothing! The work's got to be done. Get up!'

I got up and went out, feeling as though my back were broken and my skull filled with hot cinders. I did not think that I could possibly do a day's work. And yet, after only an hour in the basement, I found that I was perfectly well. It seemed that in the heat of those cellars, as in a turkish bath, one could sweat out almost any quantity of drink. *Plongeurs* know this, and count on it. The power of swallowing quarts of wine, and then sweating it out before it can do much damage, is one of the compensations of their life.

XII

By far my best time at the hotel was when I went to help the waiter on the fourth floor. We worked in a small pantry which communicated with the cafeterie by service lifts. It was delightfully cool after the cellars, and the work was chiefly polishing silver and glasses, which is a humane job. Valenti, the waiter, was a decent sort, and treated me almost as an equal when we were alone, though he had to speak roughly when there was anyone else present, for it does not do for a waiter to be friendly with *plongeurs*. He used sometimes to tip me five francs when he had had a good day. He was a comely youth, aged twenty-four but looking eighteen, and, like most waiters, he carried himself well and knew how to wear his clothes. With his black tail-coat and white tie, fresh face and sleek brown hair, he looked just like an Eton boy; yet he had earned his living since he was twelve, and worked his way up literally from the gutter. Crossing the Italian frontier without a passport, and selling chestnuts from a barrow on the northern boulevards, and being given fifty days' imprisonment in London for working without a permit, and being made love to by a rich old woman in a hotel, who gave him a diamond ring and afterwards accused him of stealing it, were among his experiences. I used to enjoy talking to him, at slack times when we sat smoking down the lift shaft.

My bad day was when I washed up for the dining-room. I had not to wash the plates, which were done in the kitchen, but only the other crockery, silver, knives and glasses; yet, even so, it meant thirteen hours' work, and I used between thirty and forty dishcloths during the day. The antiquated methods used in France double the work of washing up. Plate-racks are unheard-of, and there are no soap-flakes, only the treacly soft soap, which refuses to lather in the hard, Paris water. I worked in a dirty, crowded little den, a pantry and scullery combined, which gave straight on the dining-room. Besides washing up, I had to fetch the waiters' food and serve them at table; most of them were intolerably insolent, and I had to use my fists more than once to get common civility. The person who normally washed up was a woman, and they made her life a misery.

It was amusing to look round the filthy little scullery and think that only a double door was between us and the dining-room. There sat the customers in all their splendour—spotless table-cloths, bowls of flowers, mirrors and gilt cornices and painted cherubim; and here, just a few feet away, we in our disgusting filth. For it really was disgusting filth. There was no time to sweep the floor till evening, and we slithered about in a compound of soapy water, lettuce-leaves, torn paper and trampled food. A dozen waiters with their coats off, showing their sweaty armpits, sat at the table mixing salads and sticking their thumbs into the cream pots. The room had a dirty, mixed smell of food and sweat. Everywhere in the cupboards, behind the piles of crockery, were squalid stores of food that the waiters had stolen. There were only two sinks, and no washing basin, and it was nothing unusual for a waiter to wash his face in the water in which clean crockery was rinsing. But the customers saw nothing of this. There were a coco-nut mat and a mirror outside the dining-room door, and the waiters used to preen themselves up and go in looking the picture of cleanliness.

It is an instructive sight to see a waiter going into a hotel dining-room. As he passes the door a sudden change comes over him. The set of his shoulders alters; all the dirt and hurry and irritation have dropped off in an instant. He glides over the carpet, with a solemn priest-like air. I remember our assistant *maître d'hôtel*, a fiery Italian, pausing at the dining-room door to address an apprentice who had broken a bottle of wine. Shaking his fist above his head he yelled (luckily the door was more or less soundproof):

'*Tu me faiz—*. Do you call yourself a waiter, you young bastard? You a waiter! You're not fit to scrub floors in the brothel your mother came from. *Maquereau!*'

Words failing him, he turned to the door; and as he opened it he delivered a final insult in the same manner as Squire Western in *Tom Jones*.

Then he entered the dining-room and sailed across it dish in hand, graceful as a swan. Ten seconds later he was bowing reverently to a customer. And you could not help thinking, as you saw him bow and smile, with that benign smile of the trained waiter, that the customer was put to shame by having such an aristocrat to serve him.

This washing up was a thoroughly odious job—not hard, but boring and silly beyond words. It is dreadful to think that some people spend their whole decades at such occupations. The woman whom I replaced was quite sixty years old, and she stood at the sink thirteen hours a day, six days a week, the year round; she was, in addition, horribly bullied by the waiters. She gave out that she had once been an actress—actually, I imagine, a prostitute; most prostitutes end as charwomen. It was strange to see that in spite of her age and her life she still wore a bright blonde wig, and darkened her eyes and painted her face like a girl of twenty. So apparently even a seventy-eight-hour week can leave one with some vitality.

XIII

On my third day at the hotel the *chef du personnel*, who had generally spoken to me in quite a pleasant tone, called me up and said sharply:

'Here, you, shave that moustache off at once! *Nom de Dieu*, who ever heard of a *plongeur* with a moustache?'

I began to protest, but he cut me short. 'A *plongeur* with a moustache—nonsense! Take care I don't see you with it tomorrow.'

On the way home I asked Boris what this meant. He shrugged his shoulders. 'You must do what he says, *mon ami*. No one in the hotel wears a moustache, except the cooks. I should have thought you would have noticed it. Reason? There *is* no reason. It is the custom.'

I saw that it was an etiquette, like not wearing a white tie with a dinner-jacket, and shaved off my moustache. Afterwards I found out the explanation of the custom, which is this: waiters in good hotels do not wear moustaches, and to show their superiority they decree that *plongeurs* shall not wear them either; and the cooks wear their moustaches to show their contempt for the waiters.

This gives some idea of the elaborate caste system existing in a hotel. Our staff, amounting to about a hundred and ten, had their prestige graded as accurately as that of soldiers, and a cook or waiter was as much above a *plongeur* as a captain above a private. Highest of all came the manager, who could sack anybody, even the cooks. We never saw the *patron*, and all we knew of him was that his meals had to be prepared more carefully than that of the customers; all the discipline of the hotel depended on the manager. He was a conscientious man, and always on the lookout for slackness, but we were too clever for him. A system of service bells ran through the hotel, and the whole staff used these for signalling to one another. A long ring and a short ring, followed by two more long rings, meant that the manager was coming, and when we heard it we took care to look busy.

Below the manager came the *maître d'hôtel*. He did not serve at table, unless to a lord or someone of that kind, but directed the other waiters and helped with the catering. His tips, and his bonus from the champagne companies (it was two francs for each cork he returned to them), came to two hundred francs a day. He was in a position quite apart from the rest of the staff, and took his meals in a private room, with silver on the table and two apprentices in clean white jackets to serve him. A little below the head waiter came the head cook, drawing about five thousand francs a month; he dined in the kitchen, but at a separate table, and one of the apprentice cooks waited on him. Then came the *chef du personnel*; he drew only fifteen hundred francs a month, but he wore a black coat and did no manual work, and he could sack *plongeurs* and fine waiters. Then came the other cooks, drawing anything between three thousand and seven hundred and fifty francs a month; then the waiters, making about seventy francs a day in tips, besides a small retaining fee; then the laundresses and sewing women; then the apprentice waiters, who received no tips, but were paid seven hundred and fifty francs a month; then the *plongeurs*, also at seven hundred and fifty francs; then the chambermaids, at five or six hundred francs a month; and lastly the cafetiers, at five hundred a month. We of the cafeterie were the very dregs of the hotel, despised and *tutoied* by everyone.

There were various others—the office employees, called generally couriers, the storekeeper, the cellarman, some porters and pages, the ice man, the bakers, the night-watchman, the doorkeeper. Different jobs were done by different races. The office employees and the cooks and sewing-women were French, the waiters Italians and Germans (there is hardly such a thing as a French waiter in Paris), the *plongeurs* of every race in Europe, beside Arabs and Negroes. French was the lingua franca, even the Italians speaking it to one another.

All the departments had their special perquisites. In all Paris hotels it is the custom to sell the broken bread to bakers for eight sous a pound, and the kitchen scraps to pigkeepers for a trifle, and to divide the proceeds of this among the *plongeurs*. There was much pilfering, too. The waiters all stole food—in fact, I seldom saw a waiter trouble to eat the rations provided for him by the hotel— and the cooks did it on a larger scale in the kitchen, and we in the cafeterie swilled illicit tea and coffee. The cellarman stole brandy. By a rule of the hotel the waiters were not allowed to keep stores of spirits, but had to go to the cellarman for each drink as it was ordered. As the cellarman poured out the drinks he would set aside perhaps a teaspoonful from each glass, and he amassed quantities in this way. He would sell you the stolen brandy for five sous a swig if he thought he could trust you.

There were thieves among the staff, and if you left money in your coat pockets it was generally taken. The doorkeeper, who paid our wages and searched us for stolen food, was the greatest thief in the hotel. Out of my five hundred francs a month, this man actually managed to cheat me of a hundred and fourteen francs in six weeks. I had asked to be paid daily, so the doorkeeper paid me sixteen francs each evening, and, by not paying for Sundays (for which of course payment was due), pocketed sixty-four francs. Also, I sometimes worked on a Sunday, for which, though I did not know it, I was entitled to an extra twenty-five francs. The doorkeeper never paid me this either, and so made away with another seventy-five francs. I only realized during my last week that I was being cheated, and, as I could prove nothing, only twenty-five francs were refunded. The doorkeeper played similar tricks on any employee who was fool enough to be taken in. He called himself a Greek, but in reality he was an Armenian. After knowing him I saw the force of the proverb 'Trust a snake before a Jew and a Jew before a Greek, but don't trust an Armenian.'

There were queer characters among the waiters. One was a gentleman—a youth who had been educated at a university, and had had a well-paid job in a business office. He had caught a venereal disease, lost his job, drifted, and now considered himself lucky to be a waiter. Many of the waiters had slipped into France without passports, and one or two of them were spies—it is a common profession for a spy to adopt. One day there was a fearful row in the waiters' dining-room between Morandi, a dangerous-looking man with eyes set too far apart, and another Italian. It appeared that Morandi had taken the other man's mistress. The other man, a weakling and obviously frightened of Morandi, was threatening vaguely.

Morandi jeered at him. 'Well, what are you going to do about it? I've slept with your girl, slept with her three times. It was fine. What can you do, eh?'

'I can denounce you to the secret police. You are an Italian spy.'

Morandi did not deny it. He simply produced a razor from his tail pocket and made two swift strokes in the air, as though slashing a man's cheeks open. Whereat the other waiter took it back.

The queerest type I ever saw in the hotel was an 'extra'.

He had been engaged at twenty-five francs for the day to replace the Magyar, who was ill. He was a Serbian, a thick-set nimble fellow of about twenty-five, speaking six languages, including English. He seemed to know all about hotel work, and up till midday he worked like a slave. Then, as soon as it had struck twelve, he turned sulky, shirked his work, stole wine, and finally crowned all by loafing about openly with a pipe in his mouth. Smoking, of course, was forbidden under severe penalties. The manager himself heard of it and came down to interview the Serbian, fuming with rage.

'What the devil do you mean by smoking here?' he cried.

'What the devil do you mean by having a face like that?' answered the Serbian, calmly.

I cannot convey the blasphemy of such a remark. The head cook, if a *plongeur* had spoken to him like that, would have thrown a saucepan of hot soup in his face. The manager said instantly, 'You're sacked!' and at two o'clock the Serbian was given his twenty-five francs and duly sacked. Before he went out Boris asked him in Russian what game he was playing. He said the Serbian answered:

'Look here, *mon vieux*, they've got to pay me a day's wages if I work up to midday, haven't they? That's the law. And where's the sense of working after I get my wages? So I'll tell you what I do. I go to a hotel and get a job as an extra, and up to midday I work hard. Then, the moment it's struck twelve, I start raising such hell that they've no choice but to sack me. Neat, eh? Most days I'm sacked by half past twelve; today it was two o'clock; but I don't care, I've saved four hours' work. The only trouble is, one can't do it at the same hotel twice.'

It appeared that he had played this game at half the hotels and restaurants in Paris. It is probably quite an easy game to play during the summer, though the hotels protect themselves against it as well as they can by means of a black list.

XIV

In a few days I had grasped the main principles on which the hotel was run. The thing that would astonish anyone coming for the first time into the service quarters of a hotel would be the fearful noise and disorder during the rush hours. It is something so different from the steady work in a shop or a factory that it looks at first sight like mere bad management. But it is really quite unavoidable, and for this reason. Hotel work is not particularly hard, but by its nature it comes in rushes and cannot be economized. You cannot, for instance, grill a steak two hours before it is wanted; you have to wait till the last moment, by which time a mass of other work has accumulated, and then do it all together, in frantic haste. The result is that at mealtimes everyone is doing two men's work, which is impossible without noise and quarrelling. Indeed the quarrels are a necessary part of the process, for the pace would never be kept up if everyone did not accuse everyone else of idling. It was for this reason that during the rush hours the whole staff raged and cursed like demons. At those times there was scarcely a verb in the hotel except *foutre*. A girl in the bakery, aged sixteen, used oaths that would have defeated a cabman. (Did not Hamlet say 'cursing like a scullion'? No doubt Shakespeare had watched scullions at work.) But we are not losing our heads and wasting time; we were just stimulating one another for the effort of packing four hours' work into two hours.

What keeps a hotel going is the fact that the employees take a genuine pride in their work, beastly and silly though it is. If a man idles, the others soon find him out, and conspire against him to get him sacked. Cooks, waiters and *plongeurs* differ greatly in outlook, but they are all alike in being proud of their efficiency.

Undoubtedly the most workmanlike class, and the least servile, are the cooks. They do not earn quite so much as waiters, but their prestige is higher and their employment steadier. The cook does not look upon himself as a servant, but as a skilled workman; he is generally called '*un ouvrier*', which a waiter never is. He knows his power—knows that he alone makes or mars a restaurant, and that if he is five minutes late everything is out of gear. He despises the whole non-cooking staff, and makes it a point of honour to insult everyone below the head waiter. And he takes a genuine artistic pride in his work, which demands very great skill. It is not the cooking that is so difficult, but the doing everything to time. Between breakfast and luncheon the head cook at the Hôtel X would receive orders for several hundred dishes, all to be served at different times; he cooked few of them himself, but he gave instructions about all of them and inspected them before they were sent up. His memory was wonderful. The vouchers were pinned on a board, but the head cook seldom looked at them; everything was stored in his mind, and exactly to the minute, as each dish fell due, he would call out, '*Faites marcher une côtelette de veau*' (or whatever it was) unfailingly. He was an insufferable bully, but he was also an artist. It is for their punctuality, and not for any superiority in technique, that men cooks are preferred to women.

The waiter's outlook is quite different. He too is proud

in a way of his skill, but his skill is chiefly in being servile. His work gives him the mentality, not of a workman, but of a snob. He lives perpetually in sight of rich people, stands at their tables, listens to their conversation, sucks up to them with smiles and discreet little jokes. He has the pleasure of spending money by proxy. Moreover, there is always the chance that he may become rich himself, for, though most waiters die poor, they have long runs of luck occasionally. At some cafés on the Grand Boulevard there is so much money to be made that the waiters actually pay the *patron* for their employment. The result is that between constantly seeing money, and hoping to get it, the waiter comes to identify himself to some extent with his employers. He will take pains to serve a meal in style, because he feels that he is participating in the meal himself.

I remember Valenti telling me of some banquet at Nice at which he had once served, and of how it cost two hundred thousand francs and was talked of for months afterwards. 'It was splendid, *mon p'tit, mais magnifique!* Jesus Christ! The champagne, the silver, the orchids—I have never seen anything like them, and I have seen some things. Ah, it was glorious!'

'But,' I said, 'you were only there to wait?'

'Oh, of course. But still, it was splendid.'

The moral is, never be sorry for a waiter. Sometimes when you sit in a restaurant, still stuffing yourself half an hour after closing time, you feel that the tired waiter at your side must surely be despising you. But he is not. He is not thinking as he looks at you, 'What an overfed lout'; he is thinking, 'One day, when I have saved enough money, I shall be able to imitate that man.' He is ministering to a kind of pleasure he thoroughly understands and admires. And that is why waiters are seldom Socialists, have no effective trade union, and will work twelve hours a day—they work fifteen hours, seven days a week, in many cafés. They are snobs, and they find the servile nature of their work rather congenial.

The *plongeurs*, again, have a different outlook. Theirs is a job which offers no prospects, is intensely exhausting, and at the same time has not a trace of skill or interest; the sort of job that would always be done by women if women were strong enough. All that is required of them is to be constantly on the run, and to put up with long hours and a stuffy atmosphere. They have no way of escaping from this life, for they cannot save a penny from their wages, and working from sixty to a hundred hours a week leaves them no time to train for anything else. The best they can hope for is to find a slightly softer job as night-watchman or lavatory attendant.

And yet the *plongeurs*, low as they are, also have a kind of pride. It is the pride of the drudge—the man who is equal to no matter what quantity of work. At that level, the mere power to go on working like an ox is about the only virtue attainable. *Débrouillard* is what every *plongeur* wants to be called. A *débrouillard* is a man who, even when he is told to do the impossible, will *se débrouiller*—get it done somehow. One of the kitchen *plongeurs* at the Hôtel X, a German, was well known as a *débrouillard*. One night an English lord came to the hotel, and the waiters were in despair, for the lord had asked for peaches, and there were none in stock; it was late at night, and the shops would be shut. 'Leave it to me,' said the German. He went out, and in ten minutes he was back with four peaches. He had gone into a neighbouring restaurant and stolen them. That is what is meant by a *débrouillard*. The English lord paid for the peaches at twenty francs each.

Mario, who was in charge of the cafeterie, had the typical drudge mentality. All he thought of was getting through the '*boulot*', and he defied you to give him too much of it. Fourteen years underground had left him with about as much natural laziness as a piston rod. '*Faut être dur*,' he used to say when anyone complained. You will often hear *plongeurs* boast, '*Je suis dur*'—as though they were soldiers, not male charwomen.

Thus everyone in the hotel had his sense of honour, and when the press of work came we were all ready for a grand concerted effort to get through it. The constant war between the different departments also made for efficiency, for everyone clung to his own privileges and tried to stop the others idling and pilfering.

This is the good side of hotel work. In a hotel a huge and complicated machine is kept running by an inadequate staff, because every man has a well-defined job and does it scrupulously. But there is a weak point, and it is this—that the job the staff are doing is not necessarily what the customer pays for. The customer pays, as he sees it, for good service; the employee is paid, as he sees it, for the *boulot*—meaning, as a rule, an imitation of good service. The result is that, though hotels are miracles of punctuality, they are worse than the worst private houses in the things that matter.

Take cleanliness, for example. The dirt in the Hôtel X, as soon as one penetrated into the service quarters, was revolting. Our cafeterie had year-old filth in all the dark corners, and the bread-bin was infested with cockroaches. Once I suggested killing these beasts to Mario. 'Why kill the poor animals?' he said reproachfully. The others laughed when I wanted to wash my hands before touching the butter. Yet we were clean where we recognized cleanliness as part of the *boulot*. We scrubbed the tables and polished the brasswork regularly, because we had orders to do that; but we had no orders to be genuinely clean, and in any case we had no time for it. We were simply carrying out our duties; and as our first duty was punctuality, we saved time by being dirty.

In the kitchen the dirt was worse. It is not a figure of speech, it is a mere statement of fact to say that a French cook will spit in the soup—that is, if he is not going to drink it himself. He is an artist, but his art is not cleanliness. To a certain extent he is even dirty because he is an artist, for food, to look smart, needs dirty treatment. When a steak, for

77

instance, is brought up for the head cook's inspection, he does not handle it with a fork. He picks it up in his fingers and slaps it down, runs his thumb round the dish and licks it to taste the gravy, runs it round and licks again, then steps back and contemplates the piece of meat like an artist judging a picture, then presses it lovingly into place with his fat, pink fingers, every one of which he has licked a hundred times that morning. When he is satisfied, he takes a cloth and wipes his fingerprints from the dish, and hands it to the waiter. And the waiter, of course, dips *his* fingers into the gravy—his nasty, greasy fingers which he is for ever running through his brilliantined hair. Whenever one pays more than, say, ten francs for a dish of meat in Paris, one may be certain that it has been fingered in this manner. In very cheap restaurants it is different; there, the same trouble is not taken over the food, and it is just forked out of the pan and flung on to a plate, without handling. Roughly speaking, the more one pays for food, the more sweat and spittle one is obliged to eat with it.

Dirtiness is inherent in hotels and restaurants, because sound food is sacrificed to punctuality and smartness. The hotel employee is too busy getting food ready to remember that it is meant to be eaten. A meal is simply '*une commande*' to him, just as a man dying of cancer is simply *a case* to the doctor. A customer orders, for example, a piece of toast. Somebody, pressed with work in a cellar deep underground, has to prepare it. How can he stop and say to himself, 'This toast is to be eaten—I must make it eatable'? All he knows is that it must look right and must be ready in three minutes. Some large drops of sweat fall from his forehead on to the toast. Why should he worry? Presently the toast falls among the filthy sawdust on the floor. Why trouble to make a new piece? It is much quicker to wipe the sawdust off. On the way upstairs the toast falls again, butter side down. Another wipe is all it needs. And so with everything. The only food at the Hôtel X which was ever prepared cleanly was the staff's, and the *patron's*. The maxim, repeated by everyone, was: 'Look out for the *patron*, and as for the clients, *s'en f—pas mal!*' Everywhere in the service quarters dirt festered—a secret vein of dirt, running through the great garish hotel like the intestines through a man's body.

Apart from the dirt, the *patron* swindled the customers wholeheartedly. For the most part the materials of the food were very bad, though the cooks knew how to serve it up in style. The meat was at best ordinary, and as to the vegetables, no good housekeeper would have looked at them in the market. The cream, by a standing order, was diluted with milk. The tea and coffee were of inferior sorts, and the jam was synthetic stuff out of vast, unlabelled tins. All the cheaper wines, according to Boris, were corked *vin ordinaire*. There was a rule that employees must pay for anything they spoiled, and in consequence damaged things were seldom thrown away. Once the waiter on the third floor dropped a roast chicken down the shaft of our service lift, where it fell into a litter of broken bread, torn paper and so forth at the bottom. We simply wiped it with a cloth and sent it up again. Upstairs there were dirty tales of once-used sheets not being washed, but simply damped, ironed and put back on the beds. The *patron* was as mean to us as to the customers. Throughout the vast hotel there was not, for instance, such a thing as a brush and pan; one had to manage with a broom and a piece of cardboard. And the staff lavatory was worthy of Central Asia, and there was no place to wash one's hands, except the sinks used for washing crockery.

In spite of all this the Hôtel X was one of the dozen most expensive hotels in Paris, and the customers paid startling prices. The ordinary charge for a night's lodging, not including breakfast, was two hundred francs. All wine and tobacco were sold at exactly double shop prices, though of course the *patron* bought at the wholesale price. If a customer had a title, or was reputed to be a millionaire, all his charges went up automatically. One morning on the fourth floor an American who was on diet wanted only salt and hot water for his breakfast. Valenti was furious. 'Jesus Christ!' he said, 'what about my ten per cent? Ten per cent of salt and water!' And he charged twenty-five francs for the breakfast. The customer paid without a murmur.

According to Boris, the same kind of thing went on in all Paris hotels, or at least in all the big, expensive ones. But I imagine that the customers at the Hôtel X were especially easy to swindle, for they were mostly Americans, with a sprinkling of English—no French—and seemed to know nothing whatever about good food. They would stuff themselves with disgusting American 'cereals', and eat marmalade at tea, and drink vermouth after dinner, and order a *poulet à la reine* at a hundred francs and then souse it in Worcester sauce. One customer, from Pittsburg, dined every night in his bedroom on grape-nuts, scrambled eggs and cocoa. Perhaps it hardly matters whether such people are swindled or not.

XV

I heard queer tales in the hotel. There were tales of dope fiends, of old debauchees who frequented hotels in search of pretty page boys, of thefts and blackmail. Mario told me of a hotel in which he had been, where a chambermaid stole a priceless diamond ring from an American lady. For days the staff were searched as they left work, and two detectives searched the hotel from top to bottom, but the ring was never found. The chambermaid had a lover in the bakery, and he had baked the ring into a roll, where it lay unsuspected until the search was over.

Once Valenti, at a slack time, told me a story about himself.

'You know, *mon p'tit*, this hotel life is all very well, but it's the devil when you're out of work. I expect you know what it is to go without eating, eh? *Forcément*, otherwise you wouldn't be scrubbing dishes. Well, I'm not a poor devil of a *plongeur*; I'm a waiter, and *I* went five days without eating, once. Five days without even a crust of bread—Jesus Christ!

'I tell you, those five days were the devil. The only good thing was, I had my rent paid in advance. I was living in a dirty, cheap little hotel in the Rue Sainte Éloise up in the Latin quarter. It was called the Hôtel Suzanne May, after

81

some famous prostitute of the time of the Empire. I was starving, and there was nothing I could do; I couldn't even go to the cafés where the hotel proprietors come to engage waiters, because I hadn't the price of a drink. All I could do was to lie in bed getting weaker and weaker, and watching the bugs running about the ceiling. I don't want to go through that again, I can tell you.

'In the afternoon of the fifth day I went half mad; at least, that's how it seems to me now. There was an old faded print of a woman's head hanging on the wall of my room, and I took to wondering who it could be; and after about an hour I realized that it must be Sainte Éloise, who was the patron saint of the quarter. I had never taken any notice of the thing before, but now, as I lay staring at it, a most extraordinary idea came into my head.

'"*Écoute, mon cher*," I said to myself, "you'll be starving to death if this goes on much longer. You've got to do something. Why not try a prayer to Sainte Éloise? Go down on your knees and ask her to send you some money. After all, it can't do any harm. Try it!"

'Mad, eh? Still, a man will do anything when he's hungry. Besides, as I said, it couldn't do any harm. I got out of bed and began praying. I said:

'"Dear Sainte Éloise, if you exist, please send me some money. I don't ask for much—just enough to buy some bread and a bottle of wine and get my strength back. Three or four francs would do. You don't know how grateful I'll be, Sainte Éloise, if you help me this once. And be sure, if you send me anything, the first thing I'll do will be to go and burn a candle for you, at your church down the street. Amen."

'I put in that about the candle, because I had heard that saints like having candles burnt in their honour. I meant to keep my promise, of course. But I am an atheist and I didn't really believe that anything would come of it.

'Well, I got into bed again, and five minutes later there

came a bang at the door. It was a girl called Maria, a big fat peasant girl who lived at our hotel. She was a very stupid girl, but a good sort, and I didn't much care for her to see me in the state I was in.

'She cried out at the sight of me. "*Nom de Dieu!*" she said, "what's the matter with you? What are you doing in bed at this time of day? *Quelle mine que tu as!* You look more like a corpse than a man."

'Probably I did look a sight. I had been five days without food, most of the time in bed, and it was three days since I had had a wash or a shave. The room was a regular pigsty, too.

'"What's the matter?" said Maria again.

'"The matter!" I said; "Jesus Christ! I'm starving. I haven't eaten for five days. That's what's the matter."

'Maria was horrified. "Not eaten for five days?" she said. "But why? Haven't you any money, then?"

'"Money!" I said. "Do you suppose I should be starving if I had money? I've got just five sous in the world, and I've pawned everything. Look round the room and see if there's anything more I can sell or pawn. If you can find anything that will fetch fifty centimes, you're cleverer than I am."

'Maria began looking round the room. She poked here and there among a lot of rubbish that was lying about, and then suddenly she got quite excited. Her great thick mouth fell open with astonishment.

'"You idiot!" she cried out. "Imbecile! What's *this*, then?"

'I saw that she had picked up an empty oil *bidon* that had been lying in the corner. I had bought it weeks before, for an oil lamp I had before I sold my things.

'"That?" I said. "That's an oil *bidon*. What about it?"

'"Imbecile! Didn't you pay three francs fifty deposit on it?"

'Now, of course I had paid the three francs fifty. They always make you pay a deposit on the *bidon*, and you get it back when the *bidon* is returned. But I'd forgotten all about it.

'"Yes—" I began.

'"Idiot!" shouted Maria again. She got so excited that she began to dance about until I thought her sabots would go through the floor, "Idiot! *T'es fou! T'es fou!* What have you got to do but take it back to the shop and get your deposit back? Starving, with three francs fifty staring you in the face! Imbecile!"

'I can hardly believe now that in all those five days I had never once thought of taking the *bidon* back to the shop. As good as three francs fifty in hard cash, and it had never occurred to me! I sat up in bed. "Quick!" I shouted to Maria, "you take it for me. Take it to the grocer's at the corner—run like the devil. And bring back food!"

'Maria didn't need to be told. She grabbed the *bidon* and went clattering down the stairs like a herd of elephants and in three minutes she was back with two pounds of bread under one arm and a half-litre bottle of wine under the other. I didn't stop to thank her; I just seized the bread and sank my teeth in it. Have you noticed how bread tastes when you have been hungry for a long time? Cold, wet, doughy—like putty almost. But, Jesus Christ, how good it was! As for the wine, I sucked it all down in one draught, and it seemed to go straight into my veins and flow round my body like new blood. Ah, that made a difference!

'I wolfed the whole two pounds of bread without stopping to take breath. Maria stood with her hands on her hips, watching me eat. "Well, you feel better, eh?" she said when I had finished.

'"Better!" I said. "I feel perfect! I'm not the same man as I was five minutes ago. There's only one thing in the world I need now—a cigarette."

'Maria put her hand in her apron pocket. "You can't have it," she said. "I've no money. This is all I had left out of your three francs fifty—seven sous. It's no good; the cheapest cigarettes are twelve sous a packet."

'"Then I can have them!" I said. "Jesus Christ, what a piece of luck! I've got five sous—it's just enough."

'Maria took the twelve sous and was starting out to the tobacconist's. And then something I had forgotten all this time came into my head. There was that cursed Sainte Éloise! I had promised her a candle if she sent me money; and really, who could say that the prayer hadn't come true? "Three or four francs," I had said; and the next moment along came three francs fifty. There was no getting away from it. I should have to spend my twelve sous on a candle.

'I called Maria back. "It's no use," I said; "there is Sainte Éloise—I have promised her a candle. The twelve sous will have to go on that. Silly, isn't it? I can't have my cigarettes after all."

'"Sainte Éloise?" said Maria. "What about Sainte Éloise?"

'"I prayed to her for money and promised her a candle," I said. "She answered the prayer—at any rate, the money turned up. I shall have to buy that candle. It's a nuisance, but it seems to me I must keep my promise."

'"But what put Sainte Éloise into your head?" said Maria.

'"It was her picture," I said, and I explained the whole thing. "There she is, you see," I said, and I pointed to the picture on the wall.

'Maria looked at the picture, and then to my surprise she burst into shouts of laughter. She laughed more and more, stamping about the room and holding her fat sides as though they would burst. I thought she had gone mad. It was two minutes before she could speak.

'"Idiot!" she cried at last. "*T'es fou! T'es fou!* Do you mean to tell me you really knelt down and prayed to that picture? Who told you it was Sainte Éloise?"

'"But I made sure it was Sainte Éloise!" I said.

"'Imbecile! It isn't Sainte Éloise at all. Who do you think it is?"

"'Who?" I said.

"'It is Suzanne May, the woman this hotel is called after."

'I had been praying to Suzanne May, the famous prostitute of the Empire . . .

'But, after all, I wasn't sorry. Maria and I had a good laugh, and then we talked it over, and we made out that I didn't owe Sainte Éloise anything. Clearly it wasn't she who had answered the prayer, and there was no need to buy her a candle. So I had my packet of cigarettes after all.'

XVI

Time went on and the Auberge de Jehan Cottard showed no signs of opening. Boris and I went down there one day during our afternoon interval and found that none of the alterations had been done, except the indecent pictures, and there were three duns instead of two. The *patron* greeted us with his usual blandness, and the next instant turned to me (his prospective dishwasher) and borrowed five francs. After that I felt certain that the restaurant would never get beyond talk. The *patron*, however, again named the opening for 'exactly a fortnight from today', and introduced us to the woman who was to do the cooking, a Baltic Russian five feet tall and a yard across the hips. She told us that she had been a singer before she came down to cooking, and that she was very artistic and adored English literature, especially *La Case de l'Oncle Tom*.

In a fortnight I had got so used to the routine of a *plongeur's* life that I could hardly imagine anything different. It was a life without much variation. At a quarter to six one woke with a sudden start, tumbled into grease-stiffened clothes, and hurried out with dirty face and protesting muscles. It was dawn, and the windows were dark except for the workmen's cafés. The sky was like a vast flat wall of cobalt, with roofs and spires of black paper pasted upon it. Drowsy men were sweeping the pavements with ten-foot besoms, and ragged families picking over the dustbins. Workmen, and girls with a piece of chocolate in one hand and a *croissant* in the other, were pouring into the Métro stations. Trams, filled with more workmen, boomed gloomily past. One hastened down to the station, fought for a place—one does literally have to fight on the Paris Métro at six in the morning—and stood jammed in the swaying mass of passengers, nose to nose with some hideous French face, breathing sour wine and garlic. And then one descended into the labyrinth of the hotel basement, and forgot daylight till two o'clock, when the sun was hot and the town black with people and cars.

After my first week at the hotel I always spent the afternoon interval in sleeping, or, when I had money, in a *bistro*. Except for a few ambitious waiters who went to English classes, the whole staff wasted their leisure in this way; one seemed too lazy after the morning's work to do anything better. Sometimes half a dozen *plongeurs* would make up a party and go to an abominable brothel in the Rue de Sieyès, where the charge was only five francs twenty-five centimes—tenpence half-penny. It was nicknamed '*le prix fixe*', and they used to describe their experiences there as a great joke. It was a favourite rendezvous of hotel workers. The *plongeurs*' wages did not allow them to marry, and no doubt work in the basement does not encourage fastidious feelings.

For another four hours one was in the cellars, and then one emerged, sweating, into the cool street. It was lamplight—that strange purplish gleam of the Paris lamps—and beyond the river the Eiffel Tower flashed from top to bottom with zigzag skysigns, like enormous snakes of fire. Streams of cars glided silently to and fro, and women, exquisite-looking in the dim light, strolled up and down the arcade. Sometimes a woman would glance at Boris or me, and then, noticing our greasy clothes, look hastily away again. One fought another battle in the Métro and was home by ten. Generally from ten to midnight I went to a little *bistro* in our street, an underground place frequented by Arab navvies. It was a bad place for fights, and I sometimes saw bottles thrown, once with fearful effect, but as a rule the Arabs fought among themselves and let Christians alone. Raki, the Arab drink, was very cheap, and the *bistro* was open at all hours, for the Arabs— lucky men—had the power of working all day and drinking all night.

It was the typical life of a *plongeur*, and it did not seem a bad life at the time. I had no sensation of poverty, for even after paying my rent and setting aside enough for tobacco and journeys and my food on Sundays, I still had four francs a day for drinks, and four francs was wealth. There was—it is hard to express it—a sort of heavy contentment, the contentment a well-fed beast might feel, in a life which had become so simple. For nothing could be simpler than the life of a *plongeur*. He lives in a rhythm between work and sleep, without time to think, hardly conscious of the exterior world; his Paris has shrunk to the hotel, the Métro, a few *bistros* and his bed. If he goes afield, it is only a few streets away, on a trip with some servant-girl who sits on his knee swallowing oysters and beer. On his free day he lies in bed till noon, puts on a clean shirt, throws dice for drinks, and after lunch goes back to bed again. Nothing is quite real to him but the *boulot*, drinks and sleep; and of these sleep is the most important.

One night, in the small hours, there was a murder just beneath my window. I was woken by a fearful uproar, and, going to the window, saw a man lying flat on the stones below; I could see the murderers, three of them, flitting away at the end of the street. Some of us went down and found that the man was quite dead, his skull cracked with a piece of lead piping. I remember the colour of his blood, curiously purple, like wine; it was still on the cobbles when I came home that evening, and they said the school-children had come from miles round to see it. But the thing that strikes me in looking back is that I was in bed and asleep within three minutes of the murder. So were most of the people in the street; we just made sure that the man was done for, and went straight back to bed. We were working people, and where was the sense of wasting sleep over a murder?

Work in the hotel taught me the true value of sleep, just as being hungry had taught me the true value of food. Sleep had ceased to be a mere physical necessity; it was something voluptuous, a debauch more than a relief. I had no more trouble with the bugs. Mario had told me of a sure remedy for them, namely pepper, strewed thick over the bedclothes. It made me sneeze, but the bugs all hated it, and emigrated to other rooms.

XVII

With thirty francs a week to spend on drinks I could take part in the social life of the quarter. We had some jolly evenings, on Saturdays, in the little *bistro* at the foot of the Hôtel des Trois Moineaux.

The brick-floored room, fifteen feet square, was packed with twenty people, and the air dim with smoke. The noise was deafening, for everyone was either talking at the top of his voice or singing. Sometimes it was just a confused din of voices; sometimes everyone would burst out together in the same song—the 'Marseillaise', or the 'Internationale', or 'Madelon', or 'Les Fraises et les Framboises'. Azaya, a great clumping peasant girl who worked fourteen hours a day in a glass factory, sang a song about, '*Il a per*du *ses pantalons, tout en dan*sant *le Charleston.*' Her friend Marinette, a thin, dark Corsican girl of obstinate virtue, tied her knees together and danced the *danse du ventre*. The old Rougiers wandered in and out, cadging drinks and trying to tell a long, involved story about someone who had once cheated them over a bedstead. R., cadaverous and silent, sat in his corner quietly boozing. Charlie, drunk, half danced, half staggered to and fro with a glass of sham absinthe balanced in one fat hand, pinching the women's breasts and declaiming poetry. People played darts and diced for drinks. Manuel, a Spaniard, dragged the girls to the bar and shook the dice-box against their bellies, for luck. Madame F. stood at the bar rapidly pouring *chopines* of wine through the pewter funnel, with a wet dishcloth always handy, because every man in the room tried to make love to her. Two children, bastards of big Louis the bricklayer, sat in a corner sharing a glass of *sirop*. Everyone was very happy, overwhelmingly certain that the world was a good place and we a notable set of people.

For an hour the noise scarcely slackened. Then about midnight there was a piercing shout of '*Citoyens!*' and the sound of a chair falling over. A blond, red-faced workman had risen to his feet and was banging a bottle on the table. Everyone stopped singing; the word went round, 'Sh! Furex is starting!' Furex was a strange creature, a Limousin stone-mason who worked steadily all the week and drank himself into a kind of paroxysm on Saturdays. He had lost his memory and could not remember anything before the war, and he would have gone to pieces through drink if Madame F. had not taken care of him. On Saturday evenings at about five o'clock she would say to someone, 'Catch Furex before he spends his wages,' and when he had been caught she would take away his money, leaving him enough for one good drink. One week he escaped, and, rolling blind drunk in the Place Monge, was run over by a car and badly hurt.

The queer thing about Furex was that, though he was a Communist when sober, he turned violently patriotic when drunk. He started the evening with good Communist principles, but after four or five litres he was a rampant Chauvinist, denouncing spies, challenging all foreigners to fight, and, if he was not prevented, throwing bottles. It was at this stage that he made his speech—for he made a patriotic speech every Saturday night. The speech was always the same, word for word. It ran:

'Citizens of the Republic, are there any Frenchmen here?

If there are any Frenchmen here, I rise to remind them—to remind them in effect, of the glorious days of the war. When one looks back upon that time of comradeship and heroism—one looks back, in effect, upon that time of comradeship and heroism. When one remembers the heroes who are dead—one remembers, in effect, the heroes who are dead. Citizens of the Republic, I was wounded at Verdun—'

Here he partially undressed and showed the wound he had received at Verdun. There were shouts of applause. We thought nothing in the world could be funnier than this speech of Furex's. He was a well-known spectacle in the quarter; people used to come in from other *bistros* to watch him when his fit started.

The word was passed round to bait Furex. With a wink to the others someone called for silence, and asked him to sing the 'Marseillaise'. He sang it well, in a fine bass voice, with patriotic gurgling noises deep down in his chest when he came to '*Aux arrmes, citoyens! Forrmez vos bataillons!*' Veritable tears rolled down his cheeks; he was too drunk to see that everyone was laughing at him. Then, before he had finished, two strong workmen seized him by either arm and held him down, while Azaya shouted, '*Vive l'Allemagne!*' just out of his reach. Furex's face went purple at such infamy. Everyone in the *bistro* began shouting together, '*Vive l'Allemagne! À bas la France!*' while Furex struggled to get at them. But suddenly he spoiled the fun. His face turned pale and doleful, his limbs went limp, and before anyone could stop him he was sick on the table. Then Madame F. hoisted him like a sack and carried him up to bed. In the morning he reappeared quiet and civil, and bought a copy of *L'Humanité*.

The table was wiped with a cloth, Madame F. brought more litre bottles and loaves of bread, and we settled down to serious drinking. There were more songs. An itinerant singer came in with his banjo and performed for five-sou pieces. An Arab and a girl from the *bistro* down the street did a dance, the man wielding a painted wooden phallus the size of a rolling-pin. There were gaps in the noise now. People had begun to talk about their love-affairs, and the war, and the barbel fishing in the Seine, and the best way to *faire la révolution*, and to tell stories. Charlie, grown sober again, captured the conversation and talked about his soul for five minutes. The doors and windows were opened to cool the room. The street was emptying, and in the distance one could hear the lonely milk train thundering down the Boulevard St Michel. The air blew cold on our foreheads, and the coarse African wine still tasted good: we were still happy, but meditatively, with the shouting and hilarious mood finished.

By one o'clock we were not happy any longer. We felt the joy of the evening wearing thin, and called hastily for more bottles, but Madame F. was watering the wine now, and it did not taste the same. Men grew quarrelsome. The girls were violently kissed and hands thrust into their bosoms and they made off lest worse should happen. Big Louis, the bricklayer, was drunk, and crawled about the floor barking and pretending to be a dog. The others grew tired of him and kicked at him as he went past. People seized each other by the arm and began long rambling confessions, and were angry when these were not listened to. The crowd thinned. Manuel and another man, both gamblers, went across to the Arab *bistro*, where card-playing went on till daylight. Charlie suddenly borrowed thirty francs from Madame F. and disappeared, probably to a brothel. Men began to empty their glasses, call briefly, '*'Sieurs, dames!*' and go off to bed.

By half past one the last drop of pleasure had evaporated, leaving nothing but headaches. We perceived that we were not splendid inhabitants of a splendid world, but a crew of underpaid workmen grown squalidly and dismally drunk. We went on swallowing the wine, but it was only from habit, and the stuff seemed suddenly nauseating. One's head had swollen up like a balloon, the floor rocked, one's tongue and lips were stained purple. At last it was no use keeping it up any longer. Several men went out into the yard behind the *bistro* and were sick. We crawled up to bed, tumbled down half dressed, and stayed there ten hours.

Most of my Saturday nights went in this way. On the whole, the two hours when one was perfectly and wildly happy seemed worth the subsequent headache. For many men in the quarter, unmarried and with no future to think of, the weekly drinking-bout was the one thing that made life worth living.

XVIII

Charlie told us a good story one Saturday night in the *bistro*. Try and picture him—drunk, but sober enough to talk consecutively. He bangs on the zinc bar and yells for silence:

'Silence, *messieurs et dames*—silence, I implore you! Listen to this story, that I am about to tell you. A memorable story, an instructive story, one of the souvenirs of a refined and civilized life. Silence, *messieurs et dames*!

'It happened at a time when I was hard up. You know what that is like—how damnable, that a man of refinement should ever be in such a condition. My money had not come from home; I had pawned everything, and there was nothing open to me except to work, which is a thing I will not do. I was living with a girl at the time—Yvonne her name was—a great half-witted peasant girl like Azaya there, with yellow hair and fat legs. The two of us had eaten nothing in three days. *Mon Dieu*, what sufferings! The girl used to walk up and down the room with her hands on her belly, howling like a dog that she was dying of starvation. It was terrible.

'But to a man of intelligence nothing is impossible. I propounded to myself the question, "What is the easiest way to get money without working?" And immediately the answer came: "To get money easily one must be a woman. Has not every woman something to sell?" And then, as I lay reflecting upon the things I should do if I were a woman, an idea came into my head. I remembered the Government maternity hospitals—you know the Government maternity hospitals? They are places where women who are *enceinte* are given meals free and no questions are asked. It is done to encourage childbearing. Any woman can go there and demand a meal, and she is given it immediately.

'"*Mon Dieu!*" I thought, "if only I were a woman! I would eat at one of those places every day. Who can tell whether a woman is *enceinte* or not, without an examination?"

'I turned to Yvonne. "Stop that insufferable bawling." I said, "I have thought of a way to get food."

'"How?" she said.

'"It is simple," I said. "Go to the Government maternity hospital. Tell them you are *enceinte* and ask for food. They will give you a good meal and ask no questions."

'Yvonne was appalled. "*Mais, mon Dieu,*" she cried, "I am not *enceinte!*"

'"Who cares?" I said. "That is easily remedied. What do you need except a cushion—two cushions if necessary? It is an inspiration from heaven, *ma chère*. Don't waste it."

'Well, in the end I persuaded her, and then we borrowed a cushion and I got her ready and took her to the maternity hospital. They received her with open arms. They gave her cabbage soup, a ragoût of beef, a purée of potatoes, bread and cheese and beer, and all kinds of advice about her baby. Yvonne gorged till she almost burst her skin, and managed to slip some of the bread and cheese into her pocket for me. I took her there every day until I had money again. My intelligence had saved us.

'Everything went well until a year later. I was with Yvonne again, and one day we were walking down the Boulevard Port Royal, near the barracks. Suddenly Yvonne's mouth fell open, and she began turning red and white, and red again.

'"*Mon Dieu!*" she cried, "look at that who is coming! It is the nurse who was in charge at the maternity hospital. I am ruined!"

'"Quick!" I said, "run!" But it was too late. The nurse had recognized Yvonne, and she came straight up to us, smiling. She was a big fat woman with a gold pince-nez and red cheeks like the cheeks of an apple. A motherly, interfering kind of woman.

'"I hope you are well, *ma petite*?" she said kindly. "And your baby, is he well too? Was it a boy, as you were hoping?"

'Yvonne had begun trembling so hard that I had to grip her arm. "No," she said at last.

'"Ah, then, *évidemment*, it was a girl?"

'Thereupon Yvonne, the idiot, lost her head completely. "No," she actually said again!

'The nurse was taken aback. "*Comment!*" she exclaimed, "neither a boy nor a girl! But how can that be?"

'Figure to yourselves, *messieurs et dames*, it was a dangerous moment. Yvonne had turned the colour of a beet-root and she looked ready to burst into tears; another second and she would have confessed everything. Heaven knows what might have happened. But as for me, I had kept my head; I stepped in and saved the situation.

'"It was twins," I said calmly.

'"Twins!" exclaimed the nurse. And she was so pleased that she took Yvonne by the shoulders and embraced her on both cheeks, publicly.

'Yes, twins . . .'

XIX

One day, when we had been at the Hôtel X five or six weeks, Boris disappeared without notice. In the evening I found him waiting for me in the Rue de Rivoli. He slapped me gaily on the shoulder.

'Free at last, *mon ami*! You can give notice in the morning. The Auberge opens tomorrow.'

'Tomorrow?'

'Well, possibly we shall need a day or two to arrange things. But, at any rate, no more cafeteria! *Nous sommes lancés, mon ami*! My tail coat is out of pawn already.'

His manner was so hearty that I felt sure there was something wrong, and I did not at all want to leave my safe and comfortable job at the hotel. However, I had promised Boris, so I gave notice, and the next morning at seven went down to the Auberge de Jehan Cottard. It was locked, and I went in search of Boris, who had once more bolted from his lodgings and taken a room in the rue de la Croix Nivert. I found him asleep, together with a girl whom he had picked up the night before, and who he told me was 'of a very sympathetic temperament.' As to the restaurant, he said that it was all arranged; there were only a few little things to be seen to before we opened.

At ten I managed to get Boris out of bed, and we unlocked the restaurant. At a glance I saw what the 'few little things' amounted to. It was briefly this: that the alterations had not been touched since our last visit. The stoves for the kitchen had not arrived, the water and electricity had not been laid on, and there was all manner of painting, polishing and carpentering to be done. Nothing short of a miracle could open the restaurant within ten days, and by the look of things it might collapse without even opening. It was obvious what had happened. The *patron* was short of money, and he had engaged the staff (there were four of us) in order to use us instead of workmen. He would be getting our services almost free, for waiters are paid no wages, and though he would have to pay me, he would not be feeding me till the restaurant opened. In effect, he had swindled us of several hundred francs by sending for us before the restaurant was open. We had thrown up a good job for nothing.

Boris, however, was full of hope. He had only one idea in his head, namely, that here at last was a chance of being a waiter and wearing a tail coat once more. For this he was quite willing to do ten days' work unpaid, with the chance of being left jobless in the end. 'Patience!' he kept saying. 'That will arrange itself. Wait till the restaurant opens, and we'll get it all back. Patience, *mon ami*!'

We needed patience, for days passed and the restaurant did not even progress towards opening. We cleaned out the cellars, fixed the shelves, distempered the walls, polished the woodwork, whitewashed the ceiling, stained the floor; but the main work, the plumbing and gas-fitting and electricity, was still not done, because the *patron* could not pay the bills. Evidently he was almost penniless, for he refused the smallest charges, and he had a trick of swiftly disappearing when asked for money. His blend of shiftiness and aristocratic manners made him very hard to deal with. Melancholy duns came looking for him at all hours, and by instruction we always told them that he was at Fontainebleau, or Saint Cloud, or some other place that was safely distant. Meanwhile, I was getting hungrier and hungrier. I had left the hotel with thirty francs, and I had to go back immediately to a diet of dry bread. Boris had managed in the beginning to extract an advance of sixty francs from the *patron*, but he had spent half of it, in redeeming his waiter's clothes, and half on the girl of sympathetic temperament. He borrowed three francs a day from Jules, the second waiter, and spent it on bread. Some days we had not even money for tobacco.

Sometimes the cook came to see how things were getting on, and when she saw that the kitchen was still bare of pots and pans she usually wept. Jules, the second waiter, refused steadily to help with the work. He was a Magyar, a little dark, sharp-featured fellow in spectacles, and very talkative; he had been a medical student, but had abandoned his training for lack of money. He had a taste for talking while other people were working, and he told me all about himself and his ideas. It appeared that he was a Communist, and had various strange theories (he could prove to you by figures that it was wrong to work), and he was also, like most Magyars, passionately proud. Proud and lazy men do not make good waiters. It was Jules's dearest boast that once when a customer in a restaurant had insulted him, he had poured a plate of hot soup down the customer's neck, and then walked straight out without even waiting to be sacked.

As each day went by Jules grew more and more enraged at the trick the *patron* had played on us. He had a spluttering, oratorical way of talking. He used to walk up and down shaking his fist, and trying to incite me not to work:

'Put that brush down, you fool! You and I belong to proud races; we don't work for nothing, like these damned Russian serfs. I tell you, to be cheated like this is torture to me. There have been times in my life, when someone has cheated me even of five sous, when I have vomited—yes, vomited with rage.

'Besides, *mon vieux*, don't forget that I'm a Communist. *À bas la bourgeoisie!* Did any man alive ever see me working when I could avoid it? No. And not only I don't wear myself out working, like you other fools, but I steal, just to show my independence. Once I was in a restaurant where the *patron* thought he could treat me like a dog. Well, in revenge I found out a way to steal milk from the milk-cans and seal them up again so that no one should know. I tell you I just swilled that milk down night and morning. Every day I drank four litres of milk, besides half a litre of cream. The *patron* was at his wits' end to know where the milk was going. It wasn't that I wanted milk, you understand, because I hate the stuff; it was principle, just principle.

'Well, after three days I began to get dreadful pains in my belly, and I went to the doctor. "What have you been eating?" he said. I said: "I drink four litres of milk a day, and half a litre of cream." "Four litres!" he said. "Then stop it at once. You'll burst if you go on." "What do I care?" I said. "With me principle is everything. I shall go on drinking that milk, even if I do burst."

'Well, the next day the *patron* caught me stealing milk. "You're sacked," he said; "you leave at the end of the week." "*Pardon, monsieur,*" I said, "I shall leave this morning." "No, you won't," he said, "I can't spare you till Saturday." "Very well, *mon patron,*" I thought to myself, "we'll see who gets tired of it first." And then I set to work to smash the crockery. I broke nine plates the first day and thirteen the second; after that the *patron* was glad to see the last of me.

'Ah, I'm not one of your Russian *moujiks* . . .'

Ten days passed. It was a bad time. I was absolutely at the end of my money, and my rent was several days overdue. We loafed about the dismal empty restaurant, too hungry even to get on with the work that remained. Only Boris now believed that the restaurant would open. He had set his heart on being *maître d'hôtel*, and he invented a theory that the *patron's* money was tied up in shares and he was waiting a favourable moment for selling. On the tenth day I had nothing to eat or smoke, and I told the *patron* that I could not continue working without an advance on my wages. As blandly as usual, the *patron* promised the advance, and then, according to his custom, vanished. I walked part of the way home, but I did not feel equal to a scene with Madame F. over the rent, so I passed the night on a bench on the boulevard. It was very uncomfortable—the arm of the seat cuts into your back—and much colder than I had expected. There was plenty of time, in the long boring hours between dawn and work, to think what a fool I had been to deliver myself into the hands of these Russians.

Then, in the morning, the luck changed. Evidently the *patron* had come to an understanding with his creditors, for he arrived with money in his pockets, set the alterations going, and gave me my advance. Boris and I bought macaroni and a piece of horse's liver, and had our first hot meal in ten days.

The workmen were brought in and the alterations made, hastily and with incredible shoddiness. The tables, for instance, were to be covered with baize, but when the *patron* found that baize was expensive he bought instead disused army blankets, smelling incorrigibly of sweat. The table cloths (they were check, to go with the 'Norman' decorations) would cover them, of course. On the last night we were at work till two in the morning, getting things ready. The crockery did not arrive till eight, and, being new, had all to be washed. The cutlery did not arrive till the next morning, nor the linen either, so that we had to dry the crockery with a shirt of the *patron's* and an old pillowslip belonging to the concierge. Boris and I did all the work. Jules was skulking, and the *patron* and his wife sat in the bar with a dun and some Russian friends, drinking success to the restaurant. The cook was in the kitchen with her head on the table, crying, because she was expected to cook for fifty people, and there were not pots and pans enough for ten. About midnight there was a fearful interview with some duns, who came intending to seize eight copper saucepans which the *patron* had obtained on credit. They were bought off with half a bottle of brandy.

Jules and I missed the last Métro home and had to sleep on the floor of the restaurant. The first thing we saw in the morning were two large rats sitting on the kitchen table, eating from a ham that stood there. It seemed a bad omen, and I was surer than ever that the Auberge de Jehan Cottard would turn out a failure.

XX

The *patron* had engaged me as kitchen *plongeur*; that is, my job was to wash up, keep the kitchen clean, prepare vegetables, make tea, coffee and sandwiches, do the simpler cooking, and run errands. The terms were, as usual, five hundred francs a month and food, but I had no free day and no fixed working hours. At the Hôtel X I had seen catering at its best, with unlimited money and good organization. Now, at the Auberge, I learned how things are done in a thoroughly bad restaurant. It is worth describing, for there are hundreds of similar restaurants in Paris, and every visitor feeds in one of them occasionally.

I should add, by the way, that the Auberge was not the ordinary cheap eating-house frequented by students and workmen. We did not provide an adequate meal at less than twenty-five francs, and we were picturesque and artistic, which sent up our social standing. There were the indecent pictures in the bar, and the Norman decorations—sham beams on the walls, electric lights done up as candlesticks, 'peasant' pottery, even a mounting-block at the door—and the *patron* and the head waiter were Russian officers, and many of the customers titled Russian refugees. In short, we were decidedly chic.

Nevertheless, the conditions behind the kitchen door

were suitable for a pigsty. For this is what our service arrangements were like.

The kitchen measured fifteen feet long by eight broad, and half this space was taken up by the stoves and tables. All the pots had to be kept on shelves out of reach, and there was only room for one dustbin. This dustbin used to be crammed full by midday, and the floor was normally an inch deep in a compost of trampled food.

For firing we had nothing but three gas-stoves, without ovens, and all joints had to be sent out to the bakery.

There was no larder. Our substitute for one was a half-roofed shed in the yard, with a tree growing in the middle of it. The meat, vegetables and so forth lay there on the bare earth, raided by rats and cats.

There was no hot water laid on. Water for washing up had to be heated in pans, and, as there was no room for these on the stoves when meals were cooking, most of the plates had to be washed in cold water. This, with soft soap and the hard Paris water, meant scraping the grease off with bits of newspaper.

We were so short of saucepans that I had to wash each one as soon as it was done with, instead of leaving them till the evening. This alone wasted probably an hour a day.

Owing to some scamping of expense in the installation, the electric light usually fused at eight in the evening. The *patron* would only allow us three candles in the kitchen, and the cook said three were unlucky, so we had only two.

Our coffee-grinder was borrowed from a *bistro* near by, and our dustbin and brooms from the concierge. After the first week a quantity of linen did not come back from the wash, as the bill was not paid. We were in trouble with the inspector of labour, who had discovered that the staff included no Frenchmen; he had several private interviews with the *patron*, who, I believe, was obliged to bribe him. The electric company was still dunning us, and when the duns found that we would buy them off with *apéritifs*, they came every morning. We were in debt at the grocery, and credit would have been stopped, only the grocer's wife (a moustachio'd woman of sixty) had taken a fancy to Jules, who was sent every morning to cajole her. Similarly I had to waste an hour every day haggling over vegetables in the rue du Commerce, to save a few centimes.

These are the results of starting a restaurant on insufficient capital. And in these conditions the cook and I were expected to serve thirty or forty meals a day, and would later on be serving a hundred. From the first day it was too much for us. The cook's working hours were from eight in the morning till midnight, and mine from seven in the morning till half past twelve the next morning—seventeen and a half hours, almost without a break. We never had time to sit down till five in the afternoon, and even then there was no seat except the top of the dustbin. Boris, who lived near by and had not to catch the last Métro home, worked from eight in the morning till two the next morning—eighteen hours a day, seven days a week. Such hours, though not usual, are nothing extraordinary in Paris.

Life settled at once into a routine that made the Hôtel X seem like a holiday. Every morning at six I drove myself out of bed, did not shave, sometimes washed, hurried up to the Place d'ltalie and fought for a place on the Métro. By seven I was in the desolation of the cold, filthy kitchen, with the potato skins and bones and fishtails littered on the floor, and a pile of plates, stuck together in their grease, waiting from overnight. I could not start on the plates yet, because the water was cold, and I had to fetch milk and make coffee, for the others arrived at eight and expected to find coffee ready. Also, there were always several copper saucepans to clean. Those copper saucepans are the bane of a *plongeur's* life. They have to be scoured with sand and bunches of chain, ten minutes to each one, and then polished on the outside with Brasso. Fortunately, the art of making them has been lost and they are gradually vanishing from French kitchens, though one can still buy them secondhand.

When I had begun on the plates the cook would take me away from the plates to begin skinning onions, and when I had begun on the onions the *patron* would arrive and send me out to buy cabbages. When I came back with the cabbages the *patron's* wife would tell me to go to some shop half a mile away and buy a pot of rouge; by the time I came back there would be more vegetables waiting, and the plates were still not done. In this way our incompetence piled one job on another throughout the day, everything in arrears.

Till ten, things went comparatively easily, though we were working fast, and no one lost his temper. The cook would find time to talk about her artistic nature, and say did I not think Tolstoy was *épatant*, and sing in a fine soprano voice as she minced beef on the board. But at ten the waiters began clamouring for their lunch, which they had early, and at eleven the first customers would be arriving. Suddenly everything became hurry and bad temper. There was not the same furious rushing and yelling as at the Hôtel X, but an atmosphere of muddle, petty spite and exasperation. Discomfort was at the bottom of it. It was unbearably cramped in the kitchen, and dishes had to be put on the floor, and one had to be thinking constantly about not stepping on them. The cook's vast buttocks banged against me as she moved to and fro. A ceaseless, nagging chorus of orders streamed from her:

'Unspeakable idiot! How many times have I told you not to bleed the beetroots? Quick, let me get to the sink! Put those knives away; get on with the potatoes. What have you done with my strainer? Oh, leave those potatoes alone. Didn't I tell you to skim the *bouillon*? Take that can of water off the stove. Never mind the washing up, chop this celery. No, not like that, you fool, like this. There! Look at you letting those peas boil over! Now get to work and scale these herrings. Look, do you call this plate clean? Wipe it on your apron. Put that salad on the floor. That's right, put it where I'm bound to step in it! Look out, that pot's boiling over! Get me down that saucepan. No, the other one. Put this on the grill. Throw those potatoes away. Don't waste time, throw them on the floor. Tread them in. Now throw down some sawdust; this floor's like a skating-rink. Look, you fool, that steak's burning! *Mon Dieu*, why did they send me an idiot for a *plongeur*? Who are you talking to? Do you realize that my aunt was a Russian countess?' etc. etc. etc.

This went on till three o'clock without much variation, except that about eleven the cook usually had a *crise de nerfs* and a flood of tears. From three to five was a fairly slack time for the waiters, but the cook was still busy, and I was working my fastest, for there was a pile of dirty plates waiting, and it was a race to get them done, or partly done, before dinner began. The washing up was doubled by the primitive conditions—a cramped draining-board, tepid water, sodden cloths, and a sink that got blocked once in an hour. By five the cook and I were feeling unsteady on our feet, not having eaten or sat down since seven. We used to collapse, she on the dustbin and I on the floor, drink a bottle of beer, and apologize for some of the things we had said in the morning. Tea was what kept us going. We took care to have a pot always stewing, and drank pints during the day.

At half-past five the hurry and quarrelling began again, and now worse than before, because everyone was tired out. The cook had a *crise de nerfs* at six and another at nine; they came on so regularly that one could have told the time by them. She would flop down on the dustbin, begin weeping hysterically, and cry out that never, no, never had she thought to come to such a life as this; her nerves would not stand it; she had studied music at Vienna; she had a bedridden husband to support, etc. etc. At another time one would have been sorry for her, but, tired as we all were, her whimpering voice merely infuriated us. Jules used to stand in the doorway and mimic her weeping. The *patron's* wife nagged, and Boris and Jules quarrelled all day, because Jules shirked his work, and Boris, as head waiter, claimed the larger share of the tips. Only the second day after the restaurant opened, they came to blows in the kitchen over a two-franc tip, and the cook and I had to separate them. The only person who never forgot his manners was the *patron*. He kept the same hours as the rest of us, but he had no work to do, for it was his wife who really managed things. His sole job, besides ordering the supplies, was to stand in the bar smoking cigarettes and looking gentlemanly, and he did that to perfection.

The cook and I generally found time to eat our dinner between ten and eleven o'clock. At midnight the cook would steal a packet of food for her husband, stow it under her clothes, and make off, whimpering that these hours would kill her and she would give notice in the morning. Jules also left at midnight, usually after a dispute with Boris, who had to look after the bar till two. Between twelve and half past I did what I could to finish the washing up. There was no time to attempt doing the work properly, and I used simply to rub the grease off the plates with table-napkins. As for the dirt on the floor, I let it lie, or swept the worst of it out of sight under the stoves.

At half past twelve I would put on my coat and hurry out. The *patron*, bland as ever, would stop me as I went down the alley-way past the bar. '*Mais, mon cher monsieur*, how tired you look! Please do me the favour of accepting this glass of brandy.'

He would hand me the glass of brandy as courteously as though I had been a Russian duke instead of a *plongeur*. He treated all of us like this. It was our compensation for working seventeen hours a day.

As a rule the last Métro was almost empty—a great advantage, for one could sit down and sleep for a quarter of an hour. Generally I was in bed by half past one. Sometimes I missed the train and had to sleep on the floor of the restaurant, but it hardly mattered, for I could have slept on cobblestones at that time.

XXI

This life went on for about a fortnight, with a slight increase of work as more customers came to the restaurant. I could have saved an hour a day by taking a room near the restaurant, but it seemed impossible to find time to change lodgings—or, for that matter, to get my hair cut, look at a newspaper, or even undress completely. After ten days I managed to find a free quarter of an hour, and wrote to my friend B. in London asking him if he could get me a job of some sort—anything, so long as it allowed more than five hours sleep. I was simply not equal to going on with a seventeen-hour day, though there are plenty of people who think nothing of it. When one is overworked, it is a good cure for self-pity to think of the thousands of people in Paris restaurants who work such hours, and will go on doing it, not for a few weeks, but for years. There was a girl in a *bistro* near my hotel who worked from seven in the morning till midnight for a whole year, only sitting down to her meals. I remember once asking her to come to a dance, and she laughed and said that she had not been farther than the street corner for several months. She was consumptive, and died about the time I left Paris.

After only a week we were all neurasthenic with fatigue, except Jules, who skulked persistently. The quarrels, intermittent at first, had now become continuous. For hours' one would keep up a drizzle of useless nagging, rising into storms of abuse every few minutes. 'Get me down that saucepan, idiot!' the cook would cry (she was not tall enough to reach the shelves where the saucepans were kept). 'Get it down yourself, you old whore,' I would answer. Such remarks seemed to be generated spontaneously from the air of the kitchen.

We quarrelled over things of inconceivable pettiness. The dustbin, for instance, was an únending source of quarrels—whether it should be put where I wanted it, which was in the cook's way, or where she wanted it, which was between me and the sink. Once she nagged and nagged until at last, in pure spite, I lifted the dustbin up and put it out in the middle of the floor, where she was bound to trip over it.

'Now, you cow,' I said, 'move it yourself.'

Poor old woman, it was too heavy for her to lift, and she sat down, put her head on the table and burst out crying. And I jeered at her. This is the kind of effect that fatigue has upon one's manners.

After a few days the cook had ceased talking about Tolstoy and her artistic nature, and she and I were not on speaking terms, except for the purposes of work, and Boris and Jules were not on speaking terms, and neither of them was on speaking terms with the cook. Even Boris and I were barely on speaking terms. We had agreed beforehand that the *engueulades* of working hours did not count between times; but we had called each other things too bad to be forgotten—and besides, there were no between times. Jules grew lazier and lazier, and he stole food constantly—from a sense of duty, he said. He called the rest of us *jaune*—blackleg—when we would not join with him in stealing. He had a curious, malignant spirit. He told me, as a matter of pride, that he had sometimes wrung a dirty dishcloth into a customer's soup before taking it in, just to be revenged upon a member of the bourgeoisie.

The kitchen grew dirtier and the rats bolder, though we trapped a few of them. Looking round that filthy room, with raw meat lying among refuse on the floor, and cold, clotted saucepans sprawling everywhere, and the sink blocked and coated with grease, I used to wonder whether there could be a restaurant in the world as bad as ours. But the other three all said that they had been in dirtier places. Jules took a positive pleasure in seeings things dirty. In the afternoon, when he had not much to do, he used to stand in the kitchen doorway jeering at us for working too hard:

'Fool! Why do you wash that plate? Wipe it on your trousers. Who cares about the customers? *They* don't know what's going on. What is restaurant work? You are carving a chicken and it falls on the floor. You apologize, you bow, you go out; and in five minutes you come back by another door—with the same chicken. That is restaurant work,' etc.

And, strange to say, in spite of all this filth and incompetence, the Auberge de Jehan Cottard was actually a success. For the first few days all our customers were Russians, friends of the *patron*, and these were followed by Americans and other foreigners—no Frenchmen. Then one night there was tremendous excitement, because our first Frenchman had arrived. For a moment our quarrels were forgotten and we all united in the effort to serve a good dinner. Boris tiptoed into the kitchen, jerked his thumb over his shoulder and whispered conspiratorially:

'*Sh! Attention, un Français!*'

A moment later the *patron's* wife came and whispered:

'*Attention, un Français!* See that he gets a double portion of all vegetables.'

While the Frenchman ate, the *patron's* wife stood behind the grille of the kitchen door and watched the expression of his face. Next night the Frenchman came back with two other Frenchmen. This meant that we were earning a good name; the surest sign of a bad restaurant is to be frequented only by foreigners. Probably part of the reason for our success was that the *patron*, with the sole gleam of sense he had shown in fitting out the restaurant, had bought very sharp table-knives. Sharp knives, of course, are *the* secret of a successful restaurant. I am glad that this happened, for it destroyed one of my illusions, namely, the idea that Frenchmen know good food when they see it. Or perhaps we *were* a fairly good restaurant by Paris standards; in which case the bad ones must be past imagining.

In a very few days after I had written to B he replied to say that there was a job he could get for me. It was to look after a congenital imbecile, which sounded a splendid rest cure after the Auberge de Jehan Cottard. I pictured myself loafing in the country lanes, knocking thistle-heads off with my stick, feeding on roast lamb and treacle tart, and sleeping ten hours a night in sheets smelling of lavender. B sent me a fiver to pay my passage and get my clothes out of the pawn, and as soon as the money arrived I gave one day's notice and left the restaurant. My leaving so suddenly embarrassed the *patron*, for as usual he was penniless, and he had to pay my wages thirty francs short. However he stood me a glass of Courvoisier '48 brandy, and I think he felt that this made up the difference. They engaged a Czech, a thoroughly competent *plongeur*, in my place, and the poor old cook was sacked a few weeks later. Afterwards I heard that, with two first-rate people in the kitchen, the *plongeur's* work had been cut down to fifteen hours a day. Below that no one could have cut it, short of modernizing the kitchen.

XXII

For what they are worth I want to give my opinions about the life of a Paris *plongeur*. When one comes to think of it, it is strange that thousands of people in a great modern city should spend their waking hours swabbing dishes in hot dens underground. The question I am raising is why this life goes on—what purpose it serves, and who wants it to continue, and why I am not taking the merely rebellious, *fainéant* attitude. I am trying to consider the social significance of a *plongeur's* life.

I think one should start by saying that a *plongeur* is one of the slaves of the modern world. Not that there is any need to whine over him, for he is better off than many manual workers, but still, he is no freer than if he were bought and sold. His work is servile and without art; he is paid just enough to keep him alive; his only holiday is the sack. He is cut off from marriage, or, if he marries, his wife must work too. Except by a lucky chance, he has no escape from this life, save into prison. At this moment there are men with university degrees scrubbing dishes in Paris for ten or fifteen hours a day. One cannot say that it is mere idleness on their part, for an idle man cannot be a *plongeur*; they have simply been trapped by a routine which makes thought impossible. If *plongeurs* thought at all, they would long ago have formed a union and gone on strike for better treatment. But they do not think, because they have no leisure for it; their life has made slaves of them.

The question is, why does this slavery continue? People have a way of taking it for granted that all work is done for a sound purpose. They see somebody else doing a disagreeable job, and think that they have solved things by saying that the job is necessary. Coal-mining, for example, is hard work, but it is necessary—we must have coal. Working in the sewers is unpleasant, but somebody must work in the sewers. And similarly with a *plongeur's* work. Some people must feed in restaurants, and so other people must swab dishes for eighty hours a week. It is the work of civilization, therefore unquestionable. This point is worth considering.

Is a *plongeur's* work really necessary to civilization? We have a feeling that it must be 'honest' work, because it is hard and disagreeable, and we have made a sort of fetish of manual work. We see a man cutting down a tree, and we make sure that he is filling a social need, just because he uses his muscles; it does not occur to us that he may only be cutting down a beautiful tree to make room for a hideous statue. I believe it is the same with a *plongeur*. He earns his bread in the sweat of his brow, but it does not follow that he is doing anything useful; he may be only supplying a luxury which, very often, is not a luxury.

As an example of what I mean by luxuries which are not luxuries, take an extreme case, such as one hardly sees in Europe. Take an Indian rickshaw puller, or a gharry pony. In any Far Eastern town there are rickshaw pullers by the hundred, black wretches weighing eight stone, clad in loin-cloths. Some of them are diseased; some of them are fifty years old. For miles on end they trot in the sun or rain, head down, dragging at the shafts, with the sweat dripping from their grey moustaches. When they go too slowly the passenger calls them *bahinchut*. They earn thirty or forty rupees a month, and cough their lungs out after a few years. The gharry ponies are gaunt, vicious things that have been sold cheap as having a few years' work left in them. Their master looks on the whip as a substitute for food. Their work expresses itself in a sort of equation—whip plus food equals energy; generally it is about sixty per cent whip and forty per cent food. Sometimes their necks are encircled by one vast sore, so that they drag all day on raw flesh. It is still possible to make them work, however; it is just a question of thrashing them so hard that the pain behind outweighs the pain in front. After a few years even the whip loses its virtue, and the pony goes to the knacker. These are instances of unnecessary work, for there is no real need for gharries and rickshaws; they only exist because Orientals consider it vulgar to walk. They are luxuries, and, as anyone who has ridden in them knows, very poor luxuries. They afford a small amount of convenience, which cannot possibly balance the suffering of the men and animals.

Similarly with the *plongeur*. He is a king compared with a rickshaw puller or a gharry pony, but his case is analogous. He is the slave of a hotel or a restaurant, and his slavery is more or less useless. For, after all, where is the *real* need of big hotels and smart restaurants? They are supposed to provide luxury, but in reality they provide only a cheap, shoddy imitation of it. Nearly everyone hates hotels. Some restaurants are better than others, but it is impossible to get as good a meal in a restaurant as one can get, for the same expense, in a private house. No doubt hotels and restaurants must exist, but there is no need that they should enslave hundreds of people. What makes the work in them is not the essentials; it is the shams that are supposed to represent luxury. Smartness, as it is called, means, in effect, merely that the staff work more and the customers pay more; no one benefits except the proprietor, who will presently buy himself a striped villa at Deauville. Essentially, a 'smart' hotel is a place where a hundred people toil like devils in order that two hundred may pay through the nose for things they do not really want. If the nonsense were cut out of hotels and restaurants, and the work done with simple efficiency, *plongeurs* might work six or eight hours a day instead of ten or fifteen.

Suppose it is granted that a *plongeur's* work is more or less useless. Then the question follows, Why does anyone want him to go on working? I am trying to go beyond the immediate economic cause, and to consider what pleasure it can give anyone to think of men swabbing dishes for life. For there is no doubt that people—comfortably situated people—do find a pleasure in such thoughts. A slave, Marcus Cato said, should be working when he is not sleeping. It does not matter whether his work is needed or not, he must work, because work in itself is good—for slaves, at least. This sentiment still survives, and it has piled up mountains of useless drudgery.

I believe that this instinct to perpetuate useless work is, at bottom, simply fear of the mob. The mob (the thought runs) are such low animals that they would be dangerous if they had leisure; it is safer to keep them too busy to think. A rich man who happens to be intellectually honest, if he is questioned about the improvement of working conditions, usually says something like this:

'We know that poverty is unpleasant; in fact, since it is so remote, we rather enjoy harrowing ourselves with the thought of its unpleasantness. But don't expect us to do anything about it. We are sorry for you lower classes, just as we are sorry for a cat with the mange, but we will fight like devils against any improvement of your condition. We feel that you are much safer as you are. The present state of affairs suits us, and we are not going to take the risk of setting you free, even by an extra hour a day. So, dear brothers, since evidently you must sweat to pay for our trips to Italy, sweat and be damned to you.'

This is particularly the attitude of intelligent, cultivated people; one can read the substance of it in a hundred essays. Very few cultivated people have less than (say) four hundred pounds a year, and naturally they side with the rich, because they imagine that any liberty conceded to the poor is a threat to their own liberty. Foreseeing some dismal Marxian Utopia as the alternative, the educated man prefers to keep things as they are. Possibly he does not like his fellow-rich very much, but he supposes that even the vulgarest of them are less inimical to his pleasures, more his kind of people, than the poor, and that he had better stand by them. It is this fear of a supposedly dangerous mob that makes nearly all intelligent people conservative in their opinions.

Fear of the mob is a superstitious fear. It is based on the idea that there is some mysterious, fundamental difference between rich and poor, as though they were two different races, like Negroes and white men. But in reality there is no such difference. The mass of the rich and the poor are differentiated by their incomes and nothing else, and the average millionaire is only the average dishwasher dressed in a new suit. Change places, and handy dandy, which is the justice, which is the thief? Everyone who has mixed on equal terms with the poor knows this quite well. But the trouble is that intelligent, cultivated people, the very people who might be expected to have liberal opinions, never do mix with the poor. For what do the majority of educated people know about poverty? In my copy of Villon's poems the editor has actually thought it necessary to explain the line '*Ne pain ne voyent qu'aux fenestres*' by a footnote; so remote is even hunger from the educated man's experience.

From this ignorance a superstitious fear of the mob results quite naturally. The educated man pictures a horde of submen, wanting only a day's liberty to loot his house, burn his books, and set him to work minding a machine or sweeping out a lavatory. 'Anything,' he thinks, 'any injustice, sooner than let that mob loose.' He does not see that since there is no difference between the mass of rich and poor, there is no question of setting the mob loose. The mob is in fact loose now, and—in the shape of rich men—is using its power to set up enormous treadmills of boredom, such as 'smart' hotels.

To sum up. A *plongeur* is a slave, and a wasted slave, doing stupid and largely unnecessary work. He is kept at work, ultimately, because of a vague feeling that he would be dangerous if he had leisure. And educated people, who should be on his side, acquiesce in the process, because they know nothing about him and consequently are afraid of him. I say this of the *plongeur* because it is his case I have been considering; it would apply equally to numberless other types of worker. These are only my own ideas about the basic facts of a *plongeur's* life, made without reference to immediate economic questions, and no doubt largely platitudes. I present them as a sample of the thoughts that are put into one's head by working in an hotel.

XXIII

As soon as I left the Auberge de Jehan Cottard I went to bed and slept the clock round, all but one hour. Then I washed my teeth for the first time in a fortnight, bathed and had my hair cut, and got my clothes out of pawn. I had two glorious days of loafing. I even went in my best suit to the Auberge, leant against the bar and spent five francs on a bottle of English beer. It is a curious sensation, being a customer where you have been a slave's slave. Boris was sorry that I had left the restaurant just at the moment when we were *lancés* and there was a chance of making money. I have heard from him since, and he tells me that he is making a hundred francs a day and has set up a girl who is *très serieuse* and never smells of garlic.

I spent a day wandering about our quarter, saying good-bye to everyone. It was on this day that Charlie told me about the death of old Roucolle the miser, who had once lived in the quarter. Very likely Charlie was lying as usual, but it was a good story.

Roucolle died, aged seventy-four, a year or two before I went to Paris, but the people in the quarter still talked of him while I was there. He never equalled Daniel Dancer or anyone of that kind, but he was an interesting character. He went to Les Halles every morning to pick up damaged vegetables, and ate cat's meat, and wore newspaper instead of underclothes, and used the wainscoting of his room for firewood, and made himself a pair of trousers out of a sack—all this with half a million francs invested. I should like very much to have known him.

Like many misers, Roucolle came to a bad end through putting his money into a wildcat scheme. One day a Jew appeared in the quarter, an alert, business-like young chap who had a first-rate plan for smuggling cocaine into England. It is easy enough, of course, to buy cocaine in Paris, and the smuggling would be quite simple in itself, only there is always some spy who betrays the plan to the customs or the police. It is said that this is often done by the very people who sell the cocaine, because the smuggling trade is in the hands of a large combine, who do not want competition. The Jew, however, swore that there was no danger. He knew a way of getting cocaine direct from Vienna, not through the usual channels, and there would be no blackmail to pay. He had got into touch with Roucolle through a young Pole, a student at the Sorbonne, who was going to put four thousand francs into the scheme if Roucolle would put six thousand. For this they could buy ten pounds of cocaine, which would be worth a small fortune in England.

The Pole and the Jew had a tremendous struggle to get the money from between old Roucolle's claws. Six thousand francs was not much—he had more than that sewn into the mattress in his room—but it was agony for him to part with a sou. The Pole and the Jew were at him for weeks on end, explaining, bullying, coaxing, arguing, going down on their knees and imploring him to produce the money. The old man was half frantic between greed and fear. His bowels yearned at the thought of getting, perhaps, fifty thousand francs' profit, and yet he could not bring himself to risk the money. He used to sit in a corner with his head in his hands, groaning and sometimes yelling out in agony, and often he would kneel down (he was very pious) and pray for strength, but still he couldn't do it. But at last, more from exhaustion than anything else, he gave in quite suddenly; he slit open the mattress where his money was concealed and handed over six thousand francs to the Jew.

The Jew delivered the cocaine the same day, and promptly vanished. And meanwhile, as was not surprising after the fuss Roucolle had made, the affair had been noised all over the quarter. The very next morning the hotel was raided and searched by the police.

Roucolle and the Pole were in agonies. The police were downstairs, working their way up and searching every room in turn, and there was the great packet of cocaine on the table, with no place to hide it and no chance of escaping down the stairs. The Pole was for throwing the stuff out of the window, but Roucolle would not hear of it. Charlie told me that he had been present at the scene. He said that when they tried to take the packet from Roucolle he clasped it to his breast and struggled like a madman, although he was seventy-four years old. He was wild with fright, but he would go to prison rather than throw his money away.

At last, when the police were searching only one floor below, somebody had an idea. A man on Roucolle's floor had a dozen tins of face-powder which he was selling on commission; it was suggested that the cocaine could be put into the tins and passed off as face-powder. The powder was hastily thrown out of the window and the cocaine substituted, and the tins were put openly on Roucolle's table, as though there there were nothing to conceal. A few minutes later the police came to search Roucolle's room. They tapped the walls and looked up the chimney and turned out the drawers and examined the floor-boards, and then, just as they were about to give it up, having found nothing, the inspector noticed the tins on the table.

'*Tiens*,' he said, 'have a look at those tins. I hadn't noticed them. What's in them, eh?'

'Face-powder,' said the Pole as calmly as he could

manage. But at the same instant Roucolle let out a loud groaning noise, from alarm, and the police became suspicious immediately. They opened one of the tins and tipped out the contents, and after smelling it, the inspector said that he believed it was cocaine. Roucolle and the Pole began swearing on the names of the saints that it was only face-powder; but it was no use, the more they protested the more suspicious the police became. The two men were arrested and led off to the police station, followed by half the quarter.

At the station, Roucolle and the Pole were interrogated by the Commissaire while a tin of the cocaine was sent away to be analysed. Charlie said that the scene Roucolle made was beyond description. He wept, prayed, made contradictory statements and denounced the Pole all at once, so loud that he could be heard half a street away. The policemen almost burst with laughing at him.

After an hour a policeman came back with the tin of cocaine and a note from the analyst. He was laughing.

'This is not cocaine, *monsieur*,' he said.

'What, not cocaine?' said the Commissaire. '*Mais, alors*—what is it, then?'

'It is face-powder.'

Roucolle and the Pole were released at once, entirely exonerated but very angry. The Jew had double-crossed them. Afterwards, when the excitement was over, it turned out that he had played the same trick on two other people in the quarter.

The Pole was glad enough to escape, even though he had lost his four thousand francs, but poor old Roucolle was utterly broken down. He took to his bed at once, and all that day and half the night they could hear him thrashing about, mumbling, and sometimes yelling out at the top of his voice:

'Six thousand francs! *Nom de Jésus-Christ!* Six thousand francs!'

Three days later he had some kind of stroke, and in a fortnight he was dead—of a broken heart, Charlie said.

XXIV

I travelled to England third class via Dunkirk and Tilbury, which is the cheapest and not the worst way of crossing the Channel. You had to pay extra for a cabin, so I slept in the saloon, together with most of the third-class passengers. I find this entry in my diary for that day:

'Sleeping in the saloon, twenty-seven men, sixteen women. Of the women, not a single one has washed her face this morning. The men mostly went to the bathroom; the women merely produced vanity cases and covered the dirt with powder. *Q*. A secondary sexual difference?'

On the journey I fell in with a couple of Roumanians, mere children, who were going to England on their honeymoon trip. They asked innumerable questions about England, and I told them some startling lies. I was so pleased to be getting home, after being hard up for months in a foreign city, that England seemed to me a sort of Paradise. There are, indeed, many things in England that make you glad to get home; bathrooms, armchairs, mint sauce, new potatoes properly cooked, brown bread, marmalade, beer made with veritable hops—they are all splendid, if you can pay for them. England is a very good country when you are not poor; and, of course, with a tame imbecile to look after, I was not going to be poor. The thought of not being poor made me very patriotic. The more questions the Roumanians asked, the more I praised England; the climate, the scenery, the art, the literature, the laws—everything in England was perfect.

Was the architecture in England good? the Roumanians asked. 'Splendid!' I said. 'And you should just see the London statues! Paris is vulgar—half grandiosity and half slums. But London—'

Then the boat drew alongside Tilbury pier. The first building we saw on the waterside was one of those huge hotels, all stucco and pinnacles, which stare from the English coast like idiots staring over an asylum wall. I saw the Roumanians, too polite to say anything, cocking their eyes at the hotel. 'Built by French architects,' I assured them; and even later, when the train was crawling into London through the eastern slums, I still kept it up about the beauties of English architecture. Nothing seemed too good to say about England, now that I was coming home and was not hard up any more.

I went to B.'s office, and his first words knocked everything to ruins. 'I'm sorry,' he said; 'your employers have gone abroad, patient and all. However, they'll be back in a month. I suppose you can hang on till then?'

I was outside in the street before it even occurred to me to borrow some more money. There was a month to wait, and I had exactly nineteen and sixpence in hand. The news had taken my breath away. For a long time I could not make up my mind what to do. I loafed the day in the streets, and at night, not having the slightest notion of how to get a cheap bed in London, I went to a 'family' hotel, where the charge was seven and sixpence. After paying the bill I had ten and twopence in hand.

By the morning I had made my plans. Sooner or later I should have to go to B. for more money, but it seemed hardly decent to do so yet, and in the meantime I must exist in some hole-and-corner way. Past experience set me against pawning my best suit. I would leave all my things at the station cloak-room, except my second-best suit, which I could exchange for some cheap clothes and perhaps a pound. If I was going to live a month on thirty shillings I must have bad clothes—indeed, the worse the better. Whether thirty shillings could be made to last a month I had no idea, not knowing London as I knew Paris. Perhaps I could beg, or sell bootlaces, and I remembered articles I had read in the Sunday papers about beggars who have two thousand pounds sewn into their trou-sers. It was, at any rate, notoriously impossible to starve in London, so there was nothing to be anxious about.

To sell my clothes I went down into Lambeth, where the people are poor and there are a lot of rag shops. At the first shop I tried the proprietor was polite but unhelpful; at the second he was rude; at the third he was stone deaf, or pretended to be so. The fourth shopman was a large blond young man, very pink all over, like a slice of ham. He looked at the clothes I was wearing and felt them disparagingly between thumb and finger.

'Poor stuff,' he said, 'very poor stuff, that is.' (It was quite a good suit.) 'What yer want for 'em?'

I explained that I wanted some older clothes and as much money as he could spare. He thought for a moment, then collected some dirty-looking rags and threw them on to the counter. 'What about the money?' I said, hoping for a pound. He pursed his lips, then produced a *shilling* and laid it beside the clothes. I did not argue—I was going to argue, but as I opened my mouth he reached out as though to take up the shilling again; I saw that I was helpless. He let me change in a small room behind the shop.

The clothes were a coat, once dark brown, a pair of black dungaree trousers, a scarf and a cloth cap; I had kept my own shirt, socks and boots, and I had a comb and razor in my pocket. It gives one a very strange feeling to be wearing such clothes. I had worn bad enough things before, but nothing at all like these; they were not merely dirty and shapeless, they had—how is one to express it?—a gracelessness, a patina of antique filth, quite different from mere shabbiness. They were the sort of clothes you see on a bootlace seller, or a tramp. An hour later, in Lambeth, I saw a hang-dog man, obviously a tramp, coming towards me, and when I looked again it was myself, reflected in a shop window. The dirt was plastering my face already. Dirt is a great respecter of persons; it lets you alone when you are well dressed, but as soon as your collar is gone it flies towards you from all directions.

I stayed in the streets till late at night, keeping on the move all the time. Dressed as I was, I was half afraid that the police might arrest me as a vagabond, and I dared not speak to anyone, imagining that they must notice a disparity between my accent and my clothes. (Later I discovered that this never happened.) My new clothes had put me instantly into a new world. Everyone's demeanour seemed to have changed abruptly. I helped a hawker pick up a barrow that he had upset. 'Thanks, mate,' he said with a grin. No one had called me mate before in my life—it was the clothes that had done it. For the first time I noticed, too, how the attitude of women varies with a man's clothes. When a badly dressed man passes them they shudder away from him with a quite frank movement of disgust, as though he were a dead cat. Clothes are powerful things. Dressed in a tramp's clothes it is very difficult, at any rate for the first day, not to feel that you are genuinely degraded. You might feel the same shame, irrational but very real, your first night in prison.

At about eleven I began looking for a bed. I had read about doss-houses (they are never called doss-houses, by the way), and I supposed that one could get a bed for fourpence or thereabouts. Seeing a man, a navvy or something of the kind, standing on the kerb in the Waterloo Road, I stopped and questioned him. I said that I was stony broke and wanted the cheapest bed I could get.

'Oh,' said he, 'you go to that 'ouse across the street there, with the sign "Good Beds for Single Men". That's a good kip [sleeping place], that is. I bin there myself on and off. You'll find it cheap *and* clean.'

It was a tall, battered-looking house, with dim lights in all the windows, some of which were patched with brown paper. I entered a stone passage-way, and a little etiolated boy with sleepy eyes appeared from a door leading to a cellar. Murmurous sounds came from the cellar, and a wave of hot air and cheese. The boy yawned and held out his hand.

'Want a kip? That'll be a 'og, guv'nor.'

I paid the shilling, and the boy led me up a rickety unlighted staircase to a bedroom. It had a sweetish reek of paregoric and foul linen; the windows seemed to be tight shut, and the air was almost suffocating at first. There was a candle burning, and I saw that the room measured fifteen feet square by eight high, and had eight beds in it. Already six lodgers were in bed, queer lumpy shapes with all their own clothes, even their boots, piled on top of them. Someone was coughing in a loathsome manner in one corner.

When I got into the bed I found that it was as hard as a board, and as for the pillow, it was a mere hard cylinder like a block of wood. It was rather worse than sleeping on a table, because the bed was not six feet long, and very narrow, and the mattress was convex, so that one had to hold on to avoid falling out. The sheets stank so horribly of sweat that I could not bear them near my nose. Also, the bedclothes only consisted of the sheets and a cotton counterpane, so that though stuffy it was none too warm. Several noises recurred throughout the night. About once in an hour the man on my left—a sailor, I think—woke up, swore vilely, and lighted a cigarette. Another man, victim of a bladder disease, got up and noisily used his chamber-pot half a dozen times during the night. The man in the corner had a coughing fit once in every twenty minutes, so regularly that one came to listen for it as one listens for the next yap when a dog is baying the moon. It was an unspeakably repellent sound; a foul bubbling and retching, as though the man's bowels were being churned up within him. Once when he struck a match I saw that he was a very old man, with a grey, sunken face like that of a corpse, and he was wearing his trousers wrapped round his head as a nightcap, a thing which for some reason disgusted me very much. Every time he coughed or the other man swore, a sleepy voice from one of the other beds cried out:

'Shut up! Oh, for Christ's— *sake* shut up!'

I had about an hour's sleep in all. In the morning I was woken by a dim impression of some large brown thing coming towards me. I opened my eyes and saw that it was one of the sailor's feet, sticking out of bed close to my face. It was dark brown, quite dark brown like an Indian's, with dirt. The walls were leprous, and the sheets, three weeks from the wash, were almost raw umber colour. I got up, dressed and went downstairs. In the cellar were a row of basins and two slippery roller towels. I had a piece of soap in my pocket, and I was going to wash, when I noticed that every basin was streaked with grime—solid, sticky filth as black as boot-blacking. I went out unwashed. Altogether, the lodging-house had not come up to its description as cheap *and* clean. It was however, as I found later, a fairly representative lodging-house.

I crossed the river and walked a long way eastward, finally going into a coffee-shop on Tower Hill. An ordinary London coffee-shop, like a thousand others, it seemed queer and foreign after Paris. It was a little stuffy room with the high-backed pews that were fashionable in the 'forties, the day's menu written on a mirror with a piece of soap, and a girl of fourteen handling the dishes. Navvies were eating out of newspaper parcels, and drinking tea in vast saucerless mugs like china tumblers. In a corner by himself a Jew, muzzle down in the plate, was guiltily wolfing bacon.

'Could I have some tea and bread and butter?' I said to the girl.

She stared. 'No butter, only marg,' she said, surprised. And she repeated the order in the phrase that is to London what the eternal *coup de rouge* is to Paris: 'Large tea and two slices!'

On the wall beside my pew there was a notice saying 'Pocketing the sugar not allowed,' and beneath it some poetic customer had written:

He that takes away the sugar,
Shall be called a dirty—

but someone else had been at pains to scratch out the last word. This was England. The tea-and-two-slices cost three-pence halfpenny, leaving me with eight and twopence.

XXV

The eight shillings lasted three days and four nights. After my bad experience in the Waterloo Road* I moved eastward, and spent the next night in a lodging-house in Pennyfields. This was a typical lodging-house, like scores of others in London. It had accommodation for between fifty and a hundred men, and was managed by a 'deputy'—a deputy for the owner, that is, for these lodging-houses are profitable concerns and are owned by rich men. We slept fifteen or twenty in a dormitory; the beds were again cold and hard, but the sheets were not more than a week from the wash, which was an improvement. The charge was ninepence or a shilling (in the shilling dormitory the beds were six feet apart instead of four) and the terms were cash down by seven in the evening or out you went.*

Downstairs there was a kitchen common to all lodgers, with free firing and a supply of cooking-pots, tea-basins, and toasting-forks. There were two great clinker fires, which were kept burning day and night the year through. The work of

---

* It is a curious but well-known fact that bugs are much commoner in south than north London. For some reason they have not yet crossed the river in any great numbers.

tending the fires, sweeping the kitchen and making the beds was done by the lodgers in rotation. One senior lodger, a fine Norman-looking stevedore named Steve, was known as 'head of the house', and was arbiter of disputes and unpaid chucker-out.

I liked the kitchen. It was a low-ceiled cellar deep underground, very hot and drowsy with coke fumes, and lighted only by the fires, which cast black velvet shadows in the corners. Ragged washing hung on strings from the ceiling. Red-lit men, stevedores mostly, moved about the fires with cooking-pots; some of them were quite naked, for they had been laundering and were waiting for their clothes to dry. At night there were games of nap and draughts, and songs— 'I'm a chap what's done wrong by my parents,' was a favourite, and so was another popular song about a shipwreck. Sometimes late at night men would come in with a pail of winkles they had bought cheap, and share them out. There was a general sharing of food, and it was taken for granted to feed men who were out of work. A little pale, wizened creature, obviously dying, referred to as 'pore Brown, bin under the doctor and cut open three times,' was regularly fed by the others.

Two or three of the lodgers were old-age pensioners. Till meeting them I had never realized that there are people in England who live on nothing but the old-age pension of ten shillings a week. None of these old men had any other resource whatever. One of them was talkative, and I asked him how he managed to exist. He said:

'Well, there's ninepence a night for yer kip—that's five an' threepence a week. Then there's threepence on Saturday for a shave—that's five an' six. Then say you 'as a 'aircut once a month for sixpence—that's another three'apence a week. So you 'as about four an' four-pence for food an' bacca.'

He could imagine no other expenses. His food was bread and margarine and tea—towards the end of the week dry bread and tea without milk—and perhaps he got his clothes from charity. He seemed contented, valuing his bed and fire more than food. But, with an income of ten shillings a week, to spend money on a shave—it is awe-inspiring.

All day I loafed in the streets, east as far as Wapping, west as far as Whitechapel. It was queer after Paris; everything was so much cleaner and quieter and drearier. One missed the scream of the trams, and the noisy, festering life of the back streets, and the armed men clattering through the squares. The crowds were better dressed and the faces comelier and milder and more alike, without that fierce individuality and malice of the French. There was less drunkenness, and less dirt, and less quarrelling, and more idling. Knots of men stood at all the corners, slightly underfed, but kept going by the tea-and-two-slices which the Londoner swallows every two hours. One seemed to breathe a less feverish air than in Paris. It was the land of the tea urn and the Labour Exchange, as Paris is the land of the *bistro* and the sweatshop.

It was interesting to watch the crowds. The East London women are pretty (it is the mixture of blood, perhaps), and Limehouse was sprinkled with Orientals—Chinamen, Chittagonian lascars, Dravidians selling silk scarves, even a few Sikhs, come goodness knows how. Here and there were street meetings. In Whitechapel somebody called The Singing Evangel undertook to save you from hell for the charge of sixpence. In the East India Dock Road the Salvation Army were holding a service. They were singing 'Anybody here like sneaking Judas?' to the tune of 'What's to be done with a drunken sailor?' On Tower Hill two Mormons were trying to address a meeting. Round their platform struggled a mob of men, shouting and interrupting. Someone was denouncing them for polygamists. A lame, bearded man, evidently an atheist, had heard the word God and was heckling angrily. There was a confused uproar of voices.

'My dear friends, if you would only let us finish what we were saying—!—That's right, give 'em a say. Don't get on the argue!—No, no, you answer me. Can you *show* me God? You *show* 'im me, then I'll believe in 'im.—Oh, shut up, don't keep interrupting of 'em!—Interrupt yourself—polygamists!—Well, there's a lot to be said for polygamy. Take the—women out of industry, anyway.—My dear friends, if you would just—No, no, don't you slip out of it. 'Ave you *seen* God? 'Ave you *touched* 'im? 'Ave you shook *'ands* with 'im?—Oh, don't get on the argue, for Christ's sake don't get on the *argue*!' etc. etc. I listened for twenty minutes, anxious to learn something about Mormonism, but the meeting never got beyond shouts. It is the general fate of street meetings.

In Middlesex Street, among the crowds at the market, a draggled, down-at-heel woman was hauling a brat of five by the arm. She brandished a tin trumpet in its face. The brat was squalling.

'Enjoy yourself!' yelled the mother. 'What yer think I brought yer out 'ere for an' bought y' a trumpet an' all? D'ya want to go across my knee? You little bastard, you *shall* enjoy yerself!'

Some drops of spittle fell from the trumpet. The mother and the child disappeared, both bawling. It was all very queer after Paris.

The last night that I was in the Pennyfields lodging-house there was a quarrel between two of the lodgers, a vile scene. One of the old-age pensioners, a man of about seventy, naked to the waist (he had been laundering), was violently abusing a short, thickset stevedore, who stood with his back to the fire. I could see the old man's face in the light of the fire, and he was almost crying with grief and rage. Evidently something very serious had happened.

The old-age Pensioner: 'You—!'

The stevedore: 'Shut yer mouth, you ole—, afore I set about yer!'

The old-age Pensioner: 'Jest you try it on, you—! I'm

thirty year older'n you, but it wouldn't take much to make me give you one as'd knock you into a bucketful of piss!'

The stevedore: 'Ah, an' then p'raps I wouldn't smash you up after, you ole—!'

Thus for five minutes. The lodgers sat round, unhappy, trying to disregard the quarrel. The stevedore looked sullen, but the old man was growing more and more furious. He kept making little rushes at the other, sticking out his face and screaming from a few inches distant like a cat on a wall, and spitting. He was trying to nerve himself to strike a blow, and not quite succeeding. Finally he burst out:

'A —, that's what you are, a — —! Take that in your dirty gob and suck it, you —! By —, I'll smash you afore I've done with you. A —, that's what you are, a son of a — whore. Lick that, you —! That's what I think of you, you —, you —, you —, you — you BLACK BASTARD!'

Whereat he suddenly collapsed on a bench, took his face in his hands, and began crying. The other man seeing that public feeling was against him, went out.

Afterwards I heard Steve explaining the cause of the quarrel. It appeared that it was all about a shilling's worth of food. In some way the old man had lost his store of bread and margarine, and so would have nothing to eat for the next three days, except what the others gave him in charity. The stevedore, who was in work and well fed, had taunted him; hence the quarrel.

When my money was down to one and fourpence I went for a night to a lodging-house in Bow, where the charge was only eightpence. One went down an area and through an alley-way into a deep, stifling cellar, ten feet square. Ten men, navvies mostly, were sitting in the fierce glare of the fire. It was midnight, but the deputy's son, a pale, sticky child of five, was there playing on the navvies' knees. An old Irishman was whistling to a blind bullfinch in a tiny cage. There were other songbirds there—tiny, faded things, that had lived all their lives underground. The lodgers habitually made water in the fire, to save going across a yard to the lavatory. As I sat at the table I felt something stir near my feet, and, looking down, saw a wave of black things moving slowly across the floor; they were black-beetles.

There were six beds in the dormitory, and the sheets, marked in huge letters 'Stolen from No. — Road', smelt loathsome. In the next bed to me lay a very old man, a pavement artist, with some extraordinary curvature of the spine that made him stick right out of bed, with his back a foot or two from my face. It was bare, and marked with curious swirls of dirt, like a marble table-top. During the night a man came in drunk and was sick on the floor, close to my bed. There were bugs too—not so bad as in Paris, but enough to keep one awake. It was a filthy place. Yet the deputy and his wife were friendly people, and ready to make one a cup of tea at any hour of the day or night.

XXVI

In the morning after paying for the usual tea-and-two-slices and buying half an ounce of tobacco, I had a halfpenny left. I did not care to ask B. for more money yet, so there was nothing for it but to go to a casual ward. I had very little idea how to set about this, but I knew that there was a casual ward at Romton, so I walked out there, arriving at three or four in the afternoon. Leaning against the pigpens in Romton market-place was a wizened old Irishman, obviously a tramp. I went and leaned beside him, and presently offered him my tobacco-box. He opened the box and looked at the tobacco in astonishment:

'By God,' he said, 'dere's sixpennorth o' good baccy here! Where de hell d'you get hold o' dat? *You* ain't been on de road long.'

'What, don't you have tobacco on the road?' I said.

'Oh, we *has* it. Look.'

He produced a rusty tin which had once held Oxo Cubes. In it were twenty or thirty cigarette ends, picked up from the pavement. The Irishman said that he rarely got any other tobacco; he added that, with care, one could collect two ounces of tobacco a day on the London pavements.

'D'you come out o' one o' de London spikes [casual wards], eh?' he asked me.

I said yes, thinking this would make him accept me as a fellow tramp, and asked him what the spike at Romton was like. He said:

'Well, 'tis a cocoa spike. Dere's tay spikes, and cocoa spikes, and skilly spikes. Dey don't give you skilly in Romton, t'ank God—leastways, dey didn't de last time I was here. I been up to York and round Wales since.'

'What is skilly?' I said.

'Skilly? A can o' hot water wid some bloody oatmeal at de bottom; dat's skilly. De skilly spikes is always de worst.'

We stayed talking for an hour or two. The Irishman was a friendly old man, but he smelt very unpleasant, which was not surprising when one learned how many diseases he suffered from. It appeared (he described his symptoms fully) that taking him from top to bottom he had the following things wrong with him: on his crown, which was bald, he had eczema; he was shortsighted, and had no glasses; he had chronic bronchitis; he had some undiagnosed pain in the back; he had dyspepsia; he had urethritis; he had varicose veins, bunions and flat feet. With this assemblage of diseases he had tramped the roads for fifteen years.

At about five the Irishman said, 'Could you do wid a cup o' tay? De spike don't open till six.'

'I should think I could.'

'Well, dere's a place here where dey gives you a free cup o' tay and a bun. *Good* tay it is. Dey makes you say a lot o' bloody prayers after; but hell! It all passes de time away. You come wid me.'

He led the way to a small tin-roofed shed in a side-street, rather like a village cricket pavilion. About twenty-five other tramps were waiting. A few of them were dirty old habitual vagabonds, the majority decent-looking lads from the north, probably miners or cotton operatives out of work. Presently the door opened and a lady in a blue silk dress, wearing gold spectacles and a crucifix, welcomed us in. Inside were thirty or forty hard chairs, a harmonium, and a very gory lithograph of the Crucifixion.

Uncomfortably we took off our caps and sat down. The lady handed out the tea, and while we ate and drank she moved to and fro, talking benignly. She talked upon religious subjects—about Jesus Christ always having a soft spot for poor rough men like us, and about how quickly the time passed when you were in church, and what a difference it made to a man on the road if he said his prayers regularly. We hated it. We sat against the wall fingering our caps (a tramp feels indecently exposed with his cap off), and turning pink and trying to mumble something when the lady addressed us. There was no doubt that she meant it all kindly. As she came up to one of the north country lads with the plate of buns, she said to him:

'And you, my boy, how long is it since you knelt down and spoke with your Father in Heaven?'

Poor lad, not a word could he utter; but his belly answered for him, with a disgraceful rumbling which it set up at sight of the food. Thereafter he was so overcome with shame that he could scarcely swallow his bun. Only one man managed to answer the lady in her own style, and he was a spry, red-nosed fellow looking like a corporal who had lost his stripe for drunkenness. He could pronounce the words 'the dear Lord Jesus' with less shame than anyone I ever saw. No doubt he had learned the knack in prison.

Tea ended, and I saw the tramps looking furtively at one another. An unspoken thought was running from man to man—could we possibly make off before the prayers started? Someone stirred in his chair—not getting up actually, but with just a glance at the door, as though half suggesting the idea of departure. The lady quelled him with one look. She said in a more benign tone than ever:

'I don't think you need go *quite* yet. The casual ward doesn't open till six, and we have time to kneel down and say a few words to our Father first. I think we should all feel better after that, shouldn't we?'

The red-nosed man was very helpful, pulling the harmonium into place and handing out the prayerbooks. His back was to the lady as he did this, and it was his idea of a joke to deal the books like a pack of cards, whispering to each man as he did so, 'There y'are, mate, there's a — nap 'and for yer! Four aces and a king!' etc.

Bareheaded, we knelt down among the dirty teacups and began to mumble that we had left undone those things that we ought to have done, and done those things that we ought not to have done, and there was no health in us. The lady prayed very fervently, but her eyes roved over us all the time, making sure that we were attending. When she was not looking we grinned and winked at one another, and whispered bawdy jokes, just to show that we did not care; but it stuck in our throats a little. No one except the red-nosed man was self-possessed enough to speak the responses above a whisper. We got on better with the singing, except that one old tramp knew no tune but 'Onward, Christian soldiers', and reverted to it sometimes, spoiling the harmony.

The prayers lasted half an hour, and then, after a handshake at the door, we made off. 'Well,' said somebody as soon as we were out of hearing, 'the trouble's over. I thought them — prayers was never goin' to end.'

'You 'ad your bun,' said another; 'you got to pay for it.'

'Pray for it, you mean. Ah, you don't get much for nothing. They can't even give you a twopenny cup of tea without you go down on you — knees for it.'

There were murmurs of agreement. Evidently the tramps were not grateful for their tea. And yet it was excellent tea, as different from coffee-shop tea as good Bordeaux is from the muck called colonial claret, and we were all glad of it. I am sure too that it was given in a good spirit, without any intention of humiliating us; so in fairness we ought to have been grateful—still, we were not.

XXVII

At about a quarter to six the Irishman led me to the spike. It was a grim, smoky yellow cube of brick, standing in a corner of the workhouse grounds. With its rows of tiny, barred windows, and a high wall and iron gates separating it from the road, it looked much like a prison. Already a long queue of ragged men had formed up, waiting for the gates to open. They were of all kinds and ages, the youngest a fresh-faced boy of sixteen, the oldest a doubled-up, toothless mummy of seventy-five. Some were hardened tramps, recognizable by their sticks and billies and dust-darkened faces; some were factory hands out of work, some agricultural labourers, one a clerk in collar and tie, two certainly imbeciles. Seen in the mass, lounging there, they were a disgusting sight; nothing villainous or dangerous, but a graceless, mangy crew, nearly all ragged and palpably underfed. They were friendly, however, and asked no questions. Many offered me tobacco—cigarette ends, that is.

We leaned against the wall, smoking, and the tramps began to talk about the spikes they had been in recently. It appeared from what they said that all spikes are different, each with its peculiar merits and demerits, and it is important to know these when you are on the road. An old hand will tell you the peculiarities of every spike in England, as: at A you are allowed to smoke but there are bugs in the cells; at B the beds are comfortable but the porter is a bully; at C they let you out early in the morning but the tea is undrinkable; at D the officials steal your money if you have any—and so on interminably. There are regular beaten tracks where the spikes are within a day's march of one another. I was told that the Barnet–St Albans route is the best, and they warned me to steer clear of Billericay and Chelmsford, also Ide Hill in Kent. Chelsea was said to be the most luxurious spike in England; someone, praising it, said that the blankets there were more like prison than the spike. Tramps go far afield in summer, and in winter they circle as much as possible round the large towns, where it is warmer and there is more charity. But they have to keep moving, for you may not enter any one spike, or any two London spikes, more than once in a month, on pain of being confined for a week.

Some time after six the gates opened and we began to file in one at a time. In the yard was an office where an official entered in a ledger our names and trades and ages, also the places we were coming from and going to—this last is intended to keep a check on the movements of tramps. I gave my trade as 'painter'; I had painted water-colours—who has not? The official also asked us whether we had any money, and every man said no. It is against the law to enter the spike with more than eightpence, and any sum less than this one is supposed to hand over at the gate. But as a rule the tramps prefer to smuggle their money in, tying it tight in a piece of cloth so that it will not chink. Generally they put it in the bag of tea and sugar that every tramp carries, or among their 'papers'. The 'papers' are considered sacred and are never searched.

After registering at the office we were led into the spike by an official known as the Tramp Major (his job is to supervise casuals, and he is generally a workhouse pauper) and a

143

great bawling ruffian of a porter in a blue uniform, who treated us like cattle. The spike consisted simply of a bathroom and lavatory, and, for the rest, long double rows of stone cells, perhaps a hundred cells in all. It was a bare, gloomy place of stone and whitewash, unwillingly clean, with a smell which, somehow, I had foreseen from its appearance; a smell of soft soap, Jeyes' fluid and latrines—a cold, discouraging, prisonish smell.

The porter herded us all into the passage, and then told us to come into the bathroom six at a time, to be searched before bathing. The search was for money and tobacco, Romton being one of those spikes where you can smoke once you have smuggled your tobacco in, but it will be confiscated if it is found on you. The old hands had told us that the porter never searched below the knee, so before going in we had all hidden our tobacco in the ankles of our boots. Afterwards, while undressing, we slipped it into our coats, which we were allowed to keep, to serve as pillows.

The scene in the bathroom was extraordinarily repulsive. Fifty dirty, stark-naked men elbowing each other in a room twenty feet square, with only two bathtubs and two slimy roller towels between them all. I shall never forget the reek of dirty feet. Less than half the tramps actually bathed (I heard them saying that hot water is 'weakening' to the system), but they all washed their faces and feet, and the horrid greasy little clouts known as toe-rags which they bind round their toes. Fresh water was only allowed for men who were having a complete bath, so many men had to bathe in water where others had washed their feet. The porter shoved us to and fro, giving the rough side of his tongue when anyone wasted time. When my turn came for the bath, I asked if I might swill out the tub, which was streaked with dirt, before using it. He answered simply, 'Shut yer — mouth and get on with yer bath!' That set the social tone of the place, and I did not speak again.

When we had finished bathing, the porter tied our clothes in bundles and gave us workhouse shirts—grey cotton things of doubtful cleanliness, like abbreviated nightgowns. We were sent along to the cells at once, and presently the porter and the Tramp Major brought our supper across from the workhouse. Each man's ration was a half-pound wedge of bread smeared with margarine, and a pint of bitter sugarless cocoa in a tin billy. Sitting on the floor we wolfed this in five minutes, and at about seven o'clock the cell doors were locked on the outside, to remain locked till eight in the morning.

Each man was allowed to sleep with his mate, the cells being intended to hold two men apiece. I had no mate, and was put in with another solitary man, a thin scrubby-faced fellow with a slight squint. The cell measured eight feet by five by eight high, was made of stone, and had a tiny barred window high up in the wall and a spyhole in the door, just like a cell in a prison. In it were six blankets, a chamber-pot, a hot water pipe, and nothing else whatever. I looked round the cell with a vague feeling that there was something missing. Then, with a shock of surprise, I realized what it was, and exclaimed:

'But I say, damn it, where are the beds?'

'*Beds?*' said the other man, surprised. 'There aren't no beds! What yer expect? This is one of them spikes where you sleeps on the floor. Christ! Ain't you got used to that yet?'

It appeared that no beds was quite a normal condition in the spike. We rolled up our coats and put them against the hot-water pipe, and made ourselves as comfortable as we could. It grew foully stuffy, but it was not warm enough to allow of our putting all the blankets underneath, so that we could only use one to soften the floor. We lay a foot apart, breathing into one another's face, with our naked limbs constantly touching, and rolling against one another whenever we fell asleep. One fidgeted from side to side, but it did not do much good; whichever way one turned there would be first a dull numb feeling, then a sharp ache as the hardness of the floor wore through the blanket. One could sleep, but not for more than ten minutes on end.

About midnight the other man began making homosexual attempts upon me—a nasty experience in a locked, pitch-dark cell. He was a feeble creature and I could manage him easily, but of course it was impossible to go to sleep again. For the rest of the night we stayed awake, smoking and talking. The man told me the story of his life—he was a fitter, out of work for three years. He said that his wife had promptly deserted him when he lost his job, and he had been so long away from women that he had almost forgotten what they were like. Homosexuality is general among tramps of long standing, he said.

At eight the porter came along the passage unlocking the doors and shouting 'All out!' The doors opened, letting out a stale, fetid stink. At once the passage was full of squallid, grey-shirted figures, each chamber-pot in hand, scrambling for the bathroom. It appeared that in the morning only one tub of water was allowed for the lot of us, and when I arrived twenty tramps had already washed their faces; I took one glance at the black scum floating on the water, and went unwashed. After this we were given a breakfast identical with the previous night's supper, our clothes were returned to us, and we were ordered out into the yard to work. The work was peeling potatoes for the pauper's dinner, but it was a mere formality, to keep us occupied until the doctor came to inspect us. Most of the tramps frankly idled. The doctor turned up at about ten o'clock and we were told to go back to our cells, strip and wait in the passage for the inspection.

Naked, and shivering, we lined up in the passage. You cannot conceive what ruinous, degenerate curs we looked, standing there in the merciless morning light. A tramp's clothes are bad, but they conceal far worse things; to see him as he really is, unmitigated, you must see him naked. Flat feet, pot bellies, hollow chests, sagging muscles—every kind of physical rottenness was there. Nearly everyone was undernourished, and some clearly diseased; two men were wearing trusses, and as for the old mummy-like creature of seventy-five, one wondered how he could possibly make his daily march. Looking at our faces, unshaven and creased from the sleepless night, you would have thought that all of us were recovering from a week on the drink.

The inspection was designed merely to detect smallpox, and took no notice of our general condition. A young medical student, smoking a cigarette, walked rapidly along the line glancing us up and down, and not inquiring whether any man was well or ill. When my cell companion stripped I saw that his chest was covered with a red rash, and, having spent the night a few inches away from him, I fell into a panic about smallpox. The doctor, however, examined the rash and said that it was due merely to under-nourishment.

After the inspection we dressed and were sent into the yard, where the porter called our names over, gave us back any possessions we had left at the office, and distributed meal tickets. These were worth sixpence each, and were directed to coffee-shops on the route we had named the night before. It was interesting to see that quite a number of the tramps could not read, and had to apply to myself and other 'scholards' to decipher their tickets.

The gates were opened, and we dispersed immediately. How sweet the air does smell—even the air of a back street in the suburbs—after the shut-in, subfaecal stench of the spike! I had a mate now, for while we were peeling potatoes I had made friends with an Irish tramp named Paddy Jaques, a melancholy pale man who seemed clean and decent. He was going to Edbury spike, and suggested that we should go together. We set out, getting there at three in the afternoon. It was a twelve-mile walk, but we made it fourteen by getting lost among the desolate north London slums. Our meal tickets were directed to a coffee-shop in Ilford. When we got there, the little chit of a serving-maid, having seen our tickets and grasped that we were tramps, tossed her head in contempt and for a long time would not serve us. Finally she slapped on the table two 'large teas' and four slices of bread and dripping—that is, eightpenny-worth of food. It appeared that the shop habitually cheated the tramps of twopence or so on each ticket; having tickets instead of money, the tramps could not protest or go elsewhere.

XXVIII

Paddy was my mate for about the next fortnight, and, as he was the first tramp I had known at all well, I want to give an account of him. I believe that he was a typical tramp and there are tens of thousands in England like him.

He was a tallish man, aged about thirty-five, with fair hair going grizzled and watery blue eyes. His features were good, but his cheeks had lanked and had that greyish, dirty in the grain look that comes of a bread and margarine diet. He was dressed, rather better than most tramps, in a tweed shooting-jacket and a pair of old evening trousers with the braid still on them. Evidently the braid figured in his mind as a lingering scrap of respectability, and he took care to sew it on again when it came loose. He was careful of his appearance altogether, and carried a razor and bootbrush that he would not sell, though he had sold his 'papers' and even his pocket-knife long since. Nevertheless, one would have known him for a tramp a hundred yards away. There was something in his drifting style of walk, and the way he had of hunching his shoulders forward, essentially abject. Seeing him walk, you felt instinctively that he would sooner take a blow than give one.

He had been brought up in Ireland, served two years in

the war, and then worked in a metal polish factory, where he
had lost his job two years earlier. He was horribly ashamed
of being a tramp, but he had picked up all a tramp's ways.
He browsed the pavements unceasingly, never missing a cigarette end, or even an empty cigarette packet, as he used the
tissue paper for rolling cigarettes. On our way into Edbury
he saw a newspaper parcel on the pavement, pounced on it,
and found that it contained two mutton sandwiches, rather
frayed at the edges; these he insisted on my sharing. He never
passed an automatic machine without giving a tug at the
handle, for he said that sometimes they are out of order and
will eject pennies if you tug at them. He had no stomach for
crime, however. When we were in the outskirts of Romton,
Paddy noticed a bottle of milk on a doorstep, evidently left
there by mistake. He stopped, eyeing the bottle hungrily.

'Christ!' he said, 'dere's good food goin' to waste.
Somebody could knock dat bottle off, eh? Knock it off easy.'

I saw that he was thinking of 'knocking it off' himself.
He looked up and down the street; it was a quiet residential
street and there was nobody in sight. Paddy's sickly, chap-
fallen face yearned over the milk. Then he turned away, saying
gloomily:

'Best leave it. It don't do a man no good to steal. T'ank
God, I ain't never stolen nothin' yet.'

It was funk, bred of hunger, that kept him virtuous. With
only two or three sound meals in his belly, he would have
found courage to steal the milk.

He had two subjects of conversation, the shame and
come-down of being a tramp, and the best way of getting a
free meal. As we drifted through the streets he would keep
up a monologue in this style, in a whimpering, self-pitying
Irish voice:

'It's hell bein' on de road, eh? It breaks yer heart goin'
into dem bloody spikes. But what's a man to do else, eh? I
ain't had a good meat meal for about two months, an' me

boots is getting bad, an'—Christ! How'd it be if we was to try for a cup o' tay at one o' dem convents on de way to Edbury? Most times dey're good for a cup o' tay. Ah, what'd a man do widout religion, eh? I've took cups o' tay from de convents, an' de Baptists, an' de Church of England, an' all sorts. I'm a Catholic meself. Dat's to say, I ain't been to confession for about seventeen year, but still I got me religious feelin's, y'understand. An' dem convents is always good for a cup o' tay . . .' etc. etc. He would keep this up all day, almost without stopping.

His ignorance was limitless and appalling. He once asked me, for instance, whether Napoleon lived before Jesus Christ or after. Another time, when I was looking into a bookshop window, he grew very perturbed because one of the books was called *Of the Imitation of Christ*. He took this for blasphemy. 'What de hell do dey want to go imitatin' of *Him* for?' he demanded angrily. He could read, but he had a kind of loathing for books. On our way from Romton to Edbury I went into a public library, and, though Paddy did not want to read, I suggested that he should come in and rest his legs. But he preferred to wait on the pavement. 'No,' he said, 'de sight of all dat bloody print makes me sick.'

Like most tramps, he was passionately mean about matches. He had a box of matches when I met him, but I never saw him strike one, and he used to lecture me for extravagance when I struck mine. His method was to cadge a light from strangers, sometimes going without a smoke for half an hour rather than strike a match.

Self-pity was the clue to his character. The thought of his bad luck never seemed to leave him for an instant. He would break long silences to exclaim, apropos of nothing, 'It's hell when yer clo'es begin to go up de spout, eh?' or 'Dat tay in de spike ain't tay, it's piss,' as though there was nothing else in the world to think about. And he had a low, worm-like envy of anyone who was better off—not of the rich, for they were beyond his social horizon, but of men in work. He pined for work as an artist pines to be famous. If he saw an old man working he would say bitterly, 'Look at dat old— keepin' able-bodied men out o' work'; or if it was a boy, 'It's dem young devils what's takin' de bread out of our mouths.' And all foreigners to him were 'dem bloody dagoes'—for, according to his theory, foreigners were responsible for unemployment.

He looked at women with a mixture of longing and hatred. Young, pretty women were too much above him to enter into his ideas, but his mouth watered at prostitutes. A couple of scarlet-lipped old creatures would go past; Paddy's face would flush pale pink, and he would turn and stare hungrily after the women. 'Tarts!' he would murmur, like a boy at a sweetshop window. He told me once that he had not had to do with a woman for two years—since he had lost his job, that is—and he had forgotten that one could aim higher than prostitutes. He had the regular character of a tramp—abject, envious, a jackal's character.

Nevertheless, he was a good fellow, generous by nature and capable of sharing his last crust with a friend; indeed he did literally share his last crust with me more than once. He was probably capable of work too, if he had been well fed for a few months. But two years of bread and margarine had lowered his standards hopelessly. He had lived on this filthy imitation of food till his own mind and body were compounded of inferior stuff. It was malnutrition and not any native vice that had destroyed his manhood.

XXIX

On the way to Edbury I told Paddy that I had a friend from whom I could be sure of getting money, and suggested going straight into London rather than face another night in the spike. But Paddy had not been in Edbury spike recently, and, tramp-like, he would not waste a night's free lodging. We arranged to go into London the next morning. I had only a halfpenny, but Paddy had two shillings, which would get us a bed each and a few cups of tea.

The Edbury spike did not differ much from the one at Romton. The worst feature was that all tobacco was confiscated at the gate, and we were warned that any man caught smoking would be turned out at once. Under the Vagrancy Act tramps can be prosecuted for smoking in the spike—in fact, they can be prosecuted for almost anything; but the authorities generally save the trouble of a prosecution by turning disobedient men out of doors. There was no work to do, and the cells were fairly comfortable. We slept two in a cell, 'one up, one down'—that is, one on a wooden shelf and one on the floor, with straw palliasses and plenty of blankets, dirty but not verminous. The food was the same as at Romton, except that we had tea instead of cocoa. One could get extra tea in the morning, as the Tramp Major was selling it at a halfpenny a mug, illicitly no doubt. We were each given a hunk of bread and cheese to take away for our midday meal.

When we got into London we had eight hours to kill before the lodging-houses opened. It is curious how one does not notice things. I had been in London innumerable times, and yet till that day I had never noticed one of the worst things about London—the fact that it costs money even to sit down. In Paris, if you had no money and could not find a public bench, you would sit on the pavement. Heaven knows what sitting on the pavement would lead to in London—prison, probably. By four we had stood five hours, and our feet seemed red-hot from the hardness of the stones. We were hungry, having eaten our ration as soon as we left the spike, and I was out of tobacco—it mattered less to Paddy, who picked up cigarette ends. We tried two churches and found them locked. Then we tried a public library, but there were no seats in it. As a last hope Paddy suggested trying a Rowton House; by the rules they would not let us in before seven, but we might slip in unnoticed. We walked up to the magnificent doorway (the Rowton Houses really are magnificent) and very casually, trying to look like regular lodgers, began to stroll in. Instantly a man lounging in the doorway, a sharp-faced fellow, evidently in some position of authority, barred the way.

'You men sleep 'ere last night?'

'No.'

'Then — off.'

We obeyed, and stood two more hours on the street corner. It was unpleasant, but it taught me not to use the expression 'street corner loafer', so I gained something from it.

At six we went to a Salvation Army shelter. We could not book beds till eight and it was not certain that there would be any vacant, but an official, who called us 'Brother', let us in on the condition that we paid for two cups of tea. The main hall of the shelter was a great white-washed barn of a place, oppressively clean and bare, with no fires. Two hundred decentish, rather subdued-looking people were sitting packed on long wooden benches. One or two officers in uniform prowled up and down. On the wall were pictures of General Booth, and notices prohibiting cooking, drinking, spitting, swearing, quarrelling, and gambling. As a specimen of these notices, here is one that I copied word for word:

> Any man found gambling or playing cards will be expelled and will not be admitted under any circumstances.

> A reward will be given for information leading to the discovery of such persons.

> The officers in charge appeal to all lodgers to assist them in keeping this hostel free from the DETESTABLE EVIL OF GAMBLING.

'Gambling or playing cards' is a delightful phrase.

To my eye these Salvation Army shelters, though clean, are far drearier than the worst of the common lodging-houses. There is such a hopelessness about some of the people there—decent, broken-down types who have pawned their collars but are still trying for office jobs. Coming to a Salvation Army shelter, where it is at least clean, is their last clutch at respectability. At the next table to me were two foreigners, dressed in rags but manifestly gentlemen. They were playing chess verbally, not even writing down the moves. One of them was blind, and I heard them say that they had been saving up for a long time to buy a board, price half a crown, but could never manage it. Here and there were clerks out of work, pallid and moody. Among a group of them a tall, thin, deadly pale young man was talking excitedly. He thumped his fist on the table and boasted in a strange, feverish style. When the officers were out of hearing he broke out into startling blasphemies:

'I tell you what, boys, I'm going to get that job tomorrow. I'm not one of your bloody down-on-the-knee brigade; I can look after myself. Look at that — notice there! "The Lord will provide!" A bloody lot He's ever provided me with. You don't catch me trusting to the — Lord. You leave it to me, boys. *I'm going to get that job,*' etc. etc.

I watched him, struck by the wild, agitated way in which he talked; he seemed hysterical, or perhaps a little drunk. An hour later I went into a small room, apart from the main hall, which was intended for reading. It had no books or papers in it, so few of the lodgers went there. As I opened the door I saw the young clerk in there all alone; he was on his knees, *praying.* Before I shut the door again I had time to see his face, and it looked agonized. Quite suddenly I realized, from the expression of his face, that he was starving.

The charge for beds was eightpence. Paddy and I had fivepence left, and we spent it at the 'bar', where food was cheap, though not so cheap as in some common lodging-houses. The tea appeared to be made with tea *dust*, which I fancy had been given to the Salvation Army in charity, though they sold it at threehalfpence a cup. It was foul stuff. At ten o'clock an officer marched round the hall blowing a whistle. Immediately everyone stood up.

'What's this for?' I said to Paddy, astonished.

'Dat means you has to go off to bed. An' you has to look sharp about it, too.'

Obediently as sheep, the whole two hundred men trooped off to bed, under the command of the officers.

The dormitory was a great attic like a barrack room, with sixty or seventy beds in it. They were clean and tolerably comfortable, but very narrow and very close together, so that one breathed straight into one's neighbour's face. Two officers slept in the room, to see that there was no smoking and no talking after lights-out. Paddy and I had scarcely a wink of sleep, for there was a man near us who had some nervous trouble, shellshock perhaps, which made him cry out 'Pip!' at irregular intervals. It was a loud, startling noise, something like the toot of a small motor-horn. You never knew when it was coming, and it was a sure preventer of sleep. It appeared that Pip, as the others called him, slept regularly in the shelter, and he must have kept ten or twenty people awake every night. He was an example of the kind of thing that prevents one from ever getting enough sleep when men are herded as they are in these lodging-houses.

At seven another whistle blew, and the officers went round shaking those who did not get up at once. Since then I have slept in a number of Salvation Army shelters, and found that, though the different houses vary a little, this semi-military discipline is the same in all of them. They are certainly cheap, but they are too like workhouses for my taste. In some of them there is even a compulsory religious service once or twice a week, which the lodgers must attend or leave the house. The fact is that the Salvation Army are so in the habit of thinking themselves a charitable body that they cannot even run a lodging-house without making it stink of charity.

At ten I went to B.'s office and asked him to lend me a pound. He gave me two pounds and told me to come again when necessary, so that Paddy and I were free of money troubles for a week at least. We loitered the day in Trafalgar Square, looking for a friend of Paddy's who never turned up, and at night went to a lodging-house in a back alley near the Strand. The charge was elevenpence, but it was a dark, evil-smelling place, and a notorious haunt of the 'nancy boys'. Downstairs, in the murky kitchen, three ambiguous-looking youths in smartish blue suits were sitting on a bench apart, ignored by the other lodgers. I suppose they were 'nancy boys'. They looked the same type as the apache boys one sees in Paris, except that they wore no side-whiskers. In front of the fire a fully dressed man and a stark-naked man were bargaining.

They were newspaper sellers. The dressed man was selling his clothes to the naked man. He said:

''Ere y'are, the best rig-out you ever 'ad. A tosheroon [half a crown] for the coat, two 'ogs for the trousers, one and a tanner for the boots, and a 'og for the cap and scarf. That's seven bob.'

'You got a 'ope! I'll give yer one and a tanner for the coat, a 'og for the trousers, and two 'ogs for the rest. That's four and a tanner.'

'Take the 'ole lot for five and a tanner, chum.'

'Right y'are, off with 'em. I got to get out to sell my late edition.'

The clothed man stripped, and in three minutes their positions were reversed; the naked man dressed, and the other kilted with a sheet of the *Daily Mail*.

The dormitory was dark and close, with fifteen beds in it. There was a horrible hot reek of urine, so beastly that at first one tried to breathe in small, shallow puffs, not filling one's lungs to the bottom. As I lay down in bed a man loomed out of the darkness, leant over me and began babbling in an educated, half-drunken voice:

'An old public schoolboy, what? [He had heard me say something to Paddy.] Don't meet many of the old school here. I am an old Etonian. You know—twenty years hence this weather and all that.' He began to quaver out the Eton boating-song, not untunefully:

Jolly boating weather,
And a hay harvest—

'Stop that — noise!' shouted several lodgers.

'Low types,' said the old Etonian, 'very low types. Funny sort of place for you and me, eh? Do you know what my friends say to me? They say, "M—, you are past redemption." Quite true, I *am* past redemption. I've come down in the world; not like these —s here, who couldn't come down if they tried. We chaps who have come down ought to hang together a bit. Youth will be still in our faces—you know. May I offer you a drink?'

He produced a bottle of cherry brandy, and at the same moment lost his balance and fell heavily across my legs. Paddy, who was undressing, pulled him upright.

'Get back to yer bed, you silly ole —!'

The old Etonian walked unsteadily to his bed and crawled under the sheets with all his clothes on, even his boots. Several times in the night I heard him murmuring, 'M—, you are past redemption,' as though the phrase appealed to him. In the morning he was lying asleep fully dressed, with the bottle clasped in his arms. He was a man of about fifty, with a refined, worn face, and, curiously enough, quite fashionably dressed. It was queer to see his good patent-leather shoes sticking out of that filthy bed. It occurred to me, too, that the cherry brandy must have cost the equivalent of a fortnight's lodging, so he could not have been seriously hard up. Perhaps he frequented common lodging-houses in search of the 'nancy boys'.

The beds were not more than two feet apart. About midnight I woke up to find that the man next to me was trying to steal the money from beneath my pillow. He was pretending to be asleep while he did it, sliding his hand under the pillow as gently as a rat. In the morning I saw that he was a hunchback, with long, apelike arms. I told Paddy about the attempted theft. He laughed and said:

'Christ! You got to get used to dat. Dese lodgin' houses is full o' thieves. In some houses dere's nothin' safe but to sleep wid all yer clo'es on. I seen 'em steal a wooden leg off a cripple before now. Once I see a man—fourteen-stone man he was—come into a lodgin'-house wid four pound ten. He puts it under his mattress. "Now," he says, "any — dat touches dat money does it over my body," he says. But dey done him all de same. In de mornin' he woke up on de floor. Four fellers had took his mattress by de corners an' lifted him off as light as a feather. He never saw his four pound ten again.'

XXX

The next morning we began looking once more for Paddy's friend, who was called Bozo, and was a screever—that is, a pavement artist. Addresses did not exist in Paddy's world, but he had a vague idea that Bozo might be found in Lambeth, and in the end we ran across him on the Embankment, where he had established himself not far from Waterloo Bridge. He was kneeling on the pavement with a box of chalks, copying a sketch of Winston Churchill from a penny note-book. The likeness was not at all bad. Bozo was a small, dark, hook-nosed man, with curly hair growing low on his head. His right leg was dreadfully deformed, the foot being twisted heel forward in a way horrible to see. From his appearance one could have taken him for a Jew, but he used to deny this vigorously. He spoke of his hooknose as 'Roman', and was proud of his resemblance to some Roman Emperor—it was Vespasian, I think.

Bozo had a strange way of talking, Cockneyfied and yet very lucid and expressive. It was as though he had read good books but had never troubled to correct his grammar. For a while Paddy and I stayed on the Embankment, talking, and Bozo gave us an account of the screeving trade. I repeat what he said more or less in his own words.

'I'm what they call a serious screever. I don't draw in

blackboard chalks like these others, I use proper colours the same as what painters use; bloody expensive they are, especially the reds. I use five bobs' worth of colours in a long day, and never less than two bobs' worth.* Cartoons is my line—you know, politics and cricket and that. Look here'—he showed me his notebook—'here's likenesses of all the political blokes, what I've copied from the papers. I have a different cartoon every day. For instance, when the Budget was on I had one of Winston trying to push an elephant marked "Debt", and underneath I wrote, "Will he budge it?" See? You can have cartoons about any of the parties, but you mustn't put anything in favour of Socialism, because the police won't stand it. Once I did a cartoon of a boa constrictor marked Capital swallowing a rabbit marked Labour. The copper came along and saw it, and he says, "You rub that out, and look sharp about it," he says. I had to rub it out. The copper's got the right to move you on for loitering, and it's no good giving them a back answer.'

I asked Bozo what one could earn at screeving. He said:

'This time of year, when it don't rain, I take about three quid between Friday and Sunday—people get their wages Fridays, you see. I can't work when it rains; the colours get washed off straight away. Take the year round, I make about a pound a week, because you can't do much in the winter. Boat Race day, and Cup Final day, I've took as much as four pounds. But you have to *cut* it out of them, you know; you don't take a bob if you just sit and look at them. A halfpenny's the usual drop [gift], and you don't get even that unless you give them a bit of backchat. Once they've answered you they feel ashamed not to give you a drop. The best thing's to keep changing your picture, because when they see you drawing they'll stop and watch you. The trouble is, the beggars scatter

* Pavement artists buy their colours in the form of powder, and work them into cakes in condensed milk.

as soon as you turn round with the hat. You really want a nobber [assistant] at this game. You keep at work and get a crowd watching you, and the nobber comes casual-like round the back of them. They don't know he's the nobber. Then suddenly he pulls his cap off, and you got them between two fires like. You'll never get a drop off real toffs. It's shabby sort of blokes you get most off, and foreigners. I've had even sixpences off Japs, and blackies, and that. They're not so bloody mean as what an Englishman is. Another thing to remember is to keep your money covered up, except perhaps a penny in the hat. People won't give you anything if they see you got a bob or two already.'

Bozo had the deepest contempt for the other screevers on the Embankment. He called them 'the salmon platers'. At that time there was a screever almost every twenty-five yards along the Embankment—twenty-five yards being the recognized minimum between pitches. Bozo contemptuously pointed out an old white-bearded screever fifty yards away.

'You see that silly old fool? He's bin doing the same picture every day for ten years. "A faithful friend" he calls it. It's of a dog pulling a child out of the water. The silly old bastard can't draw any better than a child of ten. He's learned just that one picture by rule of thumb, like you learn to put a puzzle together. There's a lot of that sort about here. They come pinching my ideas sometimes; but I don't care; the silly —s can't think of anything for themselves, so I'm always ahead of them. The whole thing with cartoons is being up to date. Once a child got its head stuck in the railings of Chelsea Bridge. Well, I heard about it, and my cartoon was on the pavement before they'd got the child's head out of the railings. Prompt, I am.'

Bozo seemed an interesting man, and I was anxious to see more of him. That evening I went down to the Embankment to meet him, as he had arranged to take Paddy and myself to a lodging-house south of the river. Bozo washed his pictures off the pavement and counted his takings—it was about sixteen shillings, of which he said twelve or thirteen would be profit. We walked down into Lambeth. Bozo limped slowly, with a queer crablike gait, half sideways, dragging his smashed foot behind him. He carried a stick in each hand and slung his box of colours over his shoulder. As we were crossing the bridge he stopped in one of the alcoves to rest. He fell silent for a minute or two, and to my surprise I saw that he was looking at the stars. He touched my arm and pointed to the sky with his stick.

'Say, will you look at Aldebaran! Look at the colour. Like a — great blood orange!'

From the way he spoke he might have been an art critic in a picture gallery. I was astonished. I confessed that I did not know which Aldebaran was—indeed, I had never even noticed that the stars were of different colours. Bozo began to give me some elementary hints on astronomy, pointing out-the chief constellations. He seemed concerned at my ignorance. I said to him, surprised:

'You seem to know a lot about stars.'

'Not a great lot. I know a bit, though. I got two letters from the Astronomer Royal thanking me for writing about meteors. Now and again I go out at night and watch for meteors. The stars are a free show; it don't cost anything to use your eyes.'

'What a good idea! I should never have thought of it.'

'Well, you got to take an interest in something. It don't follow that because a man's on the road he can't think of anything but tea-and-two-slices.'

'But isn't it very hard to take an interest in things—things like stars—living this life?'

'Screeving, you mean? Not necessarily. It don't need turn you into a bloody rabbit—that is, not if you set your mind to it.'

'It seems to have that effect on most people.'

'Of course. Look at Paddy—a tea-swilling old moocher, only fit to scrounge for fag-ends. That's the way most of them go. I despise them. But you don't *need* to get like that. If you've got any education, it don't matter to you if you're on the road for the rest of your life.'

'Well, I've found just the contrary,' I said. 'It seems to me that when you take a man's money away he's fit for nothing from that moment.'

'No, not necessarily. If you set yourself to it, you can live the same life, rich or poor. You can still keep on with your books and your ideas. You just got to say to yourself, "I'm a free man in *here*"'—he tapped his forehead—'and you're all right.'

Bozo talked further in the same strain, and I listened with attention. He seemed a very unusual screever, and he was, moreover, the first person I had heard maintain that poverty did not matter. I saw a good deal of him during the next few days, for several times it rained and he could not work. He told me the history of his life, and it was a curious one.

The son of a bankrupt bookseller, he had gone to work as a house-painter at eighteen, and then served three years in France and India during the war. After the war he had found a house-painting job in Paris, and had stayed there several years. France suited him better than England (he despised the English), and he had been doing well in Paris, saving money, and engaged to a French girl. One day the girl was crushed to death under the wheels of an omnibus. Bozo went on the drink for a week, and then returned to work, rather shaky; the same morning he fell from a stage on which he was working, forty feet on to the pavement, and smashed his right foot to pulp. For some reason he received only sixty pounds compensation. He returned to England, spent his money in looking for jobs, tried hawking books in Middlesex Street market, then tried selling toys from a tray, and finally settled down as a screever. He had lived hand to mouth ever since, half starved throughout the winter, and often sleeping in the spike or on the Embankment. When I knew him he owned nothing but the clothes he stood up in, and his drawing materials and a few books. The clothes were the usual beggar's rags, but he wore a collar and tie, of which he was rather proud. The collar, a year or more old, was constantly 'going' round the neck, and Bozo used to patch it with bits cut from the tail of his shirt so that the shirt had scarcely any tail left. His damaged leg was getting worse and would probably have to be amputated, and his knees, from kneeling on the stones, had pads of skin on them as thick as boot-soles. There was, clearly, no future for him but beggary and a death in the workhouse.

With all this, he had neither fear, nor regret, nor shame, nor self-pity. He had faced his position, and made a philosophy for himself. Being a beggar, he said, was not his fault, and he refused either to have any compunction about it or to let it trouble him. He was the enemy of society, and quite ready to take to crime if he saw a good opportunity. He refused on principle to be thrifty. In the summer he saved nothing, spending his surplus earnings on drink, as he did not care about women. If he was penniless when winter came on, then society must look after him. He was ready to extract every penny he could from charity, provided that he was not expected to say thank you for it. He avoided religious charities, however, for he said it stuck in his throat to sing hymns for buns. He had various other points of honour; for instance, it was his boast that never in his life, even when starving, had he picked up a cigarette end. He considered himself in a class above the ordinary run of beggars, who, he said, were an abject lot, without even the decency to be ungrateful.

He spoke French passably, and had read some of Zola's novels, all Shakespeare's plays, *Gulliver's Travels*, and a number of essays. He could describe his adventures in words that one remembered. For instance, speaking of funerals, he said to me:

'Have you ever seen a corpse burned? I have, in India. They put the old chap on the fire, and the next moment I almost jumped out of my skin, because he'd started kicking. It was only his muscles contracting in the heat—still, it give me a turn. Well, he wriggled about for a bit like a kipper on hot coals, and then his belly blew up and went off with a bang you could have heard fifty yards away. It fair put me against cremation.'

Or, again, apropos of his accident:

'The doctor says to me, "You fell on one foot, my man. And bloody lucky for you you didn't fall on both feet," he says. "Because if you had of fallen on both feet you'd have shut up like a bloody concertina, and your thigh bones'd be sticking out of your ears!"'

Clearly the phrase was not the doctor's but Bozo's own. He had a gift for phrases. He had managed to keep his brain intact and alert, and so nothing could make him succumb to poverty. He might be ragged and cold, or even starving, but so long as he could read, think, and watch for meteors, he was, as he said, free in his own mind.

He was an embittered atheist (the sort of atheist who does not so much disbelieve in God as personally dislike Him), and took a sort of pleasure in thinking that human affairs would never improve. Sometimes, he said, when sleeping on the Embankment, it had consoled him to look up at Mars or Jupiter and think that there were probably Embankment sleepers there. He had a curious theory about this. Life on earth, he said, is harsh because the planet is poor in the necessities of existence. Mars, with its cold climate and scanty water, must be far poorer, and life correspondingly harsher. Whereas on earth you are merely imprisoned for stealing sixpence, on Mars you are probably boiled alive. This thought cheered Bozo, I do not know why. He was a very exceptional man.

XXXI

The charge at Bozo's lodging-house was ninepence a night.
It was a large, crowded place, with accommodation for five
hundred men, and a well-known rendezvous of tramps,
beggars, and petty criminals. All races, even black and white,
mixed in it on terms of equality. There were Indians there,
and when I spoke to one of them in bad Urdu he addressed
me as 'tum'—a thing to make one shudder, if it had been in
India. We had got below the range of colour prejudice. One
had glimpses of curious lives. Old 'Grandpa', a tramp of
seventy who made his living, or a great part of it, by collecting
cigarette ends and selling the tobacco at threepence an ounce.
'The Doctor'—he was a real doctor, who had been struck off
the register for some offence, and besides selling newspapers
gave medical advice at a few pence a time. A little Chittagonian
lascar, barefoot and starving, who had deserted his ship and
wandered for days through London, so vague and helpless
that he did not even know the name of the city he was in—he
thought it was Liverpool, until I told him. A begging-letter
writer, a friend of Bozo's, who wrote pathetic appeals for aid
to pay for his wife's funeral, and, when a letter had taken
effect, blew himself out with huge solitary gorges of bread
and margarine. He was a nasty, hyena-like creature. I talked

to him and found that, like most swindlers, he believed a great part of his own lies. The lodging-house was an Alsatia for types like these.

While I was with Bozo he taught me something about the technique of London begging. There is more in it than one might suppose. Beggars vary greatly, and there is a sharp social line between those who merely cadge and those who attempt to give some value for money. The amounts that one can earn by the different 'gags' also vary. The stories in the Sunday papers about beggars who die with two thousand pounds sewn into their trousers are, of course, lies; but the better-class beggars do have runs of luck, when they earn a living wage for weeks at a time. The most prosperous beggars are street acrobats and street photographers. On a good pitch—a theatre queue, for instance—a street acrobat will often earn five pounds a week. Street photographers can earn about the same, but they are dependent on fine weather. They have a cunning dodge to stimulate trade. When they see a likely victim approaching one of them runs behind the camera and pretends to take a photograph. Then as the victim reaches them, they exclaim:

'There y'are, sir, took yer photo lovely. That'll be a bob.'

'But I never asked you to take it,' protests the victim.

'What, you didn't want it took? Why, we thought you signalled with your 'and. Well, there's a plate wasted! That's cost us sixpence, that 'as.'

At this the victim usually takes pity and says he will have the photo after all. The photographers examine the plate and say that it is spoiled, and that they will take a fresh one free of charge. Of course, they have not really taken the first photo; and so, if the victim refuses, they waste nothing.

Organ-grinders, like acrobats, are considered artists rather than beggars. An organ-grinder named Shorty, a friend of Bozo's, told me all about his trade. He and his mate 'worked' the coffee-shops and public-houses round

Whitechapel and the Commercial Road. It is a mistake to think that organ-grinders earn their living in the street; nine-tenths of their money is taken in coffee-shops and pubs—only the cheap pubs, for they are not allowed into the good-class ones. Shorty's procedure was to stop outside a pub and play one tune, after which his mate, who had a wooden leg and could excite compassion, went in and passed round the hat. It was a point of honour with Shorty always to play another tune after receiving the 'drop'—an encore, as it were; the idea being that he was a genuine entertainer and not merely paid to go away. He and his mate took two or three pounds a week between them, but, as they had to pay fifteen shillings a week for the hire of the organ, they only averaged a pound a week each. They were on the streets from eight in the morning till ten at night, and later on Saturdays.

Screevers can sometimes be called artists, sometimes not. Bozo introduced me to one who was a 'real' artist—that is, he had studied art in Paris and submitted pictures to the Salon in his day. His line was copies of Old Masters, which he did marvellously, considering that he was drawing on stone. He told me how he began as a screever:

'My wife and kids were starving. I was walking home late at night, with a lot of drawings I'd been taking round the dealers, and wondering how the devil to raise a bob or two. Then, in the Strand, I saw a fellow kneeling on the pavement drawing, and people giving him pennies. As I came past he got up and went into a pub. "Damn it," I thought, "if he can make money at that, so can I." So on the impulse I knelt down and began drawing with his chalks. Heaven knows how I came to do it; I must have been lightheaded with hunger. The curious thing was that I'd never used pastels before; I had to learn the technique as I went along. Well, people began to stop and say that my drawing wasn't bad, and they gave me ninepence between them. At this moment the other fellow came out of the pub. "What in — are you doing on my pitch?"

he said. I explained that I was hungry and had to earn some-thing. "Oh," said he, "come and have a pint with me." So I had a pint, and since that day I've been a screever. I make a pound a week. You can't keep six kids on a pound a week, but luckily my wife earns a bit taking in sewing.

'The worst thing in this life is the cold, and the next worst is the interference you have to put up with. At first, not knowing any better, I used sometimes to copy a nude on the pavement. The first I did was outside St Martin's-in-the-Fields church. A fellow in black—I suppose he was a churchwarden or something—came out in a tearing rage. "Do you think we can have that obscenity outside God's holy house?" he cried. So I had to wash it out. It was a copy of Botticelli's Venus. Another time I copied the same picture on the Embankment. A policeman passing looked at it, and then, without a word, walked on to it and rubbed it out with his great flat feet.'

Bozo told the same tale of police interference. At the time when I was with him there had been a case of 'immoral conduct' in Hyde Park, in which the police had behaved rather badly. Bozo produced a cartoon of Hyde Park with policemen concealed in the trees, and the legend, 'Puzzle, find the policemen.' I pointed out to him how much more telling it would be to put, 'Puzzle, find the immoral conduct,' but Bozo would not hear of it. He said that any policeman who saw it would move him on, and he would lose his pitch for good.

Below screevers come the people who sing hymns, or sell matches, or bootlaces, or envelopes containing a few grains of lavender—called, euphemistically, perfume. All these people are frankly beggars, exploiting an appearance of misery, and none of them takes on an average more than half a crown a day. The reason why they have to pretend to sell matches and so forth instead of begging outright is that this is demanded by the absurd English laws about begging. As the law now stands, if you approach a stranger and ask him for twopence, he can call a policeman and get you seven days for begging. But if you make the air hideous by droning 'Nearer, my God, to Thee,' or scrawl some chalk daubs on the pavement, or stand about with a tray of matches—in short, if you make a nuisance of yourself—you are held to be following a legitimate trade and not begging. Match-selling and street-singing are simply legalized crimes. Not profitable crimes, however; there is not a singer or match-seller in London who can be sure of £50 a year—a poor return for standing eighty-four hours a week on the kerb, with the cars grazing your backside.

It is worth saying something about the social position of beggars, for when one has consorted with them, and found that they are ordinary human beings, one cannot help being struck by the curious attitude that society takes towards them. People seem to feel that there is some essential difference between beggars and ordinary 'working' men. They are a race apart—outcasts, like criminals and prostitutes. Working men 'work', beggars do not 'work'; they are parasites, worthless in their very nature. It is taken for granted that a beggar does not 'earn' his living, as a bricklayer or a literary critic 'earns' his. He is a mere social excrescence, tolerated because we live in a humane age, but essentially despicable.

Yet if one looks closely one sees that there is no *essential* difference between a beggar's livelihood and that of number-less respectable people. Beggars do not work, it is said; but, then, what is *work*? A navvy works by swinging a pick. An accountant works by adding up figures. A beggar works by standing out of doors in all weathers and getting varicose veins, chronic bronchitis, etc. It is a trade like any other; quite useless, of course—but, then, many reputable trades are quite useless. And as a social type a beggar compares well with scores of others. He is honest compared with the sellers of most patent medicines, high-minded compared with a Sunday newspaper proprietor, amiable compared with a hire-purchase tout—in short, a parasite, but a fairly harmless parasite. He seldom extracts more than a bare living from the community, and, what should justify him according to our ethical ideas, he pays for it over and over in suffering. I do not think there is anything about a beggar that sets him in a different class from other people, or gives most modern men the right to despise him.

Then the question arises, Why are beggars despised?—for they are despised, universally. I believe it is for the simple reason that they fail to earn a decent living. In practice nobody cares whether work is useful or useless, productive or parasitic; the sole thing demanded is that it shall be profitable. In all the modern talk about energy, efficiency, social service and the rest of it, what meaning is there except 'Get money, get it legally, and get a lot of it'? Money has become the grand test of virtue. By this test beggars fail, and for this they are despised. If one could earn even ten pounds a week at begging, it would become a respectable profession immediately. A beggar, looked at realistically, is simply a businessman, getting his living, like other businessmen, in the way that comes to hand. He has not, more than most modern people, sold his honour; he has merely made the mistake of choosing a trade at which it is impossible to grow rich.

XXXII

I want to put in some notes, as short as possible, on London slang and swearing. These (omitting the ones that everyone knows) are some of the cant words now used in London:

A gagger—beggar or street performer of any kind. A moocher—one who begs outright, without pretence of doing a trade. A nobbier—one who collects pennies for a beggar. A chanter—a street singer. A clodhopper—a street dancer. A mugfaker—a street photographer. A glimmer—one who watches vacant motor-cars. A gee (or jee—it is pronounced jee)—the accomplice of a cheapjack, who stimulates trade by pretending to buy something. A split—a detective. A flattie—a policeman. A dideki—a gypsy. A toby—a tramp.

A drop—money given to a beggar. Funkum—lavender or other perfume sold in envelopes. A boozer—a public-house. A slang—a hawker's licence. A kip—a place to sleep in, or a night's lodging. Smoke—London. A judy—a woman. The spike—the casual ward. The lump—the casual ward. A tosheroon—a half-crown. A deaner—a shilling. A hog—a shilling. A sprowsie—a sixpence. Clods—coppers. A drum—a billy can. Shackles—soup. A chat—a louse. Hard-up—tobacco made from cigarette ends. A stick or cane—a burglar's jemmy. A peter—a safe. A bly—a burglar's oxy-acetylene blow-lamp.

To bawl—to suck or swallow. To knock off—to steal. To skipper—to sleep in the open.

About half of these words are in the larger dictionaries. It is interesting to guess at the derivation of some of them, though one or two—for instance, 'funkum' and 'tosheroon'—are beyond guessing. 'Deaner' presumably comes from 'denier'. 'Glimmer' (with the verb 'to glim') may have something to do with the old word 'glim', meaning a light, or another old word 'glim', meaning a glimpse; but it is an instance of the formation of new words, for in its present sense it can hardly be older than motor-cars. 'Gee' is a curious word; conceivably it has arisen out of 'gee', meaning horse, in the sense of stalking horse. The derivation of 'screever' is mysterious. It must come ultimately from *scribo*, but there has been no similar word in English for the past hundred and fifty years; nor can it have come directly from the French, for pavement artists are unknown in France. 'Judy' and 'bawl' are East End words, not found west of Tower Bridge. 'Smoke' is a word used only by tramps. 'Kip' is Danish. Till quite recently the word 'doss' was used in this sense, but it is now quite obsolete.

London slang and dialect seem to change very rapidly. The old London accent described by Dickens and Surtees, with v for w and w for v and so forth, has now vanished utterly. The Cockney accent as we know it seems to have come up in the 'forties (it is first mentioned in an American book, Herman Melville's *White Jacket*), and Cockney is already changing; there are few people now who say 'fice' for 'face', 'nawce' for 'nice' and so forth as consistently as they did twenty years ago. The slang changes together with the accent. Twenty-five or thirty years ago, for instance, the 'rhyming slang' was all the rage in London. In the 'rhyming slang' everything was named by something rhyming with it—a 'hit or miss' for a kiss, 'plates of meat' for feet, etc. It was so common that it was even reproduced in novels; now it is almost extinct.* Perhaps all the words I have mentioned above will have vanished in another twenty years.

The swear words also change—or, at any rate, they are subject to fashions. For example, twenty years ago the London working classes habitually used the word 'bloody'. Now they have abandoned it utterly, though novelists still represent them as using it. No born Londoner (it is different with people of Scotch or Irish origin) now says 'bloody', unless he is a man of some education. The word has, in fact, moved up in the social scale and ceased to be a swear word for the purposes of the working classes. The current London adjective, now tacked on to every noun, is—.† No doubt in time —, like 'bloody', will find its way into the drawing-room and be replaced by some other word.

The whole business of swearing, especially English swearing, is mysterious. Of its very nature swearing is as irrational as magic—indeed, it is a species of magic. But there is also a paradox about it, namely this: Our intention in swearing is to shock and wound, which we do by mentioning something that should be kept secret—usually something to do with the sexual functions. But the strange thing is that when a word is well established as a swear word, it seems to lose its original meaning; that is, it loses the thing that made it into a swear word. A word becomes an oath because it means a certain thing, and, because it has become an oath, it ceases to mean that thing. For example —. The Londoners do not now use, or very seldom use, this word in its original meaning; it is on their lips from morning till night, but it is a mere expletive and means nothing. Similarly with —, which is rapidly losing its original sense. One can think of similar

---

* It survives in certain abbreviations, such as 'use your twopenny' or 'use your head.' 'Twopenny' is arrived at like this: head—loaf of bread—twopenny loaf—twopenny.

† See note on page 214.

instances in French—for example —, which is now a quite meaningless expletive. The word —, also, is still used occasionally in Paris, but the people who use it, or most of them, have no idea of what it once meant. The rule seems to be that words accepted as swear words have some magical character, which sets them apart and makes them useless for ordinary conversation.

Words used as insults seem to be governed by the same paradox as swear words. A word becomes an insult, one would suppose, because it means something bad; but in practice its insult-value has little to do with its actual meaning. For example, the most bitter insult one can offer to a Londoner is 'bastard'—which, taken for what it means, is hardly an insult at all. And the worst insult to a woman, either in London or Paris, is 'cow'; a name which might even be a compliment, for cows are among the most likeable of animals. Evidently a word is an insult simply because it is meant as an insult, without reference to its dictionary meaning; words, especially swear words, being what public opinion chooses to make them. In this connexion it is interesting to see how a swear word can change character by crossing a frontier. In England you can print '*Je m'en fous*' without protest from anybody. In France you have to print it '*Je m'en f—*'. Or, as another example, take the word 'barnshoot'—a corruption of the Hindustani word *bahinchut*. A vile and unforgivable insult in India, this word is a piece of gentle badinage in England. I have even seen it in a school text-book; it was in one of Aristophanes' plays, and the annotator suggested it as a rendering of some gibberish spoken by a Persian ambassador. Presumably the annotator knew what *bahinchut* meant. But, because it was a foreign word, it had lost its magical swear-word quality and could be printed.

One other thing is noticeable about swearing in London, and that is that the men do not usually swear in front of the women. In Paris it is quite different. A Parisian workman may prefer to suppress an oath in front of a woman, but he is not at all scrupulous about it, and the women themselves swear freely. The Londoners are more polite, or more squeamish, in this matter.

These are a few notes that I have set down more or less at random. It is a pity that someone capable of dealing with the subject does not keep a year-book of London slang and swearing, registering the changes accurately. It might throw useful light upon the formation, development, and obsolescence of words.

XXXIII

The two pounds that B. had given me lasted about ten days. That it lasted so long was due to Paddy, who had learned parsimony on the road and considered even one sound meal a day a wild extravagance. Food, to him, had come to mean simply bread and margarine—the eternal tea-and-two-slices, which will cheat hunger for an hour or two. He taught me how to live, food, bed, tobacco, and all, at the rate of half a crown a day. And he managed to earn a few extra shillings by 'glimming' in the evenings. It was a precarious job, because illegal, but it brought in a little and eked out our money.

One morning we tried for a job as sandwich men. We went at five to an alley-way behind some offices, but there was already a queue of thirty or forty men waiting, and after two hours we were told that there was no work for us. We had not missed much, for sandwich men have an unenviable job. They are paid about three shillings a day for ten hours' work—it is hard work, especially in windy weather, and there is no skulking, for an inspector comes round frequently to see that the men are on their beat. To add to their troubles, they are only engaged by the day, or sometimes for three days, never weekly, so that they have to wait hours for their job every morning. The number of unemployed men who are ready to do the work makes them powerless to fight for better treatment. The job all sandwich men covet is distributing handbills, which is paid for at the same rate. When you see a man distributing handbills you can do him a good turn by taking one, for he goes off duty when he has distributed all his bills.

Meanwhile we went on with the lodging-house life—a squalid, eventless life of crushing boredom. For days together there was nothing to do but sit in the underground kitchen, reading yesterday's newspaper, or, when one could get hold of it, a back number of the *Union Jack*. It rained a great deal at this time, and everyone who came in steamed, so that the kitchen stank horribly. One's only excitement was the periodical tea-and-two-slices. I do not know how many men are living this life in London—it must be thousands at the least. As to Paddy, it was actually the best life he had known for two years past. His interludes from tramping, the times when he had somehow laid hands on a few shillings, had all been like this; the tramping itself had been slightly worse. Listening to his whimpering voice—he was always whimpering when he was not eating—one realized what torture unemployment must be to him. People are wrong when they think that an unemployed man only worries about losing his wages; on the contrary, an illiterate man, with the work habit in his bones, needs work even more than he needs money. An educated man can put up with enforced idleness, which is one of the worst evils of poverty. But a man like Paddy, with no means of filling up time, is as miserable out of work as a dog on the chain. That is why it is such nonsense to pretend that those who have 'come down in the world' are to be pitied above all others. The man who really merits pity is the man who has been down from the start, and faces poverty with a blank, resourceless mind.

It was a dull time, and little of it stays in my mind, except for talks with Bozo. Once the lodging-house was invaded by a slumming-party. Paddy and I had been out, and, coming back in the afternoon, we heard sounds of music downstairs. We went down to find three gentle-people, sleekly dressed, holding a religious service in our kitchen. They were a grave and reverend seignior in a frock coat, a lady sitting at a portable harmonium, and a chinless youth toying with a crucifix. It appeared that they had marched in and started to hold the service, without any kind of invitation whatever.

It was a pleasure to see how the lodgers met this intrusion. They did not offer the smallest rudeness to the slummers; they just ignored them. By common consent everyone in the kitchen—a hundred men, perhaps—behaved as though the slummers had not existed. There they stood patiently singing and exhorting, and no more notice was taken of them than if they had been earwigs. The gentleman in the frock coat preached a sermon, but not a word of it was audible; it was drowned in the usual din of songs, oaths, and the clattering of pans. Men sat at their meals and card games three feet away from the harmonium, peaceably ignoring it. Presently the slummers gave it up and cleared out, not insulted in any way, but merely disregarded. No doubt they consoled themselves by thinking how brave they had been, 'freely venturing into the lowest dens,' etc. etc.

Bozo said that these people came to the lodging-house several times a month. They had influence with the police, and the 'deputy' could not exclude them. It is curious how people take it for granted that they have a right to preach at you and pray over you as soon as your income falls below a certain level.

After nine days B.'s two pounds was reduced to one and ninepence. Paddy and I set aside eighteenpence for our beds, and spent threepence on the usual tea-and-two-slices, which we shared—an appetizer rather than a meal. By the afternoon we were damnably hungry and Paddy remembered a church near King's Cross Station where a free tea was given once a week to tramps. This was the day, and we decided to go there. Bozo, though it was rainy weather and he was almost penniless, would not come, saying that churches were not his style.

Outside the church quite a hundred men were waiting, dirty types who had gathered from far and wide at the news of a free tea, like kites round a dead buffalo. Presently the doors opened and a clergyman and some girls shepherded us into a gallery at the top of the church. It was an evangelical church, gaunt and wilfully ugly, with texts about blood and fire blazoned on the walls, and a hymn-book containing twelve hundred and fifty-one hymns; reading some of the hymns, I concluded that the book would do as it stood for an anthology of bad verse. There was to be a service after the tea, and the regular congregation were sitting in the well of the church below. It was a week-day, and there were only a few dozen of them, mostly stringy old women who reminded one of boiling-fowls. We ranged ourselves in the gallery pews and were given our tea; it was a one-pound jam-jar of tea each, with six slices of bread and margarine. As soon as tea was over, a dozen tramps who had stationed themselves near the door bolted to avoid the service; the rest stayed, less from gratitude than lacking the cheek to go.

The organ let out a few preliminary hoots and the service began. And instantly, as though at a signal, the tramps began to misbehave in the most outrageous way. One would not have thought such scenes possible in a church. All round the gallery men lolled in their pews, laughed, chattered, leaned over and flicked pellets of bread among the congregation; I had to restrain the man next to me, more or less by force, from lighting a cigarette. The tramps treated the service as a purely comic spectacle. It was, indeed, a sufficiently ludicrous service—the kind where there are sudden yells of 'Hallelujah!' and endless extempore prayers—but their behaviour passed all bounds. There was one old fellow in the congregation—Brother Bootle or some such name—who was often called on to lead us in prayer, and whenever he stood up the tramps would begin stamping as though in a theatre; they said that on a previous occasion he had kept up an extempore prayer for twenty-five minutes, until the minister had interrupted him. Once when Brother Bootle stood up a tramp called out, 'Two to one 'e don't beat seven minutes!' so loud that the whole church must hear. It was not long before we were making far more noise than the minister. Sometimes somebody below would send up an indignant 'Hush!' but it made no impression. We had set ourselves to guy the service, and there was no stopping us.

It was a queer, rather disgusting scene. Below were the handful of simple, well-meaning people, trying hard to worship; and above were the hundred men whom they had fed, deliberately making worship impossible. A ring of dirty, hairy faces grinned down from the gallery, openly jeering. What could a few women and old men do against a hundred hostile tramps? They were afraid of us, and we were frankly bullying them. It was our revenge upon them for having humiliated us by feeding us.

The minister was a brave man. He thundered steadily through a long sermon on Joshua, and managed almost to ignore the sniggers and chattering from above. But in the end, perhaps goaded beyond endurance, he announced loudly:

'I shall address the last five minutes of my sermon to the *unsaved* sinners!'

Having said which, he turned his face to the gallery and kept it so for five minutes, lest there should be any doubt about who were saved and who unsaved. But much we cared! Even while the minister was threatening hell fire, we were rolling cigarettes, and at the last amen we clattered down the stairs with a yell, many agreeing to come back for another free tea next week.

The scene had interested me. It was so different from the ordinary demeanour of tramps—from the abject worm-like gratitude with which they normally accept charity. The explanation, of course, was that we outnumbered the congregation and so were not afraid of them. A man receiving charity practically always hates his benefactor—it is a fixed characteristic of human nature; and, when he has fifty or a hundred others to back him, he will show it.

In the evening, after the free tea, Paddy unexpectedly earned another eighteenpence at 'glimming'. It was exactly enough for another night's lodging, and we put it aside and went hungry till nine the next evening. Bozo, who might have given us some food, was away all day. The pavements were wet, and he had gone to the Elephant and Castle, where he knew of a pitch under shelter. Luckily I still had some tobacco, so that the day might have been worse.

At half past eight Paddy took me to the Embankment, where a clergyman was known to distribute meal tickets once a week. Under Charing Cross Bridge fifty men were waiting, mirrored in the shivering puddles. Some of them were truly appalling specimens—they were Embankment sleepers, and the Embankment dredges up worse types than the spike. One of them, I remember, was dressed in an overcoat without buttons, laced up with rope, a pair of ragged trousers, and boots exposing his toes—not a rag else. He was bearded like a fakir, and he had managed to streak his chest and shoulders with some horrible black filth resembling train oil. What one could see of his face under the dirt and hair was bleached white as paper by some malignant disease. I heard him speak, and he had a goodish accent, as of a clerk or shopwalker.

Presently the clergyman appeared and the men ranged themselves in a queue in the order in which they had arrived. The clergyman was a nice, chubby, youngish man, and, curiously enough, very like Charlie, my friend in Paris. He was shy and embarrassed, and did not speak except for a brief good evening; he simply hurried down the line of men, thrusting a ticket upon each, and not waiting to be thanked. The consequence was that, for once, there was genuine gratitude, and everyone said that the clergyman was a — good feller. Someone (in his hearing, I believe) called out: 'Well, *he'll* never be a — bishop!'—this, of course, intended as a warm compliment.

The tickets were worth sixpence each, and were directed to an eating-house not far away. When we got there we found that the proprietor, knowing that the tramps could not go elsewhere, was cheating by only giving four pennyworth of food for each ticket. Paddy and I pooled our tickets, and received food which we could have got for sevenpence or eightpence at most coffee-shops. The clergyman had distributed well over a pound in tickets, so that the proprietor was evidently swindling the tramps to the tune of seven shillings or more a week. This kind of victimization is a regular part of a tramp's life, and it will go on as long as people continue to give meal tickets instead of money.

Paddy and I went back to the lodging-house and, still hungry, loafed in the kitchen, making the warmth of the fire a substitute for food. At half-past ten Bozo arrived, tired out and haggard, for his mangled leg made walking an agony. He had not earned a penny at screeving, all the pitches under shelter being taken, and for several hours he had begged outright, with one eye on the policemen. He had amassed eightpence—a penny short of his kip. It was long past the hour for paying, and he had only managed to slip indoors when the deputy was not looking; at any moment he might be caught and turned out, to sleep on the Embankment. Bozo took the things out of his pockets and looked them over, debating what to sell. He decided on his razor, took it round the kitchen, and in a few minutes he had sold it for threepence—enough to pay his kip, buy a basin of tea, and leave a half-penny over.

Bozo got his basin of tea and sat down by the fire to dry his clothes. As he drank the tea I saw that he was laughing to himself, as though at some good joke. Surprised, I asked him what he had to laugh at.

'It's bloody funny!' he said. 'It's funny enough for *Punch*. What do you think I been and done?'

'What?'

'Sold my razor without having a shave first: Of all the — fools!'

He had not eaten since the morning, had walked several miles with a twisted leg, his clothes were drenched, and he had a halfpenny between himself and starvation. With all this, he could laugh over the loss of his razor. One could not help admiring him.

XXXIV

The next morning, our money being at an end, Paddy and I set out for the spike. We went southward by the Old Kent Road, making for Cromley; we could not go to a London spike, for Paddy had been in one recently and did not care to risk going again. It was a sixteen-mile walk over asphalt, blistering to the heels, and we were acutely hungry. Paddy browsed the pavement, laying up a store of cigarette ends against his time in the spike. In the end his perseverance was rewarded, for he picked up a penny. We bought a large piece of stale bread, and devoured it as we walked.

When we got to Cromley, it was too early to go to the spike, and we walked several miles farther, to a plantation beside a meadow, where one could sit down. It was a regular caravanserai of tramps—one could tell it by the worn grass and the sodden newspaper and rusty cans that they had left behind. Other tramps were arriving by ones and twos. It was jolly autumn weather. Near by, a deep bed of tansies was growing; it seems to me that even now I can smell the sharp reek of those tansies, warring with the reek of tramps. In the meadow two carthorse colts, raw sienna colour with white manes and tails, were nibbling at a gate. We sprawled about on the ground, sweaty and exhausted. Someone managed to find dry sticks and get a fire going, and we all had milkless tea out of a tin 'drum' which was passed round.

Some of the tramps began telling stories. One of them, Bill, was an interesting type, a genuine sturdy beggar of the old breed, strong as Hercules and a frank foe of work. He boasted that with his great strength he could get a navvying job any time he liked, but as soon as he drew his first week's wages he went on a terrific drunk and was sacked. Between whiles he 'mooched', chiefly from shopkeepers. He talked like this:

'I ain't goin' far in — Kent. Kent's a tight county, Kent is. There's too many bin' moochin' about 'ere. -- The — bakers get so as they'll throw their bread away sooner'n give it you. Now Oxford, that's the place for moochin', Oxford is. When I was in Oxford I mooched bread, and I mooched bacon, and I mooched beef, and every night I mooched tanners for my kip off of the students. The last night I was twopence short of my kip, so I goes up to a parson and mooches 'im for threepence. He give me threepence, and the next moment he turns round and gives me in charge for beggin'. "You bin beggin'," the copper says. "No I ain't," I says, "I was askin' the gentleman the time," I says. The copper starts feelin' inside my coat, and he pulls out a pound of meat and two loaves of bread. "Well, what's all this, then?" he says. "You better come 'long to the station," he says. The beak give me seven days. I don't mooch from no more — parsons. But Christ! what do I care for a lay-up of seven days?' etc. etc.

It seemed that his whole life was this—a round of mooching, drunks, and lay-ups. He laughed as he talked of it, taking it all for a tremendous joke. He looked as though he made a poor thing out of begging, for he wore only a corduroy suit, scarf, and cap—no socks or linen. Still, he was fat and jolly, and he even smelt of beer, a most unusual smell in a tramp nowadays.

Two of the tramps had been in Cromley spike recently,

and they told a ghost story connected with it. Years earlier, they said, there had been a suicide there. A tramp had managed to smuggle a razor into his cell, and there cut his throat. In the morning, when the Tramp Major came round, the body was jammed against the door, and to open it they had to break the dead man's arm. In revenge for this, the dead man haunted his cell, and anyone who slept there was certain to die within the year; there were copious instances, of course. If a cell door stuck when you tried to open it, you should avoid that cell like the plague, for it was the haunted one.

Two tramps, ex-sailors, told another grisly story. A man (they swore they had known him) had planned to stow away on a boat bound for Chile. It was laden with manufactured goods packed in big wooden crates, and with the help of a docker the stowaway had managed to hide himself in one of these. But the docker had made a mistake about the order in which the crates were to be loaded. The crane gripped the stowaway, swung him aloft, and deposited him—at the very bottom of the hold, beneath hundreds of crates. No one discovered what had happened until the end of the voyage, when they found the stowaway rotting, dead of suffocation.

Another tramp told the story of Gilderoy, the Scottish robber. Gilderoy was the man who was condemned to be hanged, escaped, captured the judge who had sentenced him, and (splendid fellow!) hanged him. The tramps liked the story, of course, but the interesting thing was to see that they had got it all wrong. Their version was that Gilderoy escaped to America, whereas in reality he was recaptured and put to death. The story had been amended, no doubt deliberately; just as children amend the stories of Samson and Robin Hood, giving them happy endings which are quite imaginary.

This set the tramps talking about history, and a very

old man declared that the 'one bite law' was a survival from days when the nobles hunted men instead of deer. Some of the others laughed at him, but he had the idea firm in his head. He had heard, too, of the Corn Laws, and the *jus primae noctis* (he believed it had really existed); also of the Great Rebellion, which he thought was a rebellion of poor against rich—perhaps he had got it mixed up with the peasant rebellions. I doubt whether the old man could read, and certainly he was not repeating newspaper articles. His scraps of history had been passed from generation to generation of tramps, perhaps for centuries in some cases. It was oral tradition lingering on, like a faint echo from the Middle Ages.

Paddy and I went to the spike at six in the evening, getting out at ten in the morning. It was much like Romton and Edbury, and we saw nothing of the ghost. Among the casuals were two young men named William and Fred, ex-fishermen from Norfolk, a lively pair and fond of singing. They had a song called 'Unhappy Bella' that is worth writing down. I heard them sing it half a dozen times during the next two days, and I managed to get it by heart, except a line or two which I have guessed. It ran:

Bella was young and Bella was fair
With bright blue eyes and golden hair,
O unhappy Bella!
Her step was light and her heart was gay,
But she had no sense, and one fine day
She got herself put in the family way
By a wicked, heartless, cruel deceiver.

Poor Bella was young, she didn't believe
That the world is hard and men deceive,
O unhappy Bella!
She said, 'My man will do what's just,

He'll marry me now, because he must';
Her heart was full of loving trust
In a wicked, heartless, cruel deceiver.

She went to his house; that dirty skunk
Had packed his bags and done a bunk,
O unhappy Bella!
Her landlady said, 'Get out, you whore,
I won't have your sort a-darkening my door.'
Poor Bella was put to affliction sore
By a wicked, heartless, cruel deceiver.

All night she tramped the cruel snows,
What she must have suffered nobody knows,
O unhappy Bella!
And when the morning dawned so red,
Alas, alas, poor Bella was dead,
Sent so young to her lonely bed
By a wicked, heartless, cruel deceiver.

So thus, you see, do what you will,
The fruits of sin are suffering still,
O unhappy Bella!
As into the grave they laid her low,
The men said, 'Alas, but life is so,'
But the women chanted, sweet and low,
'It's all the men, the dirty bastards!'

Written by a woman, perhaps.

William and Fred, the singers of this song, were thorough scallywags, the sort of men who get tramps a bad name.
They happened to know that the Tramp Major at Cromley
had a stock of old clothes, which were to be given at need
to casuals. Before going in William and Fred took off their
boots, ripped the seams and cut pieces off the soles, more

or less ruining them. Then they applied for two pairs of boots, and the Tramp Major, seeing how bad their boots were, gave them almost new pairs. William and Fred were scarcely outside the spike in the morning before they had sold these boots for one and ninepence. It seemed to them quite worth while, for one and ninepence, to make their own boots practically unwearable.

Leaving the spike, we all started southward, a long slouching procession, for Lower Binfield and Ide Hill. On the way there was a fight between two of the tramps. They had quarrelled overnight (there was some silly *casus belli* about one saying to the other, 'Bull shit', which was taken for Bolshevik—a deadly insult), and they fought it out in a field. A dozen of us stayed to watch them. The scene sticks in my mind for one thing—the man who was beaten going down, and his cap falling off and showing that his hair was quite white. After that some of us intervened and stopped the fight. Paddy had meanwhile been making inquiries, and found that the real cause of the quarrel was, as usual, a few pennyworth of food.

We got to Lower Binfield quite early, and Paddy filled in the time by asking for work at back doors. At one house he was given some boxes to chop up for firewood, and, saying he had a mate outside, he brought me in and we did the work together. When it was done the householder told the maid to take us out a cup of tea. I remember the terrified way in which she brought it out, and then, losing her courage, set the cups down on the path and bolted back to the house, shutting herself in the kitchen. So dreadful is the name of 'tramp'. They paid us sixpence each, and we bought a threepenny loaf and half an ounce of tobacco, leaving fivepence.

Paddy thought it wiser to bury our fivepence, for the Tramp Major at Lower Binfield was renowned as a tyrant and might refuse to admit us if we had any money at all. It is quite a common practice of tramps to bury their money. If they intend to smuggle at all a large sum into the spike they generally sew it into their clothes, which may mean prison if they are caught, of course. Paddy and Bozo used to tell a good story about this. An Irishman (Bozo said it was an Irishman; Paddy said an Englishman), not a tramp, and in possession of thirty pounds, was stranded in a small village where he could not get a bed. He consulted a tramp, who advised him to go to the workhouse. It is quite a regular proceeding, if one cannot get a bed elsewhere, to get one at the workhouse, paying a reasonable sum for it. The Irishman, however, thought he would be clever and get a bed for nothing, so he presented himself at the workhouse as an ordinary casual. He had sewn the thirty pounds into his clothes. Meanwhile the tramp who had advised him had seen his chance, and that night he privately asked the Tramp Major for permission to leave the spike early in the morning, as he had to see about a job. At six in the morning he was released and went out—in the Irishman's clothes. The Irishman complained of the theft, and was given thirty days for going into a casual ward under false pretences.

XXXV

Arrived at Lower Binfield, we sprawled for a long time on the green, watched by cottagers from their front gates. A clergyman and his daughter came and stared silently at us for a while, as though we had been aquarium fishes, and then went away again. There were several dozen of us waiting. William and Fred were there, still singing, and the men who had fought, and Bill the moocher. He had been mooching from bakers, and had quantities of stale bread tucked away between his coat and his bare body. He shared it out, and we were all glad of it. There was a woman among us, the first woman tramp I had ever seen. She was a fattish, battered, very dirty woman of sixty, in a long, trailing black skirt. She put on great airs of dignity, and if anyone sat down near her she sniffed and moved farther off.

'Where you bound for, missis?' one of the tramps called to her.

The woman sniffed and looked into the distance.

'Come on, missis,' he said, 'cheer up. Be chummy. We're all in the same boat 'ere.'

'Thank you,' said the woman bitterly, 'when I want to get mixed up with a set of *tramps*, I'll let you know.'

I enjoyed the way she said *tramps*. It seemed to show

you in a flash the whole of her soul; a small, blinkered, feminine soul, that had learned absolutely nothing from years on the road. She was, no doubt, a respectable widow woman, become a tramp through some grotesque accident.

The spike opened at six. This was Saturday, and we were to be confined over the week-end, which is the usual practice; why, I do not know, unless it is from a vague feeling that Sunday merits something disagreeable. When we registered I gave my trade as 'journalist'. It was truer than 'painter', for I had sometimes earned money from newspaper articles, but it was a silly thing to say, being bound to lead to questions. As soon as we were inside the spike and had been lined up for the search, the Tramp Major called my name. He was a stiff, soldierly man of forty, not looking the bully he had been represented, but with an old soldier's gruffness. He said sharply:

'Which of you is Blank?' (I forget what name I had given.) 'Me, sir.'

'So you are a journalist?'

'Yes, sir,' I said, quaking. A few questions would betray the fact that I had been lying, which might mean prison. But the Tramp Major only looked me up and down and said:

'Then you are a gentleman?'

'I suppose so.'

He gave me another long look. 'Well, that's bloody bad luck, guv'nor,' he said; 'bloody bad luck that is.' And thereafter he treated me with unfair favouritism, and even with a kind of deference. He did not search me, and in the bathroom he actually gave me a clean towel to myself—an unheard-of luxury. So powerful is the word 'gentleman' in an old soldier's ear.

By seven we had wolfed our bread and tea and were in our cells. We slept one in a cell, and there were bedsteads and straw palliasses, so that one ought to have had a good night's sleep. But no spike is perfect, and the peculiar shortcoming at Lower Binfield was the cold. The hot pipes were not working, and the two blankets we had been given were thin cotton things and almost useless. It was only autumn, but the cold was bitter. One spent the long twelve-hour night in turning from side to side, falling asleep for a few minutes and waking up shivering. We could not smoke, for our tobacco, which we had managed to smuggle in, was in our clothes and we should not get these back till the morning. All down the passage one could hear groaning noises, and sometimes a shouted oath. No one, I imagine, got more than an hour or two of sleep.

In the morning, after breakfast and the doctor's inspection, the Tramp Major herded us all into the dining-room and locked the door upon us. It was a limewashed, stone-floored room, unutterably dreary, with its furniture of deal boards and benches, and its prison smell. The barred windows were too high to look out of, and there were no ornaments save a clock and a copy of the workhouse rules. Packed elbow to elbow on the benches, we were bored already, though it was barely eight in the morning. There was nothing to do, nothing to talk about, not even room to move. The sole consolation was that one could smoke, for smoking was connived at so long as one was not caught in the act. Scotty, a little hairy tramp with a bastard accent sired by Cockney out of Glasgow, was tobaccoless, his tin of cigarette ends having fallen out of his boot during the search and been impounded. I stood him the makings of a cigarette. We smoked furtively, thrusting our cigarettes into our pockets, like schoolboys, when we heard the Tramp Major coming.

Most of the tramps spent ten continuous hours in this comfortless, soulless room. Heaven knows how they put up with it. I was luckier than the others, for at ten o'clock the Tramp Major told off a few men for odd jobs, and he picked me out to help in the workhouse kitchen, the most coveted job of all. This, like the clean towel, was a charm worked by the word 'gentleman'.

There was no work to do in the kitchen, and I sneaked off into a small shed used for storing potatoes, where some workhouse paupers were skulking to avoid the Sunday morning service. There were comfortable packing-cases to sit on, and some back numbers of the *Family Herald*, and even a copy of *Raffles* from the workhouse library. The paupers talked interestingly about workhouse life. They told me, among other things, that the thing really hated in the workhouse, as a stigma of charity, is the uniform; if the men could wear their own clothes, or even their own caps and scarves, they would not mind being paupers. I had my dinner from the workhouse table, and it was a meal fit for a boa-constrictor—the largest meal I had eaten since my first day at the Hôtel X. The paupers said that they habitually gorged to the bursting-point on Sunday and were underfed the rest of the week. After dinner the cook set me to do the washing up, and told me to throw away the food that remained. The wastage was astonishing and, in the circumstances, appalling. Half-eaten joints of meat, and bucketfuls of broken bread and vegetables, were pitched away like so much rubbish and then defiled with tea-leaves. I filled five dustbins to overflowing with quite eatable food. And while I did so fifty tramps were sitting in the spike with their bellies half filled by the spike dinner of bread and cheese, and perhaps two cold boiled potatoes each in honour of Sunday. According to the paupers, the food was thrown away from deliberate policy, rather than that it should be given to the tramps.

At three I went back to the spike. The tramps had been sitting there since eight, with hardly room to move an elbow, and they were now half mad with boredom. Even smoking was at an end, for a tramp's tobacco is picked-up cigarette ends, and he starves if he is more than a few hours away from the pavement. Most of the men were too bored even to talk;

they just sat packed on the benches, staring at nothing, their scrubby faces split in two by enormous yawns. The room stank of *ennui*.

Paddy, his backside aching from the hard bench, was in a whimpering mood, and to pass the time away I talked with a rather superior tramp, a young carpenter who wore a collar and tie and was on the road, he said, for lack of a set of tools. He kept a little aloof from the other tramps, and held himself more like a free man than a casual. He had literary tastes, too, and carried a copy of *Quentin Durward* in his pocket. He told me that he never went into a spike unless driven there by hunger, sleeping under hedges and behind ricks in preference. Along the south coast he had begged by day and slept in bathing-huts for weeks at a time.

We talked of life on the road. He criticized the system that makes a tramp spend fourteen hours a day in the spike, and the other ten in walking and dodging the police. He spoke of his own case—six months at the public charge for want of a few pounds' worth of tools. It was idiotic, he said.

Then I told him about the wastage of food in the work-house kitchen, and what I thought of it. And at that he changed his tone instantly. I saw that I had awakened the pew-renter who sleeps in every English workman. Though he had been famished along with the others, he at once saw reasons why the food should have been thrown away rather that given to the tramps. He admonished me quite severely.

'They have to do it,' he said. 'If they made these places too comfortable, you'd have all the scum of the country flocking into them. It's only the bad food as keeps all that scum away. These here tramps are too lazy to work, that's all that's wrong with them. You don't want to go encouraging of them. They're scum.'

I produced arguments to prove him wrong, but he would not listen. He kept repeating:

'You don't want to have any pity on these here tramps—scum, they are. You don't want to judge them by the same standards as men like you and me. They're scum, just scum.'

It was interesting to see the subtle way in which he disassociated himself from 'these here tramps'. He had been on the road six months, but in the sight of God, he seemed to imply, he was not a tramp. I imagine there are quite a lot of tramps who thank God they are not tramps. They are like the trippers who say such cutting things about trippers.

Three hours dragged by. At six supper arrived, and turned out to be quite uneatable; the bread, tough enough in the morning (it had been cut into slices on Saturday night), was now as hard as ship's biscuit. Luckily it was spread with dripping, and we scraped the dripping off and ate that alone, which was better than nothing. At a quarter past six we were sent to bed. New tramps were arriving, and in order not to mix the tramps of different days (for fear of infectious diseases) the new men were put in the cells and we in dormitories. Our dormitory was a barn-like room with thirty beds close together, and a tub to serve as a common chamber-pot. It stank abominably, and the older men coughed and got up all night. But being so many together kept the room warm, and we had some sleep.

We dispersed at ten in the morning, after a fresh medical inspection, with a hunk of bread and cheese for our midday dinner. William and Fred, strong in the posses-sion of a shilling, impaled their bread on the spike railings—as a protest, they said. This was the second spike in Kent that they had made too hot to hold them, and they thought it a great joke. They were cheerful souls, for tramps. The imbecile (there is an imbecile in every collection of tramps) said that he was too tired to walk and clung to the railings, until the Tramp Major had to dislodge him and start him with a kick. Paddy and I turned north, for London. Most of the others were going on to Ide Hill, said to be about the worst spike in England.*

Once again it was jolly autumn weather, and the road was quiet, with few cars passing. The air was like sweet-briar after the spike's mingled stenches of sweat, soap, and drains. We two seemed the only tramps on the road. Then I heard a hurried step behind us, and someone calling. It was little Scotty, the Glasgow tramp, who had run after us panting. He produced a rusty tin from his pocket. He wore a friendly smile, like someone repaying an obligation.

'Here y'are, mate,' he said cordially. 'I owe you some fag ends. You stood me a smoke yesterday. The Tramp Major give me back my box of fag ends when we come out this morning. One good turn deserves another—here y'are.'

And he put four sodden, debauched, loathly cigarette ends into my hand.

* I have been in it since, and it is not so bad.

XXXVI

I want to set down some general remarks about tramps. When one comes to think of it, tramps are a queer product and worth thinking over. It is queer that a tribe of men, tens of thousands in number, should be marching up and down England like so many Wandering Jews. But though the case obviously wants considering, one cannot even start to consider it until one has got rid of certain prejudices. These prejudices are rooted in the idea that every tramp, *ipso facto*, is a black-guard. In childhood we have been taught that tramps are blackguards, and consequently there exists in our minds a sort of ideal or typical tramp—a repulsive, rather dangerous creature, who would die rather than work or wash, and wants nothing but to beg, drink, and rob hen-houses. This tramp-monster is no truer to life than the sinister Chinaman of the magazine stories, but he is very hard to get rid of. The very word 'tramp' evokes his image. And the belief in him obscures the real questions of vagrancy.

To take a fundamental question about vagrancy: Why do tramps exist at all? It is a curious thing, but very few people know what makes a tramp take to the road. And, because of the belief in the tramp-monster, the most fantastic reasons are suggested. It is said, for instance, that tramps tramp to avoid work, to beg more easily, to seek opportunities for crime, even—least probable of reasons—because they like tramping. I have even read in a book of criminology that the tramp is an atavism, a throw-back to the nomadic stage of humanity. And meanwhile the quite obvious cause of vagrancy is staring one in the face. Of course a tramp is not a nomadic atavism—one might as well say that a commercial traveller is an atavism. A tramp tramps, not because he likes it, but for the same reason as a car keeps to the left; because there happens to be a law compelling him to do so. A destitute man, if he is not supported by the parish, can only get relief at the casual wards, and as each casual ward will only admit him for one night, he is automatically kept moving. He is a vagrant because, in the state of the law, it is that or starve. But people have been brought up to believe in the tramp-monster, and so they prefer to think that there must be some more or less villainous motive for tramping.

As a matter of fact, very little of the tramp-monster will survive inquiry. Take the generally accepted idea that tramps are dangerous characters. Quite apart from experience, one can say *a priori* that very few tramps are dangerous, because if they were dangerous they would be treated accordingly. A casual ward will often admit a hundred tramps in one night, and these are handled by a staff of at most three porters. A hundred ruffians could not be controlled by three unarmed men. Indeed, when one sees how tramps let themselves be bullied by the workhouse officials, it is obvious that they are the most docile, broken-spirited creatures imaginable. Or take the idea that all tramps are drunkards—an idea ridiculous on the face of it. No doubt many tramps would drink if they got the chance, but in the nature of things they cannot get the chance. At this moment a pale watery stuff called beer is sevenpence a pint in England. To be drunk on it would cost at least half a crown, and a man who can command half a crown at all often is not a tramp. The idea that tramps are impudent social parasites ('sturdy beggars') is not absolutely unfounded, but it is only true in a few per cent of the cases. Deliberate, cynical parasitism, such as one reads of in Jack London's books on American tramping, is not in the English character. The English are a conscience-ridden race, with a strong sense of the sinfulness of poverty. One cannot imagine the average Englishman deliberately turning parasite, and this national character does not necessarily change because a man is thrown out of work. Indeed, if one remembers that a tramp is only an Englishman out of work, forced by law to live as a vagabond, then the tramp-monster vanishes. I am not saying, of course, that most tramps are ideal characters; I am only saying that they are ordinary human beings, and that if they are worse than other people it is the result and not the cause of their way of life.

It follows that the 'Serve them damned well right' attitude that is normally taken towards tramps is no fairer than it would be towards cripples or invalids. When one has realized that, one begins to put oneself in a tramp's place and understand what his life is like. It is an extraordinarily futile, acutely unpleasant life. I have described the casual ward—the routine of a tramp's day—but there are three especial evils that need insisting upon. The first is hunger, which is the almost general fate of tramps. The casual ward gives them a ration which is probably not even meant to be sufficient, and anything beyond this must be got by begging—that is, by breaking the law. The result is that nearly every tramp is rotted by malnutrition; for proof of which one need only look at the men lining up outside any casual ward. The second great evil of a tramp's life—it seems much smaller at first sight, but it is a good second—is that he is entirely cut off from contact with women. This point needs elaborating.

Tramps are cut off from women, in the first place, because there are very few women at their level of society. One might imagine that among destitute people the sexes would be as equally balanced as elsewhere. But it is not so; in fact, one can almost say that below a certain level society is entirely male. The following figures, published by the L.C.C. from a night census taken on February 13th, 1931, will show the relative numbers of destitute men and destitute women:

Spending the night in the streets, 60 men, 18 women.*

In shelters and homes not licensed as common lodging-houses, 1,057 men, 137 women.

In the crypt of St Martin's-in-the-Fields Church, 88 men, 12 women.

In L.C.C. casual wards and hostels, 674 men, 15 women.

It will be seen from these figures that at the charity level men outnumber women by something like ten to one. The cause is presumably that unemployment affects women less than men; also that any presentable woman can, in the last resort, attach herself to some man. The result, for a tramp, is that he is condemned to perpetual celibacy. For of course it goes without saying that if a tramp finds no women at his own level, those above—even a very little above—are as far out of his reach as the moon. The reasons are not worth discussing, but there is no doubt that women never, or hardly ever, condescend to men who are much poorer than themselves. A tramp, therefore, is a celibate from the moment when he takes to the road. He is absolutely without hope of getting a wife, a mistress, or any kind of woman except—very rarely, when he can raise a few shillings—a prostitute.

It is obvious what the results of this must be: homosexuality, for instance, and occasional rape cases. But deeper than these there is the degradation worked in a man who knows that he is not even considered fit for marriage. The sexual

---

* This must be an underestimate. Still, the proportions probably hold good.

impulse, not to put it any higher, is a fundamental impulse, and starvation of it can be almost as demoralizing as physical hunger. The evil of poverty is not so much that it makes a man suffer as that it rots him physically and spiritually. And there can be no doubt that sexual starvation contributes to this rotting process. Cut off from the whole race of women, a tramp feels himself degraded to the rank of a cripple or a lunatic. No humiliation could do more damage to a man's self-respect.

The other great evil of a tramp's life is enforced idleness. By our vagrancy laws things are so arranged that when he is not walking the road he is sitting in a cell; or, in the intervals, lying on the ground waiting for the casual ward to open. It is obvious that this is a dismal, demoralizing way of life, especially for an uneducated man.

Besides these one could enumerate scores of minor evils—to name only one, discomfort, which is inseparable from life on the road; it is worth remembering that the average tramp has no clothes but what he stands up in, wears boots that are ill-fitting, and does not sit in a chair for months together. But the important point is that a tramp's sufferings are entirely useless. He lives a fantastically disagreeable life, and lives it to no purpose whatever. One could not, in fact, invent a more futile routine than walking from prison to prison, spending perhaps eighteen hours a day in the cell and on the road. There must be at the least several tens of thousands of tramps in England. Each day they expend innumerable foot-pounds of energy—enough to plough thousands of acres, build miles of road, put up dozens of houses—in mere, useless walking. Each day they waste between them possibly ten years of time in staring at cell walls. They cost the country at least a pound a week a man, and give nothing in return for it. They go round and round, on an endless boring game of general post, which is of no use, and is not even meant to be of any use to any person whatever. The law keeps this process going, and we have got so accustomed to it that we are not surprised. But it is very silly.

Granting the futility of a tramp's life, the question is whether anything could be done to improve it. Obviously it would be possible, for instance, to make the casual wards a little more habitable, and this is actually being done in some cases. During the last year some of the casual wards have been improved—beyond recognition, if the accounts are true—and there is talk of doing the same to all of them. But this does not go to the heart of the problem. The problem is how to turn the tramp from a bored, half alive vagrant into a self-respecting human being. A mere increase of comfort cannot do this. Even if the casual wards became positively luxurious (they never will)* a tramp's life would still be wasted. He would still be a pauper, cut off from marriage and home life, and a dead loss to the community. What is needed is to depauperize him, and this can only be done by finding him work—not work for the sake of working, but work of which he can enjoy the benefit. At present, in the great majority of casual wards, tramps do no work whatever. At one time they were made to break stones for their food, but this was stopped when they had broken enough stone for years ahead and put the stone-breakers out of work. Nowadays they are kept idle, because there is seemingly nothing for them to do. Yet there is a fairly obvious way of making them useful, namely this: Each workhouse could run a small farm, or at least a kitchen garden, and every able-bodied tramp who presented himself could be made to do a sound day's work. The produce of the farm or garden could be used for feeding the tramps, and at the worst it would be better than the filthy diet of bread and margarine and tea. Of course, the casual wards could never be quite self-supporting, but they could go a long way towards it, and the rates would probably benefit in the long run. It must be remembered that under the present system tramps are as dead a loss to the country as they could possibly be, for they do not only do no work, but they live on a diet that is bound to undermine their health; the system, therefore, loses lives as well as money. A scheme which fed them decently, and made them produce at least a part of their own food, would be worth trying.[*]

It may be objected that a farm or even a garden could not be run with casual labour. But there is no real reason why tramps should only stay a day at each casual ward; they might stay a month or even a year, if there were work for them to do. The constant circulation of tramps is something quite artificial. At present a tramp is an expense to the rates, and the object of each workhouse is therefore to push him on to the next; hence the rule that he can stay only one night. If he returns within a month he is penalized by being confined for a week, and, as this is much the same as being in prison, naturally he keeps moving. But if he represented labour to the workhouse, and the workhouse represented sound food to him, it would be another matter. The workhouses would develop into partially self-supporting institutions, and the tramps, settling down here or there according as they were needed, would cease to be tramps. They would be doing something comparatively useful, getting decent food, and living a settled life. By degrees, if the scheme worked well, they might even cease to be regarded as paupers, and be able to marry and take a respectable place in society.

This is only a rough idea, and there are some obvious objections to it. Nevertheless, it does suggest a way of improving the status of tramps without piling new burdens on the rates. And the solution must, in any case, be something of this kind. For the question is, what to do with men who are underfed and idle; and the answer—to make them grow their own food—imposes itself automatically.

---

[*] In fairness, it must be added that a few of the casual wards have been improved recently, at least from the point of view of sleeping accommodation. But most of them are the same as ever, and there has been no real improvement in the food.

XXXVII

A word about the sleeping accommodation open to a homeless person in London. At present it is impossible to get a *bed* in any non-charitable institution in London for less than seven-pence a night. If you cannot afford sevenpence for a bed, you must put up with one of the following substitutes:

1. The Embankment. Here is the account that Paddy gave me of sleeping on the Embankment:

'De whole t'ing wid de Embankment is gettin' to sleep early. You got to be on your bench by eight o'clock, because dere ain't too many benches and sometimes dey're all taken. And you got to try to get to sleep at once. 'Tis too cold to sleep much after twelve o'clock, an' de police turns you off at four in de mornin'. It ain't easy to sleep, dough, wid dem bloody trams flyin' past your head all de time, an' dem sky-signs across de river flickin' on an' off in your eyes. De cold's cruel. Dem as sleeps dere generally wraps demselves up in newspaper, but it don't do much good. You'd be bloody lucky if you got t'ree hours' sleep.'

I have slept on the Embankment and found that it corresponded to Paddy's description. It is, however, much better than not sleeping at all, which is the alternative if you spend the night in the streets, elsewhere than on the

Embankment. According to the law in London, you may sit down for the night, but the police must move you on if they see you asleep; the Embankment and one or two odd corners (there is one behind the Lyceum Theatre) are special exceptions. This law is evidently a piece of wilful offensiveness. Its object, so it is said, is to prevent people from dying of exposure; but clearly if a man has no home and is going to die of exposure, die he will, asleep or awake. In Paris there is no such law. There, people sleep by the score under the Seine bridges, and in doorways, and on benches in the squares, and round the ventilating shafts of the Métro, and even inside the Métro stations. It does no apparent harm. No one will spend a night in the street if he can possibly help it, and if he is going to stay out of doors he might as well be allowed to sleep, if he can.

2. The Twopenny Hangover. This comes a little higher than the Embankment. At the Twopenny Hangover, the lodgers sit in a row on a bench; there is a rope in front of them, and they lean on this as though leaning over a fence. A man, humorously called the valet, cuts the rope at five in the morning. I have never been there myself, but Bozo had been there often. I asked him whether anyone could possibly sleep in such an attitude, and he said that it was more comfortable than it sounded—at any rate, better than bare floor. There are similar shelters in Paris, but the charge there is only twenty-five centimes (a halfpenny) instead of twopence.

3. The Coffin, at fourpence a night. At the Coffin you sleep in a wooden box, with a tarpaulin for covering. It is cold, and the worst thing about it are the bugs, which, being enclosed in a box, you cannot escape.

Above this come the common lodging-houses, with charges varying between sevenpence and one and a penny a night. The best are the Rowton Houses, where the charge is a shilling, for which you get a cubicle to yourself, and the use of excellent bathrooms. You can also pay half a crown for a 'special', which is practically hotel accommodation. The Rowton Houses are splendid buildings, and the only objection to them is the strict discipline, with rules against cooking, card-playing, etc. Perhaps the best advertisement for the Rowton Houses is the fact that they are always full to over-flowing. The Bruce Houses, at one and a penny, are also excellent.

Next best, in point of cleanliness, are the Salvation Army hostels, at sevenpence or eightpence. They vary (I have been in one or two that were not very unlike common lodging-houses), but most of them are clean, and they have good bathrooms; you have to pay extra for a bath, however. You can get a cubicle for a shilling. In the eightpenny dormitories the beds are comfortable, but there are so many of them (as a rule at least forty to a room), and so close together, that it is impossible to get a quiet night. The numerous restrictions stink of prison and charity. The Salvation Army hostels would only appeal to people who put cleanliness before anything else.

Beyond this there are the ordinary common lodging-houses. Whether you pay sevenpence or a shilling, they are all stuffy and noisy, and the beds are uniformly dirty and uncomfortable. What redeems them are their *laissez-faire* atmosphere and the warm home-like kitchens where one can lounge at all hours of the day or night. They are squalid dens, but some kind of social life is possible in them. The women's lodging-houses are said to be generally worse than the men's, and there are very few houses with accommodation for married couples. In fact, it is nothing out of the common for a homeless man to sleep in one lodging-house and his wife in another.

At this moment at least fifteen thousand people in London are living in common lodging-houses. For an unattached man earning two pounds a week, or less, a lodging-house is a great convenience. He could hardly get a furnished room so cheaply, and the lodging-house gives him free firing, a bathroom of sorts, and plenty of society. As for the dirt, it is a minor evil. The really bad fault of lodging-houses is that they are places in which one pays to sleep, and in which sound sleep is impossible. All one gets for one's money is a bed measuring five feet six by two feet six, with a hard convex mattress and a pillow like a block of wood, covered by one cotton counterpane and two grey, stinking sheets. In winter there are blankets, but never enough. And this bed is in a room where there are never less than five, and sometimes fifty or sixty beds, a yard or two apart. Of course, no one can sleep soundly in such circumstances. The only other places where people are herded like this are barracks and hospitals. In the public wards of a hospital no one even hopes to sleep well. In barracks the soldiers are crowded, but they have good beds, and they are healthy; in a common lodging-house nearly all the lodgers have chronic coughs, and a large number have bladder diseases which make them get up at all the hours of the night. The result is a perpetual racket, making sleep impossible. So far as my observation goes, no one in a lodging-house sleeps more than five hours a night—a damnable swindle when one has paid sevenpence or more.

Here legislation could accomplish something. At present there is all manner of legislation by the L.C.C. about lodging-houses, but it is not done in the interests of the lodgers. The L.C.C. only exert themselves to forbid drinking, gambling, fighting, etc. etc. There is no law to say that the beds in a lodging-house must be comfortable. This would be quite an easy thing to enforce—much easier, for instance, than restrictions upon gambling. The lodging-house keepers should be compelled to provide adequate bedclothes and better mattresses, and above all to divide their dormitories into cubicles. It does not matter how small a cubicle is, the important thing is that a man should be alone when he sleeps. These few changes, strictly enforced, would make an enormous difference. It is not impossible to make a lodging-house reasonably comfortable at the usual rates of payment. In the Croydon municipal lodging-house, where the charge is only ninepence, there are cubicles, good beds, chairs (a very rare luxury in lodging-houses), and kitchens above ground instead of in a cellar. There is no reason why every ninepenny lodging-house should not come up to this standard.

Of course, the owners of lodging-houses would be opposed *en bloc* to any improvement, for their present business is an immensely profitable one. The average house takes five or ten pounds a night, with no bad debts (credit being strictly forbidden), and except for rent the expenses are small. Any improvement would mean less crowding, and hence less profit. Still, the excellent municipal lodging-house at Croydon shows how well one *can* be served for ninepence. A few well-directed laws could make these conditions general. If the authorities are going to concern themselves with lodging-houses at all, they ought to start by making them more comfortable, not by silly restrictions that would never be tolerated in a hotel.

XXXVIII

After we left the spike at Lower Binfield, Paddy and I earned half a crown at weeding and sweeping in somebody's garden, stayed the night at Cromley, and walked back to London. I parted from Paddy a day or two later. B. lent me a final two pounds, and, as I had only another eight days to hold out, that was the end of my troubles. My tame imbecile turned out worse than I had expected, but not bad enough to make me wish myself back in the spike or the Auberge de Jehan Cottard.

Paddy set out for Portsmouth, where he had a friend who might conceivably find work for him, and I have never seen him since. A short time ago I was told that he had been run over and killed, but perhaps my informant was mixing him up with someone else. I had news of Bozo only three days ago. He is in Wandsworth—fourteen days for begging. I do not suppose prison worries him very much.

My story ends here. It is a fairly trivial story, and I can only hope that it has been interesting in the same way as a travel diary is interesting. I can at least say, Here is the world that awaits you if you are ever penniless. Some days I want to explore that world more thoroughly. I should like to know people like Mario and Paddy and Bill the moocher, not from casual encounters, but intimately; I should like to understand what really goes on in the souls of *plongeurs* and tramps and Embankment sleepers. At present I do not feel that I have seen more than the fringe of poverty.

Still I can point to one or two things I have definitely learned by being hard up. I shall never again think that all tramps are drunken scoundrels, nor expect a beggar to be grateful when I give him a penny, nor be surprised if men out of work lack energy, nor subscribe to the Salvation Army, nor pawn my clothes, nor refuse a handbill, nor enjoy a meal at a smart restaurant. That is a beginning.

The blanks in this edition appeared in the original publication, due to concerns regarding obscenity at the time.

CLASSIC LITERATURE: WORDS AND PHRASES
adapted from the Collins English Dictionary

Accoucheur NOUN a male midwife or doctor ❏ *I think my sister must have had some general idea that I was a young offender whom an Accoucheur Policemen had taken up (on my birthday) and delivered over to her* (*Great Expectations* by Charles Dickens)

addled ADJ confused and unable to think properly ❏ *But she counted and counted till she got that addled* (*The Adventures of Huckleberry Finn* by Mark Twain)

admiration NOUN amazement or wonder ❏ *lifting up his hands and eyes by way of admiration* (*Gulliver's Travels* by Jonathan Swift)

afeard ADJ afeard means afraid ❏ *shake it—and don't be afeard* (*The Adventures of Huckleberry Finn* by Mark Twain)

affected VERB affected means to assume the appearance of ❏ *Hadst thou affected sweet divinity* (*Doctor Faustus 5.2* by Christopher Marlowe)

aground ADV when a boat runs aground, it touches the ground in a shallow part of the water and gets stuck ❏ *what kep' you?—boat get aground?* (*The Adventures of Huckleberry Finn* by Mark Twain)

ague NOUN a fever in which the patient has alternate hot and cold shivering fits ❏ *his exposure to the wet and cold had brought on fever and ague* (*Oliver Twist* by Charles Dickens)

alchemy ADJ false or worthless ❏ *all wealth alchemy* (*The Sun Rising* by John Donne)

all alike PHRASE the same all the time ❏ *Love, all alike* (*The Sun Rising* by John Donne)

alow and aloft PHRASE alow means in the lower part or bottom, and aloft means on the top, so alow and aloft means on the top and in the bottom or throughout ❏ *Someone's turned the chest out alow and aloft* (*Treasure Island* by Robert Louis Stevenson)

ambuscade NOUN ambuscade is not a proper word. Tom means an ambush, which is when a group of people attack their enemies, after hiding and waiting for them ❏ *and so we would lie in ambuscade, as he called it* (*The Adventures of Huckleberry Finn* by Mark Twain)

amiable ADJ likeable or pleasant ❏ *Such amiable qualities must speak for themselves* (*Pride and Prejudice* by Jane Austen)

amulet NOUN an amulet is a charm thought to drive away evil spirits. ❏ *uttered phrases at once occult and familiar, like the amulet worn on the heart* (*Silas Marner* by George Eliot)

amusement NOUN here amusement means a strange and disturbing puzzle ❏ *this was an amusement the other way* (*Robinson Crusoe* by Daniel Defoe)

ancient NOUN an ancient was the flag displayed on a ship to show which country it belongs to. It is also called the ensign ❏ *her ancient and pendants out* (*Robinson Crusoe* by Daniel Defoe)

antic ADJ here antic means horrible or grotesque ❏ *armed and dressed after a very antic manner* (*Gulliver's Travels* by Jonathan Swift)

antics NOUN antics is an old word meaning clowns, or people who do silly things to make other people laugh ❏ *And point like antics at his triple crown* (*Doctor Faustus 3.2* by Christopher Marlowe)

appanage NOUN an appanage is a living allowance ❏ *As if loveliness were not the special prerogative of woman–her legitimate appanage and heritage!* (*Jane Eyre* by Charlotte Brontë)

appended VERB appended means attached or added to ❏ *and these words appended* (*Treasure Island* by Robert Louis Stevenson)

approver NOUN an approver is someone who gives evidence against someone he used to work with ❏ *Mr. Noah Claypole: receiving a free pardon from the Crown in consequence of being admitted approver against Fagin* (*Oliver Twist* by Charles Dickens)

areas NOUN the areas is the space, below street level, in front of the basement of a house ❏ *The Dodger had a vicious propensity, too, of pulling the caps from the heads of small boys and tossing them down areas* (*Oliver Twist* by Charles Dickens)

argument NOUN theme or important idea or subject which runs through a piece of writing ❏ *Thrice needful to the argument which now* (*The Prelude* by William Wordsworth)

artificially ADV artfully or cleverly ❏ *and he with a sharp flint sharpened very artificially* (*Gulliver's Travels* by Jonathan Swift)

artist NOUN here artist means a skilled workman ❏ *This man was a most ingenious artist* (*Gulliver's Travels* by Jonathan Swift)

assizes NOUN assizes were regular court sessions which a visiting judge was in charge of ❏ *you shall hang at the next assizes* (*Treasure Island* by Robert Louis Stevenson)

attraction NOUN gravitation, or Newton's theory of gravitation ❏ *he predicted the same fate to attraction* (*Gulliver's Travels* by Jonathan Swift)

aver VERB to aver is to claim something strongly ❏ *for Jem Rodney, the mole catcher, averred that one evening as he was returning homeward* (*Silas Marner* by George Eliot)

baby NOUN here baby means doll, which is a child's toy that looks like a small person ❏ *and skilful dressing her baby* (*Gulliver's Travels* by Jonathan Swift)

bagatelle NOUN bagatelle is a game rather like billiards and pool ❏ *Breakfast had been ordered at a pleasant little tavern, a mile or so away upon the rising ground beyond the green; and there was a bagatelle board in the room, in case we should desire to unbend our minds after the solemnity.* (*Great Expectations* by Charles Dickens)

bah EXCLAM Bah is an exclamation of frustration or anger ❏ *"Bah," said Scrooge.* (*A Christmas Carol* by Charles Dickens)

bairn NOUN a northern word for child ❏ *Who has taught you those fine words, my bairn?* (*Wuthering Heights* by Emily Brontë)

bait VERB to bait means to stop on a journey to take refreshment ❏ *So, when they stopped to bait the horse, and ate and drank and enjoyed themselves, I could touch nothing that they touched, but kept my fast unbroken.* (*David Copperfield* by Charles Dickens)

balustrade NOUN a balustrade is a row of vertical columns that form railings ❏ *but I mean to say you might have got a hearse up that staircase, and taken it broadwise, with the splinter-bar towards the wall, and the door towards the balustrades: and done it easy* (*A Christmas Carol* by Charles Dickens)

bandbox NOUN a large lightweight box for carrying bonnets or hats ❏ *I am glad I bought my bonnet, if it is only for the fun of having another bandbox* (*Pride and Prejudice* by Jane Austen)

barren NOUN a barren here is a stretch or expanse of barren land ❏ *a line of upright stones, continued the* *length of the barren* (*Wuthering Heights* by Emily Brontë)

basin NOUN a basin was a cup without a handle ❑ *who is drinking his tea out of a basin* (*Wuthering Heights* by Emily Brontë)

battalia NOUN the order of battle ❑ *till I saw part of his army in battalia* (*Gulliver's Travels* by Jonathan Swift)

battery NOUN a Battery is a fort or a place where guns are positioned ❑ *You bring the lot to me, at that old Battery over yonder* (*Great Expectations* by Charles Dickens)

battledore and shuttlecock NOUN The game battledore and shuttlecock was an early version of the game now known as badminton. The aim of the early game was simply to keep the shuttlecock from hitting the ground. ❑ *Battledore and shuttlecock's a wery good game vhen you an't the shuttlecock and two lawyers the battledores, in which case it gets too excitin' to be pleasant* (*Pickwick Papers* by Charles Dickens)

beadle NOUN a beadle was a local official who had power over the poor ❑ *But these impertinences were speedily checked by the evidence of the surgeon, and the testimony of the beadle* (*Oliver Twist* by Charles Dickens)

bearings NOUN the bearings of a place are the measurements or directions that are used to find or locate it ❑ *the bearings of the island* (*Treasure Island* by Robert Louis Stevenson)

beaufet NOUN a beaufet was a sideboard ❑ *and sweet-cake from the beaufet* (*Emma* by Jane Austen)

beck NOUN a beck is a small stream ❑ *a beck which follows the bend of the glen* (*Wuthering Heights* by Emily Brontë)

bedight VERB decorated ❑ *and bedight with Christmas holly stuck into the top.* (*A Christmas Carol* by Charles Dickens)

Bedlam NOUN Bedlam was a lunatic asylum in London which had statues carved by Caius Gabriel Cibber at its entrance ❑ *Bedlam, and those carved maniacs at the gates* (*The Prelude* by William Wordsworth)

beeves NOUN oxen or castrated bulls which are animals used for pulling vehicles or carrying things ❑ *to deliver in every morning six beeves* (*Gulliver's Travels* by Jonathan Swift)

begot VERB created or caused ❑ *Begot in thee* (*On His Mistress* by John Donne)

behoof NOUN behoof means benefit ❑ *"Yes, young man," said he, releasing the handle of the article in question, retiring a step or two from my table, and speaking for the behoof of the landlord and waiter at the door* (*Great Expectations* by Charles Dickens)

berth NOUN a berth is a bed on a boat ❑ *this is the berth for me* (*Treasure Island* by Robert Louis Stevenson)

bevers NOUN a bever was a snack, or small portion of food, eaten between main meals ❑ *that buys me thirty meals a day and ten bevers* (*Doctor Faustus 2.1* by Christopher Marlowe)

bilge water NOUN the bilge is the widest part of a ship's bottom, and the bilge water is the dirty water that collects there ❑ *no gush of bilge-water had turned it to fetid puddle* (*Jane Eyre* by Charlotte Brontë)

bills NOUN bills is an old term meaning prescription. A prescription is the piece of paper on which your doctor writes an order for medicine and which you give to a chemist to get the medicine ❑ *Are not thy bills hung up as monuments* (*Doctor Faustus 1.1* by Christopher Marlowe)

black cap NOUN a judge wore a black cap when he was about to sentence a prisoner to death ❑ *The judge assumed the black cap, and the prisoner still stood with the same air and gesture.* (*Oliver Twist* by Charles Dickens)

boot-jack NOUN a wooden device to help take boots off ❑ *The speaker appeared to throw a boot-jack, or some such article, at the person he addressed* (*Oliver Twist* by Charles Dickens)

booty NOUN booty means treasure or prizes ❑ *would be inclined to give up their booty in payment of the dead man's debts* (*Treasure Island* by Robert Louis Stevenson)

Bow Street runner PHRASE Bow Street runners were the first British police force, set up by the author Henry Fielding in the eighteenth century ❑ *as would have convinced a judge or a Bow Street runner* (*Treasure Island* by Robert Louis Stevenson)

brawn NOUN brawn is a dish of meat which is set in jelly ❑ *Heaped up upon the floor, to form a kind of throne, were turkeys, geese, game, poultry, brawn, great joints of meat, suckling-pigs* (*A Christmas Carol* by Charles Dickens)

bray VERB when a donkey brays, it makes a loud, harsh sound ❑ *and she doesn't bray like a jackass* (*The Adventures of Huckleberry Finn* by Mark Twain)

break VERB in order to train a horse you first have to break it ❑ *"If a high-mettled creature like this," said he, "can't be broken by fair means, she will never be good for anything"* (*Black Beauty* by Anna Sewell)

bullyragging VERB bullyragging is an old word which means bullying. To bullyrag someone is to threaten or force someone to do something they don't want to do ❑ *and a lot of loafers bullyragging him for sport* (*The Adventures of Huckleberry Finn* by Mark Twain)

but PREP except for (this) ❑ *but this, all pleasures fancies be* (*The Good-Morrow* by John Donne)

by hand PHRASE by hand was a common expression of the time meaning that baby had been fed either using a spoon or a bottle rather than by breast-feeding ❑ *My sister, Mrs. Joe Gargery, was more than twenty years older than I, and had established a great reputation with herself . . . because she had bought me up "by hand"* (*Great Expectations* by Charles Dickens)

bye-spots NOUN bye-spots are lonely places ❑ *and bye-spots of tales rich with indigenous produce* (*The Prelude* by William Wordsworth)

calico NOUN calico is plain white fabric made from cotton ❑ *There was two old dirty calico dresses* (*The Adventures of Huckleberry Finn* by Mark Twain)

camp-fever NOUN camp-fever was another word for the disease typhus ❑ *during a severe camp-fever* (*Emma* by Jane Austen)

cant NOUN cant is insincere or empty talk ❑ *"Man," said the Ghost, "if man you be in heart, not adamant, forbear that wicked cant until you have discovered What the surplus is, and Where it is."* (*A Christmas Carol* by Charles Dickens)

canty ADJ canty means lively, full of life ❑ *My mother lived til eighty, a canty dame to the last* (*Wuthering Heights* by Emily Brontë)

canvas VERB to canvas is to discuss ❑ *We think so very differently on this point Mr Knightley, that there can be no use in canvassing it* (*Emma* by Jane Austen)

capital ADJ capital means excellent or extremely good ❑ *for it's capital, so shady, light, and big* (*Little Women* by Louisa May Alcott)

capstan NOUN a capstan is a device used on a ship to lift sails and anchors ❑ *capstans going, ships going out to sea, and unintelligible sea creatures roaring curses over the* *bulwarks at respondent lightermen* (*Great Expectations* by Charles Dickens)

case-bottle NOUN a square bottle designed to fit with others into a case ❏ *The spirit being set before him in a huge case-bottle, which had originally come out of some ship's locker* (*The Old Curiosity Shop* by Charles Dickens)

casement NOUN casement is a word meaning window. The teacher in *Nicholas Nickleby* misspells window showing what a bad teacher he is ❏ *W-i-n, win, d-e-r, der, winder, a casement.* (*Nicholas Nickleby* by Charles Dickens)

cataleptic ADJ a cataleptic fit is one in which the victim goes into a trancelike state and remains still for a long time ❏ *It was at this point in their history that Silas's cataleptic fit occurred during the prayer-meeting* (*Silas Marner* by George Eliot)

cauldron NOUN a cauldron is a large cooking pot made of metal ❏ *stirring a large cauldron which seemed to be full of soup* (*Alice's Adventures in Wonderland* by Lewis Carroll)

cephalic ADJ cephalic means to do with the head ❏ *with ink composed of a cephalic tincture* (*Gulliver's Travels* by Jonathan Swift)

chaise and four NOUN a closed four-wheel carriage pulled by four horses ❏ *he came down on Monday in a chaise and four to see the place* (*Pride and Prejudice* by Jane Austen)

chamberlain NOUN the main servant in a household ❏ *In those times a bed was always to be got there at any hour of the night, and the chamberlain, letting me in at his ready wicket, lighted the candle next in order on his shelf* (*Great Expectations* by Charles Dickens)

characters NOUN distinguishing marks ❏ *Impressed upon all forms the characters* (*The Prelude* by William Wordsworth)

chary ADJ cautious ❏ *I should have been chary of discussing my guardian too freely even with her* (*Great Expectations* by Charles Dickens)

cherishes VERB here cherishes means cheers or brightens ❏ *some philosophic song of Truth that cherishes our daily life* (*The Prelude* by William Wordsworth)

chickens' meat PHRASE chickens' meat is an old term which means chickens' feed or food ❏ *I had shook a bag of chickens' meat out in that place* (*Robinson Crusoe* by Daniel Defoe)

chimeras NOUN a chimera is an unrealistic idea or a wish which is unlikely to be fulfilled ❏ *with many other wild impossible chimeras* (*Gulliver's Travels* by Jonathan Swift)

chines NOUN chine is a cut of meat that includes part or all of the backbone of the animal ❏ *and they found hams and chines uncut* (*Silas Marner* by George Eliot)

chits NOUN chits is a slang word which means girls ❏ *I hate affected, niminy-piminy chits!* (*Little Women* by Louisa May Alcott)

chopped VERB chopped means come suddenly or accidentally ❏ *if I had chopped upon them* (*Robinson Crusoe* by Daniel Defoe)

chute NOUN a narrow channel ❏ *One morning about day-break, I found a canoe and crossed over a chute to the main shore* (*The Adventures of Huckleberry Finn* by Mark Twain)

circumspection NOUN careful observation of events and circumstances; caution ❏ *I honour your circumspection* (*Pride and Prejudice* by Jane Austen)

clambered VERB clambered means to climb somewhere with difficulty, usually using your hands and your feet ❏ *he clambered up and down stairs* (*Treasure Island* by Robert Louis Stevenson)

GEORGE ORWELL

clime NOUN climate ❑ *no season knows nor clime* (*The Sun Rising* by John Donne)

clinched VERB clenched ❑ *the tops whereof I could but just reach with my fist clinched* (*Gulliver's Travels* by Jonathan Swift)

close chair NOUN a close chair is a sedan chair, which is an covered chair which has room for one person. The sedan chair is carried on two poles by two men, one in front and one behind ❑ *persuaded even the Empress herself to let me hold her in her close chair* (*Gulliver's Travels* by Jonathan Swift)

clown NOUN clown here means peasant or person who lives off the land ❑ *In ancient days by emperor and clown* (*Ode on a Nightingale* by John Keats)

coalheaver NOUN a coalheaver loaded coal onto ships using a spade ❑ *Good, strong, wholesome medicine, as was given with great success to two Irish labourers and a coalheaver* (*Oliver Twist* by Charles Dickens)

coal-whippers NOUN men who worked at docks using machines to load coal onto ships ❑ *here, were colliers by the score and score, with the coal-whippers plunging off stages on deck* (*Great Expectations* by Charles Dickens)

cobweb NOUN a cobweb is the net which a spider makes for catching insects ❑ *the walls and ceilings were all hung round with cobwebs* (*Gulliver's Travels* by Jonathan Swift)

coddling VERB coddling means to treat someone too kindly or protect them too much ❑ *and I've been coddling the fellow as if I'd been his grandmother* (*Little Women* by Louisa May Alcott)

coil NOUN coil means noise or fuss or disturbance ❑ *What a coil is there?* (*Doctor Faustus 4.7* by Christopher Marlowe)

collared VERB to collar something is a slang term which means to capture.

In this sentence, it means he stole it [the money] ❑ *he collared it* (*The Adventures of Huckleberry Finn* by Mark Twain)

colling VERB colling is an old word which means to embrace and kiss ❑ *and no clasping and colling at all* (*Tess of the D'Urbervilles* by Thomas Hardy)

colloquies NOUN colloquy is a formal conversation or dialogue ❑ *Such colloquies have occupied many a pair of pale-faced weavers* (*Silas Marner* by George Eliot)

comfit NOUN sugar-covered pieces of fruit or nut eaten as sweets ❑ *and pulled out a box of comfits* (*Alice's Adventures in Wonderland* by Lewis Carroll)

coming out VERB when a girl came out in society it meant she was of marriageable age. In order to "come out" girls were expecting to attend balls and other parties during a season ❑ *The younger girls formed hopes of coming out a year or two sooner than they might otherwise have done* (*Pride and Prejudice* by Jane Austen)

commit VERB commit means arrest or stop ❑ *Commit the rascals* (*Doctor Faustus 4.7* by Christopher Marlowe)

commodious ADJ commodious means convenient ❑ *the most commodious and effectual ways* (*Gulliver's Travels* by Jonathan Swift)

commons NOUN commons is an old term meaning food shared with others ❑ *his pauper assistants ranged themselves behind him; the gruel was served out; and a long grace was said over the short commons.* (*Oliver Twist* by Charles Dickens)

complacency NOUN here complacency means a desire to please others. To-day complacency means feeling pleased with oneself without good reason. ❑ *Twas thy power that raised the first complacency in me* (*The Prelude* by William Wordsworth)

complaisance NOUN complaisance was eagerness to please ❑ *we cannot wonder at his complaisance* (*Pride and Prejudice* by Jane Austen)

complaisant ADJ complaisant means polite ❑ *extremely cheerful and complaisant to their guest* (*Gulliver's Travels* by Jonathan Swift)

conning VERB conning means learning by heart ❑ *Or conning more* (*The Prelude* by William Wordsworth)

consequent NOUN consequence ❑ *as avarice is the necessary consequent of old age* (*Gulliver's Travels* by Jonathan Swift)

consorts NOUN concerts ❑ *The King, who delighted in music, had frequent consorts at Court* (*Gulliver's Travels* by Jonathan Swift)

conversible ADJ conversible meant easy to talk to, companionable ❑ *He can be a conversible companion* (*Pride and Prejudice* by Jane Austen)

copper NOUN a copper is a large pot that can be heated directly over a fire ❑ *He gazed in stupefied astonishment on the small rebel for some seconds, and then clung for support to the copper* (*Oliver Twist* by Charles Dickens)

copper-stick NOUN a copper-stick is the long piece of wood used to stir washing in the copper (or boiler) which was usually the biggest cooking pot in the house ❑ *It was Christmas Eve, and I had to stir the pudding for next day, with a copper-stick, from seven to eight by the Dutch clock* (*Great Expectations* by Charles Dickens)

counting-house NOUN a counting-house is a place where accountants work ❑ *Once upon a time–of all the good days in the year, on Christmas Eve–old Scrooge sat busy in his counting-house* (*A Christmas Carol* by Charles Dickens)

courtier NOUN a courtier is someone who attends the king or queen–a member of the court ❑ *next the ten courtiers;* (*Alice's Adventures in Wonderland* by Lewis Carroll)

covies NOUN covies were flocks of partridges ❑ *and will save all of the best covies for you* (*Pride and Prejudice* by Jane Austen)

cowed VERB cowed means frightened or intimidated ❑ *it cowed me more than the pain* (*Treasure Island* by Robert Louis Stevenson)

cozened VERB cozened means tricked or deceived ❑ *Do you remember, sir, how you cozened me* (*Doctor Faustus 4.7* by Christopher Marlowe)

cravats NOUN a cravat is a folded cloth that a man wears wrapped around his neck as a decorative item of clothing ❑ *we'd 'a' slept in our cravats to-night* (*The Adventures of Huckleberry Finn* by Mark Twain)

crock and dirt PHRASE crock and dirt is an old expression meaning soot and dirt ❑ *and the mare catching cold at the door, and the boy grimed with crock and dirt* (*Great Expectations* by Charles Dickens)

crockery NOUN here crockery means pottery ❑ *By one of the parrots was a cat made of crockery* (*The Adventures of Huckleberry Finn* by Mark Twain)

crooked sixpence PHRASE it was considered unlucky to have a bent sixpence ❑ *You've got the beauty, you see, and I've got the luck, so you must keep me by you for your crooked sixpence* (*Silas Marner* by George Eliot)

croquet NOUN croquet is a traditional English summer game in which players try to hit wooden balls through hoops ❑ *and once she remembered trying to box her own ears for having cheated herself in a game of croquet* (*Alice's Adventures in Wonderland* by Lewis Carroll)

cross PREP across ❑ *The two great streets, which run cross and divide it into four quarters* (*Gulliver's Travels* by Jonathan Swift)

culpable ADJ if you are culpable for something it means you are to blame ❑ *deep are the sorrows that spring from false ideas for which no man is culpable.* (*Silas Marner* by George Eliot)

cultured ADJ cultivated ❑ *Nor less when spring had warmed the cultured Vale* (*The Prelude* by William Wordsworth)

cupidity NOUN cupidity is greed ❑ *These people hated me with the hatred of cupidity and disappointment.* (*Great Expectations* by Charles Dickens)

curricle NOUN an open two-wheeled carriage with one seat for the driver and space for a single passenger ❑ *and they saw a lady and a gentleman in a curricle* (*Pride and Prejudice* by Jane Austen)

cynosure NOUN a cynosure is something that strongly attracts attention or admiration ❑ *Then I thought of Eliza and Georgiana; I beheld one the cynosure of a ballroom, the other the inmate of a convent cell* (*Jane Eyre* by Charlotte Brontë)

dalliance NOUN someone's dalliance with something is a brief involvement with it ❑ *nor sporting in the dalliance of love* (*Doctor Faustus Chorus* by Christopher Marlowe)

darkling ADV darkling is an archaic way of saying in the dark ❑ *Darkling I listen* (*Ode on a Nightingale* by John Keats)

delf-case NOUN a sideboard for holding dishes and crockery ❑ *at the pewter dishes and delf-case* (*Wuthering Heights* by Emily Brontë)

determined ■ VERB here determined means ended ❑ *and be out of vogue when that was determined* (*Gulliver's Travels* by Jonathan Swift) ■ VERB determined can mean to have been learned or found especially by investigation or experience ❑ *All the sensitive feelings it wounded so cruelly, all the shame and misery it kept alive within my breast, became more poignant as I thought of this; and I determined that the life was unendurable* (*David Copperfield* by Charles Dickens)

Deuce NOUN a slang term for the Devil ❑ *Ah, I dare say I did. Deuce take me, he added suddenly, I know I did. I find I am not quite unscrewed yet.* (*Great Expectations* by Charles Dickens)

diabolical ADJ diabolical means devilish or evil ❑ *and with a thousand diabolical expressions* (*Treasure Island* by Robert Louis Stevenson)

direction NOUN here direction means address ❑ *Elizabeth was not surprised at it, as Jane had written the direction remarkably ill* (*Pride and Prejudice* by Jane Austen)

discover VERB to make known or announce ❑ *the Emperor would discover the secret while I was out of his power* (*Gulliver's Travels* by Jonathan Swift)

dissemble VERB hide or conceal ❑ *Dissemble nothing* (*On His Mistress* by John Donne)

dissolve VERB dissolve here means to release from life, to die ❑ *Fade far away, dissolve, and quite forget* (*Ode on a Nightingale* by John Keats)

distrain VERB to distrain is to seize the property of someone who is in debt in compensation for the money owed ❑ *for he's threatening to distrain for it* (*Silas Marner* by George Eliot)

Divan NOUN a Divan was originally a Turkish council of state–the name was transferred to the couches they sat on and is used to mean this in English ❑ *Mr Brass applauded this picture very much, and the bed being soft and comfortable, Mr Quilp determined to use it, both as a sleeping place by night and as a kind of Divan by day.* (*The Old Curiosity Shop* by Charles Dickens)

divorcement NOUN separation ❑ *By all pains which want and divorcement* *hath* (*On His Mistress* by John Donne)

dog in the manger, PHRASE this phrase describes someone who prevents you from enjoying something that they themselves have no need for ❑ *You are a dog in the manger, Cathy, and desire no one to be loved but yourself* (*Wuthering Heights* by Emily Brontë)

dolorifuge NOUN dolorifuge is a word which Thomas Hardy invented. It means pain-killer or comfort ❑ *as a species of dolorifuge* (*Tess of the D'Urbervilles* by Thomas Hardy)

dome NOUN building ❑ *that river and that mouldering dome* (*The Prelude* by William Wordsworth)

domestic NOUN here domestic means a person's management of the house ❑ *to give some account of my domestic* (*Gulliver's Travels* by Jonathan Swift)

dunce NOUN a dunce is another word for idiot ❑ *Do you take me for a dunce? Go on?* (*Alice's Adventures in Wonderland* by Lewis Carroll)

Ecod EXCLAM a slang exclamation meaning "oh God!" ❑ *"Ecod," replied Wemmick, shaking his head, "that's not my trade."* (*Great Expectations* by Charles Dickens)

egg-hot NOUN an egg-hot (see also "flip" and "negus") was a hot drink made from beer and eggs, sweetened with nutmeg ❑ *She fainted when she saw me return, and made a little jug of egg-hot afterwards to console us while we talked it over.* (*David Copperfield* by Charles Dickens)

encores NOUN an encore is a short extra performance at the end of a longer one, which the entertainer gives because the audience has enthusiastically asked for it ❑ *we want a little something to answer encores with, anyway* (*The Adventures of Huckleberry Finn* by Mark Twain)

equipage NOUN an elegant and impressive carriage ❑ *and besides, the equipage did not answer to any of*

their neighbours (*Pride and Prejudice* by Jane Austen)

exordium NOUN an exordium is the opening part of a speech ❑ *"Now, Handel," as if it were the grave beginning of a portentous business exordium, he had suddenly given up that tone* (*Great Expectations* by Charles Dickens)

expect VERB here expect means to wait for ❑ *to expect his farther commands* (*Gulliver's Travels* by Jonathan Swift)

familiars NOUN familiars means spirits or devils who come to someone when they are called ❑ *I'll turn all the lice about thee into familiars* (*Doctor Faustus 1.4* by Christopher Marlowe)

fantods NOUN a fantod is a person who fidgets or can't stop moving nervously ❑ *It most give me the fantods* (*The Adventures of Huckleberry Finn* by Mark Twain)

farthing NOUN a farthing is an old unit of British currency which was worth a quarter of a penny ❑ *Not a farthing less. A great many back-payments are included in it, I assure you.* (*A Christmas Carol* by Charles Dickens)

farthingale NOUN a hoop worn under a skirt to extend it ❑ *A bell with an old voice–which I dare say in its time had often said to the house, Here is the green farthingale* (*Great Expectations* by Charles Dickens)

favours NOUN here favours is an old word which means ribbons ❑ *A group of humble mourners entered the gate: wearing white favours* (*Oliver Twist* by Charles Dickens)

feigned VERB pretend or pretending ❑ *not my feigned page* (*On His Mistress* by John Donne)

fence ■ NOUN a fence is someone who receives and sells stolen goods ❑ *What are you up to? Ill-treating the boys, you covetous, avaricious, in-sa-ti-a-ble old fence?* (*Oliver Twist* by

223

Charles Dickens) ■ NOUN defence or protection ❑ *but honesty hath no fence against superior cunning* (*Gulliver's Travels* by Jonathan Swift)

fess ADJ fess is an old word which means pleased or proud ❑ *You'll be fess enough, my poppet* (*Tess of the D'Urbervilles* by Thomas Hardy)

fettered ADJ fettered means bound in chains or chained ❑ *"You are fettered," said Scrooge, trembling. "Tell me why?"* (*A Christmas Carol* by Charles Dickens)

fidges VERB fidges means fidgets, which is to keep moving your hands slightly because you are nervous or excited ❑ *Look, Jim, how my fingers fidges* (*Treasure Island* by Robert Louis Stevenson)

finger-post NOUN a finger-post is a sign-post showing the direction to different places ❑ *"The gallows," continued Fagin, "the gallows, my dear, is an ugly finger-post, which points out a very short and sharp turning that has stopped many a bold fellow's career on the broad highway."* (*Oliver Twist* by Charles Dickens)

fire-irons NOUN fire-irons are tools kept by the side of the fire to either cook with or look after the fire ❑ *the fire-irons came first* (*Alice's Adventures in Wonderland* by Lewis Carroll)

fire-plug NOUN a fire-plug is another word for a fire hydrant ❑ *The pony looked with great attention into a fire-plug, which was near him, and appeared to be quite absorbed in contemplating it* (*The Old Curiosity Shop* by Charles Dickens)

flank NOUN flank is the side of an animal ❑ *And all her silken flanks with garlands dressed* (*Ode on a Grecian Urn* by John Keats)

flip NOUN a flip is a drink made from warmed ale, sugar, spice and beaten egg ❑ *The events of the day, in combination with the twins, if not with the flip, had made Mrs.*

Micawber hysterical, and she shed tears as she replied (*David Copperfield* by Charles Dickens)

flit VERB flit means to move quickly ❑ *and if he had meant to flit to Thrushcross Grange* (*Wuthering Heights* by Emily Brontë)

floorcloth NOUN a floorcloth was a hard-wearing piece of canvas used instead of carpet ❑ *This avenging phantom was ordered to be on duty at eight on Tuesday morning in the hall (it was two feet square, as charged for floorcloth)* (*Great Expectations* by Charles Dickens)

fly-driver NOUN a fly-driver is a carriage drawn by a single horse ❑ *The fly-drivers, among whom I inquired next, were equally jocose and equally disrespectful* (*David Copperfield* by Charles Dickens)

fob NOUN a small pocket in which a watch is kept ❑ *"Certain," replied the man, drawing a gold watch from his fob* (*Oliver Twist* by Charles Dickens)

folly NOUN folly means foolishness or stupidity ❑ *the folly of beginning a work* (*Robinson Crusoe* by Daniel Defoe)

fond ADJ fond means foolish ❑ *Fond worldling* (*Doctor Faustus 5.2* by Christopher Marlowe)

fondness NOUN silly or foolish affection ❑ *They have no fondness for their colts or foals* (*Gulliver's Travels* by Jonathan Swift)

for his fancy PHRASE for his fancy means for his liking or as he wanted ❑ *and as I did not obey quick enough for his fancy* (*Treasure Island* by Robert Louis Stevenson)

forlorn ADJ lost or very upset ❑ *you are from that day forlorn* (*Gulliver's Travels* by Jonathan Swift)

foster-sister NOUN a foster-sister was someone brought up by the same nurse or in the same household ❑ *I had been his foster-sister* (*Wuthering Heights* by Emily Brontë)

fox-fire NOUN fox-fire is a weak glow that is given off by decaying, rotten wood ❑ *what we must have was a lot of them rotten chunks that's called fox-fire* (*The Adventures of Huckleberry Finn* by Mark Twain)

frozen sea PHRASE the Arctic Ocean ❑ *into the frozen sea* (*Gulliver's Travels* by Jonathan Swift)

gainsay VERB to gainsay something is to say it isn't true or to deny it ❑ *"So she had," cried Scrooge. "You're right. I'll not gainsay it, Spirit. God forbid!"* (*A Christmas Carol* by Charles Dickens)

gaiters NOUN gaiters were leggings made of a cloth or piece of leather which covered the leg from the knee to the ankle ❑ *Mr Knightley was hard at work upon the lower buttons of his thick leather gaiters* (*Emma* by Jane Austen)

galluses NOUN galluses is an old spelling of gallows, and here means suspenders. Suspenders are straps worn over someone's shoulders and fastened to their trousers to prevent the trousers falling down ❑ *and home-knit galluses* (*The Adventures of Huckleberry Finn* by Mark Twain)

galoot NOUN a sailor but also a clumsy person ❑ *and maybe a galoot on it chopping* (*The Adventures of Huckleberry Finn* by Mark Twain)

gayest ADJ gayest means the most lively and bright or merry ❑ *Beth played her gayest march* (*Little Women* by Louisa May Alcott)

gem NOUN here gem means jewellery ❑ *the mountain shook off turf and flower, had only heath for raiment and crag for gem* (*Jane Eyre* by Charlotte Brontë)

giddy ADJ giddy means dizzy ❑ *and I wish you wouldn't keep appearing and vanishing so suddenly; you make one quite giddy.* (*Alice's Adventures in Wonderland* by Lewis Carroll)

gig NOUN a light two-wheeled carriage ❑ *when a gig drove up to the garden gate: out of which there jumped a fat gentleman* (*Oliver Twist* by Charles Dickens)

gladsome ADJ gladsome is an old word meaning glad or happy ❑ *Nobody ever stopped him in the street to say, with gladsome looks* (*A Christmas Carol* by Charles Dickens)

glen NOUN a glen is a small valley; the word is used commonly in Scotland ❑ *a beck which follows the bend of the glen* (*Wuthering Heights* by Emily Brontë)

gravelled VERB gravelled is an old term which means to baffle or defeat someone ❑ *Gravelled the pastors of the German Church* (*Doctor Faustus 1.1* by Christopher Marlowe)

grinder NOUN a grinder was a private tutor ❑ *but that when he had had the happiness of marrying Mrs Pocket very early in his life, he had impaired his prospects and taken up the calling of a Grinder* (*Great Expectations* by Charles Dickens)

gruel NOUN gruel is a thin, watery cornmeal or oatmeal soup ❑ *and the little saucepan of gruel (Scrooge had a cold in his head) upon the hob.* (*A Christmas Carol* by Charles Dickens)

guinea, half a NOUN half a guinea was ten shillings and sixpence ❑ *but lay out half a guinea at Ford's* (*Emma* by Jane Austen)

gull VERB gull is an old term which means to fool or deceive someone ❑ *Hush, I'll gull him supernaturally* (*Doctor Faustus 3.4* by Christopher Marlowe)

gunnel NOUN the gunnel, or gunwale, is the upper edge of a boat's side ❑ *But he put his foot on the gunnel and rocked her* (*The Adventures of Huckleberry Finn* by Mark Twain)

gunwale NOUN the side of a ship ❑ *He dipped his hand in the water over the boat's gunwale* (*Great Expectations* by Charles Dickens)

Gytrash NOUN a Gytrash is an omen of misfortune to the superstitious, usually taking the form of a hound ❏ *I remembered certain of Bessie's tales, wherein figured a North-of-England spirit, called a "Gytrash"* (*Jane Eyre* by Charlotte Brontë)

hackney-cabriolet NOUN a two-wheeled carriage with four seats for hire and pulled by a horse ❏ *A hackney-cabriolet was in waiting; with the same vehemence which she had exhibited in addressing Oliver, the girl pulled him in with her, and drew the curtains close.* (*Oliver Twist* by Charles Dickens)

hackney-coach NOUN a four-wheeled horse-drawn vehicle for hire ❏ *The twilight was beginning to close in, when Mr. Brownlow alighted from a hackney-coach at his own door, and knocked softly.* (*Oliver Twist* by Charles Dickens)

haggler NOUN a haggler is someone who travels from place to place selling small goods and items ❏ *when I be plain Jack Durbeyfield, the haggler* (*Tess of the D'Urbervilles* by Thomas Hardy)

halter NOUN a halter is a rope or strap used to lead an animal or to tie it up ❏ *I had of course long been used to a halter and a headstall* (*Black Beauty* by Anna Sewell)

hamlet NOUN a hamlet is a small village or a group of houses in the countryside ❏ *down from the hamlet* (*Treasure Island* by Robert Louis Stevenson)

hand-barrow NOUN a hand-barrow is a device for carrying heavy objects. It is like a wheelbarrow except that it has handles, rather than wheels, for moving the barrow ❏ *his sea chest following behind him in a hand-barrow* (*Treasure Island* by Robert Louis Stevenson)

handspike NOUN a handspike was a stick which was used as a lever ❏ *a bit of stick like a handspike* (*Treasure Island* by Robert Louis Stevenson)

haply ADV haply means by chance or perhaps ❏ *And haply the Queen-Moon is on her throne* (*Ode on a Nightingale* by John Keats)

harem NOUN the harem was the part of the house where the women lived ❏ *mostly they hang round the harem* (*The Adventures of Huckleberry Finn* by Mark Twain)

hautboys NOUN hautboys are oboes ❏ *sausages and puddings resembling flutes and hautboys* (*Gulliver's Travels* by Jonathan Swift)

hawker NOUN a hawker is someone who sells goods to people as he travels rather than from a fixed place like a shop ❏ *to buy some stockings from a hawker* (*Treasure Island* by Robert Louis Stevenson)

hawser NOUN a hawser is a rope used to tie up or tow a ship or boat ❏ *Again among the tiers of shipping, in and out, avoiding rusty chain-cables, frayed hempen hawsers* (*Great Expectations* by Charles Dickens)

headstall NOUN the headstall is the part of the bridle or halter that goes around a horse's head ❏ *I had of course long been used to a halter and a headstall* (*Black Beauty* by Anna Sewell)

hearken VERB hearken means to listen ❏ *though we sometimes stopped to lay hold of each other and hearken* (*Treasure Island* by Robert Louis Stevenson)

heartless ADJ here heartless means without heart or dejected ❏ *I am not heartless* (*The Prelude* by William Wordsworth)

hebdomadal ADJ hebdomadal means weekly ❏ *It was the hebdomadal treat to which we all looked forward from Sabbath to Sabbath* (*Jane Eyre* by Charlotte Brontë)

highwaymen NOUN highwaymen were people who stopped travellers and robbed them ❏ *We are high-waymen* (*The Adventures of Huckleberry Finn* by Mark Twain)

hinds NOUN hinds means farm hands, or people who work on a farm ❏ *He called his hinds about him* (*Gulliver's Travels* by Jonathan Swift)

histrionic ADJ if you refer to someone's behaviour as histrionic, you are being critical of it because it is dramatic and exaggerated ❏ *But the histrionic muse is the darling* (*The Adventures of Huckleberry Finn* by Mark Twain)

hogs NOUN hogs is another word for pigs ❏ *Tom called the hogs "ingots"* (*The Adventures of Huckleberry Finn* by Mark Twain)

horrors NOUN the horrors are a fit, called delirium tremens, which is caused by drinking too much alcohol ❏ *I'll have the horrors* (*Treasure Island* by Robert Louis Stevenson)

huffy ADJ huffy means to be obviously annoyed or offended about something ❏ *They will feel that more than angry speeches or huffy actions* (*Little Women* by Louisa May Alcott)

hulks NOUN hulks were prison-ships ❏ *The miserable companion of thieves and ruffians, the fallen outcast of low haunts, the associate of the scourings of the jails and hulks* (*Oliver Twist* by Charles Dickens)

humbug NOUN humbug means nonsense or rubbish ❏ *"Bah," said Scrooge. "Humbug!"* (*A Christmas Carol* by Charles Dickens)

humours NOUN it was believed that there were four fluids in the body called humours which decided the temperament of a person depending on how much of each fluid was present ❏ *other peccant humours* (*Gulliver's Travels* by Jonathan Swift)

husbandry NOUN husbandry is farming animals ❏ *bad husbandry were plentifully anointing their wheels* (*Silas Marner* by George Eliot)

huswife NOUN a huswife was a small sewing kit ❏ *but I had put my huswife on it* (*Emma* by Jane Austen)

ideal ADJ ideal in this context means imaginary ❏ *I discovered the yell was not ideal* (*Wuthering Heights* by Emily Brontë)

If our two PHRASE if both our ❏ *If our two loves be one* (*The Good-Morrow* by John Donne)

ignis-fatuus NOUN ignis-fatuus is the light given out by burning marsh gases, which lead careless travellers into danger ❏ *it is madness in all women to let a secret love kindle within them, which, if unreturned and unknown, must devour the life that feeds it; and, if discovered and responded to, must lead ignis-fatuus-like, into miry wilds whence there is no extrication.* (*Jane Eyre* by Charlotte Brontë)

imaginations NOUN here imaginations means schemes or plans ❏ *soon drove out those imaginations* (*Gulliver's Travels* by Jonathan Swift)

impressible ADJ impressible means open or impressionable ❏ *for Marner had one of those impressible, self-doubting natures* (*Silas Marner* by George Eliot)

in good intelligence PHRASE friendly with each other ❏ *that these two persons were in good intelligence with each other* (*Gulliver's Travels* by Jonathan Swift)

inanity NOUN inanity is silliness or dull stupidity ❏ *Do we not wile away moments of inanity* (*Silas Marner* by George Eliot)

incivility NOUN incivility means rudeness or impoliteness ❏ *if it's only for a piece of incivility like to-night's* (*Treasure Island* by Robert Louis Stevenson)

indigenae NOUN indigenae means natives or people from that area ❏ *an exotic that the surly indigenae will not recognise for kin* (*Wuthering Heights* by Emily Brontë)

indocible ADJ unteachable ❏ *so they were the most restive and indocible* (*Gulliver's Travels* by Jonathan Swift)

ingenuity NOUN inventiveness ❑ *entreated me to give him something as an encouragement to ingenuity* (*Gulliver's Travels* by Jonathan Swift)

ingots NOUN an ingot is a lump of a valuable metal like gold, usually shaped like a brick ❑ *Tom called the hogs "ingots"* (*The Adventures of Huckleberry Finn* by Mark Twain)

inkstand NOUN an inkstand is a pot which was put on a desk to contain either ink or pencils and pens ❑ *throwing an inkstand at the Lizard as she spoke* (*Alice's Adventures in Wonderland* by Lewis Carroll)

inordinate ADJ without order. To-day inordinate means "excessive". ❑ *Though yet untutored and inordinate* (*The Prelude* by William Wordsworth)

intellectuals NOUN here intellectuals means the minds (of the workmen) ❑ *those instructions they give being too refined for the intellectuals of their workmen* (*Gulliver's Travels* by Jonathan Swift)

interview NOUN meeting ❑ *By our first strange and fatal interview* (*On His Mistress* by John Donne)

jacks NOUN jacks are rods for turning a spit over a fire ❑ *It was a small bit of pork suspended from the kettle hanger by a string passed through a large door key, in a way known to primitive housekeepers unpossessed of jacks* (*Silas Marner* by George Eliot)

jews-harp NOUN a jews-harp is a small, metal, musical instrument that is played by the mouth ❑ *A jews-harp's plenty good enough for a rat* (*The Adventures of Huckleberry Finn* by Mark Twain)

jorum NOUN a large bowl ❑ *while Miss Skiffins brewed such a jorum of tea, that the pig in the back premises became strongly excited* (*Great Expectations* by Charles Dickens)

jostled VERB jostled means bumped or pushed by someone or some people ❑ *being jostled himself into the kennel* (*Gulliver's Travels* by Jonathan Swift)

keepsake NOUN a keepsake is a gift which reminds someone of an event or of the person who gave it to them. ❑ *books and ornaments they had in their boudoirs at home: keepsakes that different relations had presented to them* (*Jane Eyre* by Charlotte Brontë)

kenned VERB kenned means knew ❑ *though little kenned the lamplighter that he had any company but Christmas!* (*A Christmas Carol* by Charles Dickens)

kennel NOUN kennel means gutter, which is the edge of a road next to the pavement, where rain water collects and flows away ❑ *being jostled himself into the kennel* (*Gulliver's Travels* by Jonathan Swift)

knock-knee ADJ knock-knee means slanted, at an angle. ❑ *LOT 1 was marked in whitewashed knock-knee letters on the brewhouse* (*Great Expectations* by Charles Dickens)

ladylike ADJ to be ladylike is to behave in a polite, dignified and graceful way ❑ *No, winking isn't ladylike* (*Little Women* by Louisa May Alcott)

lapse NOUN flow ❑ *Stealing with silent lapse to join the brook* (*The Prelude* by William Wordsworth)

larry NOUN larry is an old word which means commotion or noisy celebration ❑ *That was all a part of the larry!* (*Tess of the D'Urbervilles* by Thomas Hardy)

laths NOUN laths are strips of wood ❑ *The panels shrunk, the windows cracked; fragments of plaster fell out of the ceiling, and the naked laths were shown instead* (*A Christmas Carol* by Charles Dickens)

leer NOUN a leer is an unpleasant smile ❑ *with a kind of leer* (*Treasure Island* by Robert Louis Stevenson)

lenitives NOUN these are different kinds of drugs or medicines: lenitives and palliatives were pain relievers; aperitives were laxatives; abstersives caused vomiting; corrosives destroyed human tissue; restringents caused constipation; cephalalgics stopped headaches; icterics were used as medicine for jaundice; apophlegmatics were cough medicine, and acoustics were cures for the loss of hearing ❑ *lenitives, aperitives, abstersives, corrosives, restringents, palliatives, laxatives, cephalalgics, icterics, apophlegmatics, acoustics* (*Gulliver's Travels* by Jonathan Swift)

lest CONJ in case. If you do something lest something (usually) unpleasant happens you do it to try to prevent it happening ❑ *She went in without knocking, and hurried upstairs, in great fear lest she should meet the real Mary Ann* (*Alice's Adventures in Wonderland* by Lewis Carroll)

levee NOUN a levee is an old term for a meeting held in the morning, shortly after the person holding the meeting has got out of bed ❑ *I used to attend the King's levee once or twice a week* (*Gulliver's Travels* by Jonathan Swift)

life-preserver NOUN a club which had lead inside it to make it heavier and therefore more dangerous ❑ *and with no more suspicious articles displayed to view than two or three heavy bludgeons which stood in a corner, and a "life-preserver" that hung over the chimney-piece.* (*Oliver Twist* by Charles Dickens)

lighterman NOUN a lighterman is another word for sailor ❑ *in and out, hammers going in ship-builders' yards, saws going at timber, clashing engines going at things unknown, pumps going in leaky ships, capstans going, ships going out to sea, and unintelligible sea creatures roaring curses over the bulwarks at respondent lightermen* (*Great Expectations* by Charles Dickens)

livery NOUN servants often wore a uniform known as a livery ❑ *suddenly a footman in livery came running out of the wood* (*Alice's Adventures in Wonderland* by Lewis Carroll)

livid ADJ livid means pale or ash coloured. Livid also means very angry ❑ *a dirty, livid white* (*Treasure Island* by Robert Louis Stevenson)

lottery-tickets NOUN a popular card game ❑ *and Mrs. Philips protested that they would have a nice comfortable noisy game of lottery tickets* (*Pride and Prejudice* by Jane Austen)

lower and upper world PHRASE the earth and the heavens are the lower and upper worlds ❑ *the changes in the lower and upper world* (*Gulliver's Travels* by Jonathan Swift)

lustres NOUN lustres are chandeliers. A chandelier is a large, decorative frame which holds light bulbs or candles and hangs from the ceiling ❑ *the lustres, lights, the carving and the guilding* (*The Prelude* by William Wordsworth)

lynched VERB killed without a criminal trial by a crowd of people ❑ *He'll never know how nigh he come to getting lynched* (*The Adventures of Huckleberry Finn* by Mark Twain)

malingering VERB if someone is malingering they are pretending to be ill to avoid working ❑ *And you stand there malingering* (*Treasure Island* by Robert Louis Stevenson)

managing PHRASE treating with consideration ❑ *to think the honour of my own kind not worth managing* (*Gulliver's Travels* by Jonathan Swift)

manhood PHRASE manhood means human nature ❑ *concerning the nature of manhood* (*Gulliver's Travels* by Jonathan Swift)

man-trap NOUN a man-trap is a set of steel jaws that snap shut when trodden on and trap a person's leg

❏ *"Don't go to him,"* I called out of the window, *"he's an assassin! A man-trap!"* (*Oliver Twist* by Charles Dickens)

maps NOUN charts of the night sky ❏ *Let maps to others, worlds on worlds have shown* (*The Good-Morrow* by John Donne)

mark VERB look at or notice ❏ *Mark but this flea, and mark in this* (*The Flea* by John Donne)

maroons NOUN A maroon is someone who has been left in a place which it is difficult for them to escape from, like a small island ❏ *if schooners, islands, and maroons* (*Treasure Island* by Robert Louis Stevenson)

mast NOUN here mast means the fruit of forest trees ❏ *a quantity of acorns, dates, chestnuts, and other mast* (*Gulliver's Travels* by Jonathan Swift)

mate VERB defeat ❏ *Where Mars did mate the warlike Carthigens* (*Doctor Faustus Chorus* by Christopher Marlowe)

mealy ADJ Mealy when used to describe a face meant pallid, pale or colourless ❏ *I only know two sorts of boys. Mealy boys, and beef-faced boys* (*Oliver Twist* by Charles Dickens)

middling ADV fairly or moderately ❏ *she worked me middling hard for about an hour* (*The Adventures of Huckleberry Finn* by Mark Twain)

mill NOUN a mill, or treadmill, was a device for hard labour or punishment in prison ❏ *Was you never on the mill?* (*Oliver Twist* by Charles Dickens)

milliner's shop NOUN a milliner's sold fabrics, clothing, lace and accessories; as time went on they specialized more and more in hats ❏ *to pay their duty to their aunt and to a milliner's shop just over the way* (*Pride and Prejudice* by Jane Austen)

minching un' munching PHRASE how people in the north of England used to describe the way people

from the south speak ❏ *Minching un' munching!* (*Wuthering Heights* by Emily Brontë)

mine NOUN gold ❏ *Whether both th'Indias of spice and mine* (*The Sun Rising* by John Donne)

mire NOUN mud ❏ *Tis my fate to be always ground into the mire under the iron heel of oppression* (*The Adventures of Huckleberry Finn* by Mark Twain)

miscellany NOUN a miscellany is a collection of many different kinds of things ❏ *under that, the miscellany began* (*Treasure Island* by Robert Louis Stevenson)

mistarshers NOUN mistarshers means moustache, which is the hair that grows on a man's upper lip ❏ *when he put his hand up to his mistarshers* (*Tess of the D'Urbervilles* by Thomas Hardy)

morrow NOUN here good-morrow means tomorrow and a new and better life ❏ *And now good-morrow to our waking souls* (*The Good-Morrow* by John Donne)

mortification NOUN mortification is an old word for gangrene which is when part of the body decays or "dies" because of disease ❏ *Yes, it was a mortification–that was it* (*The Adventures of Huckleberry Finn* by Mark Twain)

mought VERB mought is an old spelling of might ❏ *what you mought call me? You mought call me captain* (*Treasure Island* by Robert Louis Stevenson)

move VERB move me not means do not make me angry ❏ *Move me not, Faustus* (*Doctor Faustus 2.1* by Christopher Marlowe)

muffin-cap NOUN a muffin-cap is a flat cap made from wool ❏ *the old one, remained stationary in the muffin-cap and leathers* (*Oliver Twist* by Charles Dickens)

mulatter NOUN a mulatter was another word for mulatto, which is a person with parents who are from different races ❏ *a mulatter, most as white as a white man* (*The Adventures of Huckleberry Finn* by Mark Twain)

mummery NOUN mummery is an old word that meant meaningless (or pretentious) ceremony ❏ *When they were all gone, and when Trabb and his men–but not his boy: I looked for him–had crammed their mummery into bags, and were gone too, the house felt wholesomer.* (*Great Expectations* by Charles Dickens)

nap NOUN the nap is the woolly surface on a new item of clothing. Here the surface has been worn away so it looks bare ❏ *like an old hat with the nap rubbed off* (*The Adventures of Huckleberry Finn* by Mark Twain)

natural ◼ NOUN a natural is a person born with learning difficulties ❏ *though he had been left to his particular care by their deceased father, who thought him almost a natural.* (*David Copperfield* by Charles Dickens) ◼ ADJ natural meant illegitimate ❏ *Harriet Smith was the natural daughter of somebody* (*Emma* by Jane Austen)

navigator NOUN a navigator was originally someone employed to dig canals. It is the origin of the word "navvy" meaning a labourer ❏ *She ascertained from me in a few words what it was all about, comforted Dora, and gradually convinced her that I was not a labourer–from my manner of stating the case I believe Dora concluded that I was a navigator, and went balancing myself up and down a plank all day with a wheelbarrow–and so brought us together in peace.* (*David Copperfield* by Charles Dickens)

necromancy NOUN necromancy means a kind of magic where the magician speaks to spirits or ghosts to find out what will happen in the future ❏ *He surfeits upon cursed necromancy* (*Doctor Faustus chorus* by Christopher Marlowe)

negus NOUN a negus is a hot drink made from sweetened wine and water ❏ *He sat placidly perusing the newspaper, with his little head on one side, and a glass of warm sherry negus at his elbow.* (*David Copperfield* by Charles Dickens)

nice ADJ discriminating. Able to make good judgements or choices ❏ *consequently a claim to be nice* (*Emma* by Jane Austen)

nigh ADV nigh means near ❏ *He'll never know how nigh he come to getting lynched* (*The Adventures of Huckleberry Finn* by Mark Twain)

nimbleness NOUN nimbleness means being able to move very quickly or skilfully ❏ *and with incredible accuracy and nimbleness* (*Treasure Island* by Robert Louis Stevenson)

noggin NOUN a noggin is a small mug or a wooden cup ❏ *you'll bring me one noggin of rum* (*Treasure Island* by Robert Louis Stevenson)

none ADJ neither ❏ *none can die* (*The Good-Morrow* by John Donne)

notices NOUN observations ❏ *Arch are his notices* (*The Prelude* by William Wordsworth)

occiput NOUN occiput means the back of the head ❏ *saw off the occiput of each couple* (*Gulliver's Travels* by Jonathan Swift)

officiously ADV kindly ❏ *the governess who attended Glumdalclitch very officiously lifted me up* (*Gulliver's Travels* by Jonathan Swift)

old salt PHRASE old salt is a slang term for an experienced sailor ❏ *a "true sea-dog", and a "real old salt"* (*Treasure Island* by Robert Louis Stevenson)

or ere PHRASE before ❏ *or ere the Hall was built* (*The Prelude* by William Wordsworth)

ostler NOUN one who looks after horses at an inn ❏ *The bill paid, and the waiter remembered, and the ostler not forgotten, and the chambermaid taken into consideration* (*Great Expectations* by Charles Dickens)

ostry NOUN an ostry is an old word for a pub or hotel ❏ *lest I send you into the ostry with a vengeance* (*Doctor Faustus 2.2* by Christopher Marlowe)

outrunning the constable PHRASE outrunning the constable meant spending more than you earn ❏ *but I shall by this means be able to check your bills and to pull you up if I find you outrunning the constable.* (*Great Expectations* by Charles Dickens)

over ADV across ❏ *It is in length six yards, and in the thickest part at least three yards over* (*Gulliver's Travels* by Jonathan Swift)

over the broomstick PHRASE this is a phrase meaning "getting married without a formal ceremony" ❏ *They both led tramping lives, and this woman in Gerrard-street here, had been married very young, over the broomstick (as we say), to a tramping man, and was a perfect fury in point of jealousy.* (*Great Expectations* by Charles Dickens)

own VERB own means to admit or to acknowledge ❏ *It's my old girl that advises. She has the head. But I never own to it before her. Discipline must be maintained* (*Bleak House* by Charles Dickens)

page NOUN here page means a boy employed to run errands ❏ *not my feigned page* (*On His Mistress* by John Donne)

paid pretty dear PHRASE paid pretty dear means paid a high price or suffered quite a lot ❏ *I paid pretty dear for my monthly fourpenny piece* (*Treasure Island* by Robert Louis Stevenson)

pannikins NOUN pannikins were small tin cups ❏ *of lifting light glasses and cups to his lips, as if they were clumsy pannikins* (*Great Expectations* by Charles Dickens)

pards NOUN pards are leopards ❏ *Not charioted by Bacchus and his pards* (*Ode on a Nightingale* by John Keats)

parlour boarder NOUN a pupil who lived with the family ❏ *and somebody had lately raised her from the condition of scholar to parlour boarder* (*Emma* by Jane Austen)

particular, a London PHRASE London in Victorian times and up to the 1950s was famous for having very dense fog–which was a combination of real fog and the smog of pollution from factories ❏ *This is a London particular . . . A fog, miss* (*Bleak House* by Charles Dickens)

patten NOUN pattens were wooden soles which were fixed to shoes by straps to protect the shoes in wet weather ❏ *carrying a basket like the Great Seal of England in plaited straw, a pair of pattens, a spare shawl, and an umbrella, though it was a fine bright day* (*Great Expectations* by Charles Dickens)

paviour NOUN a paviour was a labourer who worked on the street pavement ❏ *the paviour his pickaxe* (*Oliver Twist* by Charles Dickens)

peccant ADJ peccant means unhealthy ❏ *other peccant humours* (*Gulliver's Travels* by Jonathan Swift)

penetralium NOUN penetralium is a word used to describe the inner rooms of the house ❏ *and I had no desire to aggravate his impatience previous to inspecting the penetralium* (*Wuthering Heights* by Emily Brontë)

pensive ADV pensive means deep in thought or thinking seriously about something ❏ *and she was leaning pensive on a tomb-stone on her right elbow* (*The Adventures of Huckleberry Finn* by Mark Twain)

penury NOUN penury is the state of being extremely poor ❏ *Distress, if not penury, loomed in the distance* (*Tess of the D'Urbervilles* by Thomas Hardy)

perspective NOUN telescope ❏ *a pocket perspective* (*Gulliver's Travels* by Jonathan Swift)

phaeton NOUN a phaeton was an open carriage for four people ❏ *often* *condescends to drive by my humble abode in her little phaeton and ponies* (*Pride and Prejudice* by Jane Austen)

phantasm NOUN a phantasm is an illusion, something that is not real. It is sometimes used to mean ghost ❑ *Experience had bred no fancies in him that could raise the phantasm of appetite* (*Silas Marner* by George Eliot)

physic NOUN here physic means medicine ❑ *there I studied physic two years and seven months* (*Gulliver's Travels* by Jonathan Swift)

pinioned VERB to pinion is to hold both arms so that a person cannot move them ❑ *But the relentless Ghost pinioned him in both his arms, and forced him to observe what happened next.* (*A Christmas Carol* by Charles Dickens)

piquet NOUN piquet was a popular card game in the C18th ❑ *Mr Hurst and Mr Bingley were at piquet* (*Pride and Prejudice* by Jane Austen)

plaister NOUN a plaister is a piece of cloth on which an apothecary (or pharmacist) would spread ointment. The cloth is then applied to wounds or bruises to treat them ❑ *Then, she gave the knife a final smart wipe on the edge of the plaister, and then sawed a very thick round off the loaf: which she finally, before separating from the loaf, hewed into two halves, of which Joe got one, and I the other.* (*Great Expectations* by Charles Dickens)

plantations NOUN here plantations means colonies, which are countries controlled by a more powerful country ❑ *besides our plantations in America* (*Gulliver's Travels* by Jonathan Swift)

plastic ADJ here plastic is an old term meaning shaping or a power that was forming ❑ *A plastic power abode with me* (*The Prelude* by William Wordsworth)

players NOUN actors ❑ *of players which upon the world's stage be* (*On His Mistress* by John Donne)

plump ADV all at once, suddenly ❑ *But it took a bit of time to get it well round, the change come so uncommon plump, didn't it? (Great Expectations* by Charles Dickens)

plundered VERB to plunder is to rob or steal from ❑ *These crosses stand for the names of ships or towns that they sank or plundered* (*Treasure Island* by Robert Louis Stevenson)

pommel ■ VERB to pommel someone is to hit them repeatedly with your fists ❑ *hug him round the neck, pommel his back, and kick his legs in irrepressible affection! (A Christmas Carol* by Charles Dickens) ■ NOUN a pommel is the part of a saddle that rises up at the front ❑ *He had his gun across his pommel* (*The Adventures of Huckleberry Finn* by Mark Twain)

poor's rates NOUN poor's rates were property taxes which were used to support the poor ❑ *"Oh!" replied the undertaker; "why, you know, Mr. Bumble, I pay a good deal towards the poor's rates." (Oliver Twist* by Charles Dickens)

popular ADJ popular means ruled by the people, or Republican, rather than ruled by a monarch ❑ *With those of Greece compared and popular Rome* (*The Prelude* by William Wordsworth)

porringer NOUN a porringer is a small bowl ❑ *Of this festive composition each boy had one porringer, and no more* (*Oliver Twist* by Charles Dickens)

postboy NOUN a postboy was the driver of a horse-drawn carriage ❑ *He spoke to a postboy who was dozing under the gateway* (*Oliver Twist* by Charles Dickens)

post-chaise NOUN a fast carriage for two or four passengers ❑ *Looking round, he saw that it was a post-chaise, driven at great speed* (*Oliver Twist* by Charles Dickens)

postern NOUN a small gate usually at the back of a building ❑ *The little servant happening to be entering the* fortress with two hot rolls, I passed through the postern and crossed the drawbridge, in her company (*Great Expectations* by Charles Dickens)

pottle NOUN a pottle was a small basket ❏ *He had a paper-bag under each arm and a pottle of strawberries in one hand . . .* (*Great Expectations* by Charles Dickens)

pounce NOUN pounce is a fine powder used to prevent ink spreading on untreated paper ❏ *in that grim atmosphere of pounce and parchment, red-tape, dusty wafers, ink-jars, brief and draft paper, law reports, writs, declarations, and bills of costs* (*David Copperfield* by Charles Dickens)

pox NOUN pox means sexually transmitted diseases like syphilis ❏ *how the pox in all its consequences and denominations* (*Gulliver's Travels* by Jonathan Swift)

prelibation NOUN prelibation means a foretaste of or an example of something to come ❏ *A prelibation to the mower's scythe* (*The Prelude* by William Wordsworth)

prentice NOUN an apprentice ❏ *and Joe, sitting on an old gun, had told me that when I was 'prentice to him regularly bound, we would have such Larks there!* (*Great Expectations* by Charles Dickens)

presently ADV immediately ❏ *I presently knew what they meant* (*Gulliver's Travels* by Jonathan Swift)

pumpion NOUN pumpkin ❏ *for it was almost as large as a small pumpion* (*Gulliver's Travels* by Jonathan Swift)

punctual ADJ kept in one place ❏ *was not a punctual presence, but a spirit* (*The Prelude* by William Wordsworth)

quadrille ■ NOUN a quadrille is a dance invented in France which is usually performed by four couples ❏ *However, Mr Swiveller had Miss Sophy's hand for the first quadrille (country-dances being low, were utterly proscribed)* (*The Old Curiosity Shop* by Charles Dickens) ■ NOUN quadrille was a card game for four people ❏ *to make up her pool of quadrille in the evening* (*Pride and Prejudice* by Jane Austen)

quality NOUN gentry or upper-class people ❏ *if you are with the quality* (*The Adventures of Huckleberry Finn* by Mark Twain)

quick parts PHRASE quick-witted ❏ *Mr Bennet was so odd a mixture of quick parts* (*Pride and Prejudice* by Jane Austen)

quid NOUN a quid is something chewed or kept in the mouth, like a piece of tobacco ❏ *rolling his quid* (*Treasure Island* by Robert Louis Stevenson)

quit VERB quit means to avenge or to make even ❏ *But Faustus's death shall quit my infamy* (*Doctor Faustus 4.3* by Christopher Marlowe)

rags NOUN divisions ❏ *Nor hours, days, months, which are the rags of time* (*The Sun Rising* by John Donne)

raiment NOUN raiment means clothing ❏ *the mountain shook off turf and flower, had only heath for raiment and crag for gem* (*Jane Eyre* by Charlotte Brontë)

rain cats and dogs PHRASE an expression meaning rain heavily. The origin of the expression is unclear ❏ *But it'll perhaps rain cats and dogs to-morrow* (*Silas Marner* by George Eliot)

raised Cain PHRASE raised Cain means caused a lot of trouble. Cain is a character in the Bible who killed his brother Abel ❏ *and every time he got drunk he raised Cain around town* (*The Adventures of Huckleberry Finn* by Mark Twain)

rambling ADJ rambling means confused and not very clear ❏ *my head began to be filled very early with rambling thoughts* (*Robinson Crusoe* by Daniel Defoe)

raree-show NOUN a raree-show is an old term for a peep-show or a fairground entertainment ❑ *A raree-show is here, with children gathered round* (*The Prelude* by William Wordsworth)

recusants NOUN people who resisted authority ❑ *hardy recusants* (*The Prelude* by William Wordsworth)

redounding VERB eddying. An eddy is a movement in water or air which goes round and round instead of flowing in one direction ❑ *mists and steam-like fogs redounding everywhere* (*The Prelude* by William Wordsworth)

redundant ADJ here redundant means overflowing but Wordsworth also uses it to mean excessively large or too big ❑ *A tempest, a redundant energy* (*The Prelude* by William Wordsworth)

reflex NOUN reflex is a shortened version of reflexion, which is an alternative spelling of reflection ❑ *To cut across the reflex of a star* (*The Prelude* by William Wordsworth)

Reformatory NOUN a prison for young offenders/criminals ❑ *Even when I was taken to have a new suit of clothes, the tailor had orders to make them like a kind of Reformatory, and on no account to let me have the free use of my limbs.* (*Great Expectations* by Charles Dickens)

remorse NOUN pity or compassion ❑ *by that remorse* (*On His Mistress* by John Donne)

render VERB in this context render means give. ❑ *and Sarah could render no reason that would be sanctioned by the feeling of the community.* (*Silas Marner* by George Eliot)

repeater NOUN a repeater was a watch that chimed the last hour when a button was pressed–as a result it was useful in the dark ❑ *And his watch is a gold repeater, and worth a hundred pound if it's worth a*

penny. (*Great Expectations* by Charles Dickens)

repugnance NOUN repugnance means a strong dislike of something or someone ❑ *overcoming a strong repugnance* (*Treasure Island* by Robert Louis Stevenson)

reverence NOUN reverence means bow. When you bow to someone, you briefly bend your body towards them as a formal way of showing them respect ❑ *made my reverence* (*Gulliver's Travels* by Jonathan Swift)

reverie NOUN a reverie is a daydream ❑ *I can guess the subject of your reverie* (*Pride and Prejudice* by Jane Austen)

revival NOUN a religious meeting held in public ❑ *well I'd ben a-running' a little temperance revival thar' bout a week* (*The Adventures of Huckleberry Finn* by Mark Twain)

revolt VERB revolt means turn back or stop your present course of action and go back to what you were doing before ❑ *Revolt, or I'll in piecemeal tear thy flesh* (*Doctor Faustus 5.1* by Christopher Marlowe)

rheumatics/rheumatism NOUN rheumatics [rheumatism] is an illness that makes your joints or muscles stiff and painful ❑ *a new cure for the rheumatics* (*Treasure Island* by Robert Louis Stevenson)

riddance NOUN riddance is usually used in the form good riddance which you say when you are pleased that something has gone or been left behind ❑ *I'd better go into the house, and die and be a riddance* (*David Copperfield* by Charles Dickens)

rimy ADJ rimy is an adjective which means covered in ice or frost ❑ *It was a rimy morning, and very damp* (*Great Expectations* by Charles Dickens)

riper ADJ riper means more mature or older ❑ *At riper years to Wittenberg he went* (*Doctor Faustus chorus* by Christopher Marlowe)

GEORGE ORWELL

rubber NOUN a set of games in whist or backgammon ❏ *her father was sure of his rubber* (*Emma* by Jane Austen)

ruffian NOUN a ruffian is a person who behaves violently ❏ *and when the ruffian had told him* (*Treasure Island* by Robert Louis Stevenson)

sadness NOUN sadness is an old term meaning seriousness ❏ *But I prithee tell me, in good sadness* (*Doctor Faustus 2.2* by Christopher Marlowe)

sailed before the mast PHRASE this phrase meant someone who did not look like a sailor ❏ *he had none of the appearance of a man that sailed before the mast* (*Treasure Island* by Robert Louis Stevenson)

scabbard NOUN a scabbard is the covering for a sword or dagger ❏ *Girded round its middle was an antique scabbard; but no sword was in it, and the ancient sheath was eaten up with rust* (*A Christmas Carol* by Charles Dickens)

schooners NOUN A schooner is a fast, medium-sized sailing ship ❏ *if schooners, islands, and maroons* (*Treasure Island* by Robert Louis Stevenson)

science NOUN learning or knowledge ❏ *Even Science, too, at hand* (*The Prelude* by William Wordsworth)

scrouge VERB to scrouge means to squeeze or to crowd ❏ *to scrouge in and get a sight* (*The Adventures of Huckleberry Finn* by Mark Twain)

scrutore NOUN a scrutore, or escritoire, was a writing table ❏ *set me gently on my feet upon the scrutore* (*Gulliver's Travels* by Jonathan Swift)

scutcheon/escutcheon NOUN an escutcheon is a shield with a coat of arms, or the symbols of a family name, engraved on it ❏ *On the scutcheon we'll have a bend* (*The Adventures of Huckleberry Finn* by Mark Twain)

sea-dog PHRASE sea-dog is a slang term for an experienced sailor or pirate

❏ *a "true sea-dog", and a "real old salt,"* (*Treasure Island* by Robert Louis Stevenson)

see the lions PHRASE to see the lions was to go and see the sights of London. Originally the phrase referred to the menagerie in the Tower of London and later in Regent's Park ❏ *We will go and see the lions for an hour or two–it's something to have a fresh fellow like you to show them to, Copperfield* (*David Copperfield* by Charles Dickens)

self-conceit NOUN self-conceit is an old term which means having too high an opinion of oneself, or deceiving yourself ❏ *Till swollen with cunning, of a self-conceit* (*Doctor Faustus chorus* by Christopher Marlowe)

seneschal NOUN a steward ❏ *where a grey-headed seneschal sings a funny chorus with a funnier body of vassals* (*Oliver Twist* by Charles Dickens)

sensible ADJ if you were sensible of something you are aware or conscious of something ❏ *If my children are silly I must hope to be always sensible of it* (*Pride and Prejudice* by Jane Austen)

sessions NOUN court cases were heard at specific times of the year called sessions ❏ *He lay in prison very ill, during the whole interval between his committal for trial, and the coming round of the Sessions.* (*Great Expectations* by Charles Dickens)

shabby ADJ shabby places look old and in bad condition ❏ *a little bit of a shabby village named Pikesville* (*The Adventures of Huckleberry Finn* by Mark Twain)

shay-cart NOUN a shay-cart was a small cart drawn by one horse ❏ *"I were at the Bargemen t'other night, Pip;" whenever he subsided into affection, he called me Pip, and whenever he relapsed into politeness he called me Sir; "when there come up in his* *shay-cart Pumblechook."* (*Great Expectations* by Charles Dickens)

shilling NOUN a shilling is an old unit of currency. There were twenty shillings in every British pound ❑ *"Ten shillings too much," said the gentleman in the white waistcoat.* (*Oliver Twist* by Charles Dickens)

shines NOUN tricks or games ❑ *well, it would make a cow laugh to see the shines that old idiot cut* (*The Adventures of Huckleberry Finn* by Mark Twain)

shirking VERB shirking means not doing what you are meant to be doing, or evading your duties ❑ *some of you shirking lubbers* (*Treasure Island* by Robert Louis Stevenson)

shiver my timbers PHRASE shiver my timbers is an expression which was used by sailors and pirates to express surprise ❑ *why, shiver my timbers, if I hadn't forgotten my score!* (*Treasure Island* by Robert Louis Stevenson)

shoe-roses NOUN shoe-roses were roses made from ribbons which were stuck on to shoes as decoration ❑ *the very shoe-roses for Netherfield were got by proxy* (*Pride and Prejudice* by Jane Austen)

singular ADJ singular means very great and remarkable or strange ❑ *"Singular dream," he says* (*The Adventures of Huckleberry Finn* by Mark Twain)

sire NOUN sire is an old word which means lord or master or elder ❑ *She also defied her sire* (*Little Women* by Louisa May Alcott)

sixpence NOUN a sixpence was half of a shilling ❑ *if she had only a shilling in the world, she would be very lilkely to give away sixpence of it* (*Emma* by Jane Austen)

slavey NOUN the word slavey was used when there was only one servant in a house or boarding-house–so she had to perform all the duties of a larger staff ❑ *Two distinct knocks, sir, will produce the slavey at any*

time (*The Old Curiosity Shop* by Charles Dickens)

slender ADJ weak ❑ *In slender accents of sweet verse* (*The Prelude* by William Wordsworth)

slop-shops NOUN slop-shops were shops where cheap ready-made clothes were sold. They mainly sold clothes to sailors ❑ *Accordingly, I took the jacket off, that I might learn to do without it; and carrying it under my arm, began a tour of inspection of the various slop-shops.* (*David Copperfield* by Charles Dickens)

sluggard NOUN a lazy person ❑ *"Stand up and repeat ''Tis the voice of the sluggard,'" said the Gryphon.* (*Alice's Adventures in Wonderland* by Lewis Carroll)

smallpox NOUN smallpox is a serious infectious disease ❑ *by telling the men we had smallpox aboard* (*The Adventures of Huckleberry Finn* by Mark Twain)

smalls NOUN smalls are short trousers ❑ *It is difficult for a large-headed, small-eyed youth, of lumbering make and heavy countenance, to look dignified under any circum- stances; but it is more especially so, when superadded to these personal attractions are a red nose and yellow smalls* (*Oliver Twist* by Charles Dickens)

sneeze-box NOUN a box for snuff was called a sneeze-box because sniffing snuff makes the user sneeze ❑ *To think of Jack Dawkins—lummy Jack —the Dodger—the Artful Dodger— going abroad for a common twopen- ny-halfpenny sneeze-box!* (*Oliver Twist* by Charles Dickens)

snorted VERB slept ❑ *Or snorted we in the Seven Sleepers' den?* (*The Good- Morrow* by John Donne)

snuff NOUN snuff is tobacco in powder form which is taken by sniffing ❑ *as he thrust his thumb and fore- finger into the proffered snuff-box of the undertaker: which was an ingenious little model of a patent*

coffin. (*Oliver Twist* by Charles Dickens)

soliloquized VERB to soliloquize is when an actor in a play speaks to himself or herself rather than to another actor ❏ *"A new servitude! There is something in that," I soliloquized (mentally, be it understood; I did not talk aloud)* (*Jane Eyre* by Charlotte Brontë)

sough NOUN a sough is a drain or a ditch ❏ *as you may have noticed the sough that runs from the marshes* (*Wuthering Heights* by Emily Brontë)

spirits NOUN a spirit is the nonphysical part of a person which is believed to remain alive after their death ❏ *that I might raise up spirits when I please* (*Doctor Faustus 1.5* by Christopher Marlowe)

spleen ■ NOUN here spleen means a type of sadness or depression which was thought to only affect the wealthy ❏ *yet here I could plainly discover the true seeds of spleen* (*Gulliver's Travels* by Jonathan Swift) ■ NOUN irritability and low spirits ❏ *Adieu to disappointment and spleen* (*Pride and Prejudice* by Jane Austen)

spondulicks NOUN spondulicks is a slang word which means money ❏ *not for all his spondulicks and as much more on top of it* (*The Adventures of Huckleberry Finn* by Mark Twain)

stalled of VERB to be stalled of something is to be bored with it ❏ *I'm stalled of doing naught* (*Wuthering Heights* by Emily Brontë)

stanchion NOUN a stanchion is a pole or bar that stands upright and is used as a building support ❏ *and slid down a stanchion* (*The Adventures of Huckleberry Finn* by Mark Twain)

stang NOUN stang is another word for pole which was an old measurement ❏ *These fields were intermingled with woods of half a stang* (*Gulliver's Travels* by Jonathan Swift)

starlings NOUN a starling is a wall built around the pillars that support a bridge to protect the pillars ❏ *There were states of the tide when, having been down the river, I could not get back through the eddy-chafed arches and starlings of old London Bridge* (*Great Expectations* by Charles Dickens)

startings NOUN twitching or night-time movements of the body ❏ *with midnight's startings* (*On His Mistress* by John Donne)

stomacher NOUN a panel at the front of a dress ❏ *but send her aunt the pattern of a stomacher* (*Emma* by Jane Austen)

stoop VERB swoop ❏ *Once a kite hovering over the garden made a stoop at me* (*Gulliver's Travels* by Jonathan Swift)

succedaneum NOUN a succedaneum is a substitute ❏ *But as a succedaneum* (*The Prelude* by William Wordsworth)

suet NOUN a hard animal fat used in cooking ❏ *and your jaws are too weak For anything tougher than suet* (*Alice's Adventures in Wonderland* by Lewis Carroll)

sultry ADJ sultry weather is hot and damp. Here sultry means unpleasant or risky ❏ *for it was getting pretty sultry for us* (*The Adventures of Huckleberry Finn* by Mark Twain)

summerset NOUN summerset is an old spelling of somersault. If someone does a somersault, they turn over completely in the air ❏ *I have seen him do the summerset* (*Gulliver's Travels* by Jonathan Swift)

supper NOUN supper was a light meal taken late in the evening. The main meal was dinner which was eaten at four or five in the afternoon ❏ *and the supper table was all set out* (*Emma* by Jane Austen)

surfeits VERB to surfeit in something is to have far too much of it, or to overindulge in it to an unhealthy degree ❏ *He surfeits upon cursed* necromancy (*Doctor Faustus chorus* by Christopher Marlowe)

surtout NOUN a surtout is a long close-fitting overcoat ❑ *He wore a long black surtout reaching nearly to his ankles* (*The Old Curiosity Shop* by Charles Dickens)

swath NOUN swath is the width of corn cut by a scythe ❑ *while thy hook Spares the next swath* (*Ode to Autumn* by John Keats)

sylvan ADJ sylvan means belonging to the woods ❑ *Sylvan historian* (*Ode on a Grecian Urn* by John Keats)

taction NOUN taction means touch. This means that the people had to be touched on the mouth or the ears to get their attention ❑ *without being roused by some external taction upon the organs of speech and hearing* (*Gulliver's Travels* by Jonathan Swift)

Tag and Rag and Bobtail PHRASE the riff-raff, or lower classes. Used in an insulting way ❑ *"No," said he; "not till it got about that there was no protection on the premises, and it come to be considered dangerous, with convicts and Tag and Rag and Bobtail going up and down."* (*Great Expectations* by Charles Dickens)

tallow NOUN tallow is hard animal fat that is used to make candles and soap ❑ *and a lot of tallow candles* (*The Adventures of Huckleberry Finn* by Mark Twain)

tan VERB to tan means to beat or whip ❑ *and if I catch you about that school I'll tan you good* (*The Adventures of Huckleberry Finn* by Mark Twain)

tanyard NOUN the tanyard is part of a tannery, which is a place where leather is made from animal skins ❑ *hid in the old tanyard* (*The Adventures of Huckleberry Finn* by Mark Twain)

tarry ADJ tarry means the colour of tar or black ❑ *his tarry pig-tail*

(*Treasure Island* by Robert Louis Stevenson)

thereof PHRASE from there ❑ *By all desires which thereof did ensue* (*On His Mistress* by John Donne)

thick with, be PHRASE if you are "thick with someone" you are very close, sharing secrets–it is often used to describe people who are planning something secret ❑ *Hasn't he been thick with Mr Heathcliff lately?* (*Wuthering Heights* by Emily Brontë)

thimble NOUN a thimble is a small cover used to protect the finger while sewing ❑ *The paper had been sealed in several places by a thimble* (*Treasure Island* by Robert Louis Stevenson)

thirtover ADJ thirtover is an old word which means obstinate or that someone is very determined to do want they want and can not be persuaded to do something in another way ❑ *I have been living on in a thirtover, lackadaisical way* (*Tess of the D'Urbervilles* by Thomas Hardy)

timbrel NOUN timbrel is a tambourine ❑ *What pipes and timbrels?* (*Ode on a Grecian Urn* by John Keats)

tin NOUN tin is slang for money/cash ❑ *Then the plain question is, an't it a pity that this state of things should continue, and how much better would it be for the old gentleman to hand over a reasonable amount of tin, and make it all right and comfortable* (*The Old Curiosity Shop* by Charles Dickens)

tincture NOUN a tincture is a medicine made with alcohol and a small amount of a drug ❑ *with ink composed of a cephalic tincture* (*Gulliver's Travels* by Jonathan Swift)

tithe NOUN a tithe is a tax paid to the church ❑ *and held farms which, speaking from a spiritual point of view, paid highly-desirable tithes* (*Silas Marner* by George Eliot)

towardly ADJ a towardly child is dutiful or obedient ❏ *and a towardly child* (*Gulliver's Travels* by Jonathan Swift)

toys NOUN trifles are things which are considered to have little importance, value, or significance ❏ *purchase my life from them bysome bracelets, glass rings, and other toys* (*Gulliver's Travels* by Jonathan Swift)

tract NOUN a tract is a religious pamphlet or leaflet ❏ *and Joe Harper got a hymn-book and a tract* (*The Adventures of Huckleberry Finn* by Mark Twain)

train-oil NOUN train-oil is oil from whale blubber ❏ *The train-oil and gunpowder were shoved out of sight in a minute* (*Wuthering Heights* by Emily Brontë)

tribulation NOUN tribulation means the suffering or difficulty you experience in a particular situation ❏ *Amy was learning this distinction through much tribulation* (*Little Women* by Louisa May Alcott)

trivet NOUN a trivet is a three-legged stand for resting a pot or kettle ❏ *a pocket-knife in his right; and a pewter pot on the trivet* (*Oliver Twist* by Charles Dickens)

trot line NOUN a trot line is a fishing line to which a row of smaller fishing lines are attached ❏ *when he got along I was hard at it taking up a trot line* (*The Adventures of Huckleberry Finn* by Mark Twain)

troth NOUN oath or pledge ❏ *I wonder, by my troth* (*The Good-Morrow* by John Donne)

truckle NOUN a truckle bedstead is a bed that is on wheels and can be slid under another bed to save space ❏ *It rose under my hand, and the door yielded. Looking in, I saw a lighted candle on a table, a bench, and a mattress on a truckle bedstead.* (*Great Expectations* by Charles Dickens)

trump NOUN a trump is a good, reliable person who can be trusted ❏ *This lad Hawkins is a trump, I perceive* (*Treasure Island* by Robert Louis Stevenson)

tucker NOUN a tucker is a frilly lace collar which is worn around the neck ❏ *Whereat Scrooge's niece's sister—the plump one with the lace tucker: not the one with the roses—blushed.* (*A Christmas Carol* by Charles Dickens)

tureen NOUN a large bowl with a lid from which soup or vegetables are served ❏ *Waiting in a hot tureen!* (*Alice's Adventures in Wonderland* by Lewis Carroll)

turnkey NOUN a prison officer; jailer ❏ *As we came out of the prison through the lodge, I found that the great importance of my guardian was appreciated by the turnkeys, no less than by those whom they held in charge.* (*Great Expectations* by Charles Dickens)

turnpike NOUN the upkeep of many roads of the time was paid for by tolls (fees) collected at posts along the road. There was a gate to prevent people travelling further along the road until the toll had been paid. ❏ *Traddles, whom I have taken up by appointment at the turnpike, presents a dazzling combination of cream colour and light blue; and both he and Mr. Dick have a general effect about them of being all gloves.* (*David Copperfield* by Charles Dickens)

twas PHRASE it was ❏ *twas but a dream of thee* (*The Good-Morrow* by John Donne)

tyrannized VERB tyrannized means bullied or forced to do things against their will ❏ *for people would soon cease coming there to be tyrannized over and put down* (*Treasure Island* by Robert Louis Stevenson)

'un NOUN 'un is a slang term for one—usually used to refer to a person ❏ *She's been thinking the old 'un* (*David Copperfield* by Charles Dickens)

undistinguished ADJ undiscriminating or incapable of making a distinction between good and bad things ❏

their undistinguished appetite to devour everything (*Gulliver's Travels* by Jonathan Swift)

use NOUN habit ❏ *Though use make you apt to kill me* (*The Flea* by John Donne)

vacant ADJ vacant usually means empty, but here Wordsworth uses it to mean carefree ❏ *To vacant musing, unreproved neglect* (*The Prelude* by William Wordsworth)

valetudinarian NOUN one too concerned with his or her own health. ❏ *for having been a valetudinarian all his life* (*Emma* by Jane Austen)

vamp VERB vamp means to walk or tramp to somewhere ❏ *Well, vamp on to Marlott, will 'ee* (*Tess of the D'Urbervilles* by Thomas Hardy)

vapours NOUN the vapours is an old term which means unpleasant and strange thoughts, which make the person feel nervous and unhappy ❏ *and my head was full of vapours* (*Robinson Crusoe* by Daniel Defoe)

vegetables NOUN here vegetables means plants ❏ *the other vegetables are in the same proportion* (*Gulliver's Travels* by Jonathan Swift)

venturesome ADJ if you are venturesome you are willing to take risks ❏ *he must be either hopelessly stupid or a venturesome fool* (*Wuthering Heights* by Emily Brontë)

verily ADV verily means really or truly ❏ *though I believe verily* (*Robinson Crusoe* by Daniel Defoe)

vicinage NOUN vicinage is an area or the residents of an area ❏ *and to his thought the whole vicinage was haunted by her.* (*Silas Marner* by George Eliot)

victuals NOUN victuals means food ❏ *grumble a little over the victuals* (*The Adventures of Huckleberry Finn* by Mark Twain)

vintage NOUN vintage in this context means wine ❏ *Oh, for a draught of*

vintage! (*Ode on a Nightingale* by John Keats)

virtual ADJ here virtual means powerful or strong ❏ *had virtual faith* (*The Prelude* by William Wordsworth)

vittles NOUN vittles is a slang word which means food ❏ *There never was such a woman for givin' away vittles and drink* (*Little Women* by Louisa May Alcott)

voided straight PHRASE voided straight is an old expression which means emptied immediately ❏ *see the rooms be voided straight* (*Doctor Faustus 4.1* by Christopher Marlowe)

wainscot NOUN wainscot is wood panel lining in a room so wainscoted means a room lined with wooden panels ❏ *in the dark wainscoted parlor* (*Silas Marner* by George Eliot)

walking the plank PHRASE walking the plank was a punishment in which a prisoner would be made to walk along a plank on the side of the ship and fall into the sea, where they would be abandoned ❏ *about hanging, and walking the plank* (*Treasure Island* by Robert Louis Stevenson)

want VERB want means to be lacking or short of ❏ *The next thing wanted was to get the picture framed* (*Emma* by Jane Austen)

wanting ADJ wanting means lacking or missing ❏ *wanting two fingers of the left hand* (*Treasure Island* by Robert Louis Stevenson)

wanting, I was not PHRASE I was not wanting means I did not fail ❏ *I was not wanting to lay a foundation of religious knowledge in his mind* (*Robinson Crusoe* by Daniel Defoe)

ward NOUN a ward is, usually, a child who has been put under the protection of the court or a guardian for his or her protection ❏ *I call the Wards in Jarndcye. They*

are caged up with all the others.
(*Bleak House* by Charles Dickens)

waylay VERB to waylay someone is to lie in wait for them or to intercept them ❏ *I must go up the road and waylay him* (*The Adventures of Huckleberry Finn* by Mark Twain)

weazen NOUN weazen is a slang word for throat. It actually means shrivelled ❏ *You with a uncle too! Why, I knowed you at Gargery's when you was so small a wolf that I could have took your weazen betwixt this finger and thumb and chucked you away dead* (*Great Expectations* by Charles Dickens)

wery ■ ADV very ❏ *Be wery careful o' vidders all your life* (*Pickwick Papers* by Charles Dickens) ■ *See* wibrated

wherry NOUN wherry is a small swift rowing boat for one person ❏ *It was flood tide when Daniel Quilp sat himself down in the wherry to cross to the opposite shore.* (*The Old Curiosity Shop* by Charles Dickens)

whether PREP whether means which of the two in this example ❏ *we came in full view of a great island or continent (for we knew not whether)* (*Gulliver's Travels* by Jonathan Swift)

whetstone NOUN a whetstone is a stone used to sharpen knives and other tools ❏ *I dropped pap's whetstone there too* (*The Adventures of Huckleberry Finn* by Mark Twain)

wibrated VERB in Dickens's use of the English language "w" often replaces "v" when he is reporting speech. So here "wibrated" means "vibrated". In *Pickwick Papers* a judge asks Sam Weller (who constantly confuses the two letters) "Do you spell it with a 'v' or a 'w'?" to which Weller replies "That depends upon the taste and fancy of the speller, my Lord" ❏ *There are strings . . . in the human heart that had better not be wibrated* (*Barnaby Rudge* by Charles Dickens)

wicket NOUN a wicket is a little door in a larger entrance ❏ *Having rested* here, *for a minute or so, to collect a good burst of sobs and an imposing show of tears and terror, he knocked loudly at the wicket* (*Oliver Twist* by Charles Dickens)

without CONJ without means unless ❏ *You don't know about me, without you have read a book by the name of The Adventures of Tom Sawyer* (*The Adventures of Huckleberry Finn* by Mark Twain)

wittles ■ NOUN wittles is a slang word which means food ❏ *I live on broken wittles–and I sleep on the coals* (*David Copperfield* by Charles Dickens) ■ *See* wibrated

woo VERB courts or forms a proper relationship with ❏ *before it woo* (*The Flea* by John Donne)

words, to have PHRASE if you have words with someone you have a disagreement or an argument ❏ *I do not want to have words with a young thing like you.* (*Black Beauty* by Anna Sewell)

workhouse NOUN workhouses were places where the homeless were given food and a place to live in return for doing very hard work ❏ *And the Union workhouses? demanded Scrooge. Are they still in operation?* (*A Christmas Carol* by Charles Dickens)

yawl NOUN a yawl is a small boat kept on a bigger boat for short trips. Yawl is also the name for a small fishing boat ❏ *She sent out her yawl, and we went aboard* (*The Adventures of Huckleberry Finn* by Mark Twain)

yeomanry NOUN the yeomanry was a collective term for the middle classes involved in agriculture ❏ *The yeomanry are precisely the order of people with whom I feel I can have nothing to do* (*Emma* by Jane Austen)

yonder ADV yonder means over there ❏ *all in the same second we seem to hear low voices in yonder!* (*The Adventures of Huckleberry Finn* by Mark Twain)